LAST TO DIE

LAST
TO
DIE

A Defeated Empire, a Forgotten Mission,
and the Last American Killed in World War II

STEPHEN HARDING

Da Capo Press
A member of the Perseus Books Group

Designed by Trish Wilkinson
Set in 10.5 point Palatino by The Perseus Books Group

Library of Congress Cataloging-in-Publication Data

Harding, Stephen, 1952–
    Last to die : a defeated empire, a forgotten mission, and the last American killed in World War II / Stephen Harding.
        pages   cm
    Includes bibliographical references and index.
    ISBN 978-0-306-82338-1 (hardcover : alk. paper) — ISBN 978-0-306-82339-8 (e-book : alk. paper) 1. Marchione, Anthony James, 1925–1945. 2. United States. Army Air Forces. Photo Reconnaissance Squadron, 20th—Biography. 3. United States. Army Air Forces—Aerial gunners—Biography. 4. World War, 1939–1945 —Aerial operations, American. 5. World War, 1939–1945—Reconnaissance operations, American. 6. World War, 1939–1945—Campaigns—Japan—Tokyo. 7. Pottstown (Pa.)—Biography. I. Title.
    D790.264.H373 2015
    940.54'252135—dc23

                                                                    2015003486

Published by Da Capo Press
A Member of the Perseus Books Group
www.dacapopress.com

Da Capo Press books are available at special discounts for bulk purchases in the U.S. by corporations, institutions, and other organizations. For more information, please contact the Special Markets Department at the Perseus Books Group, 2300 Chestnut Street, Suite 200, Philadelphia, PA 19103, or call (800) 810-4145, ext. 5000, or e-mail special.markets@perseusbooks.com.

10 9 8 7 6 5 4 3 2 1

*As always,
for Mari, with love*

CONTENTS

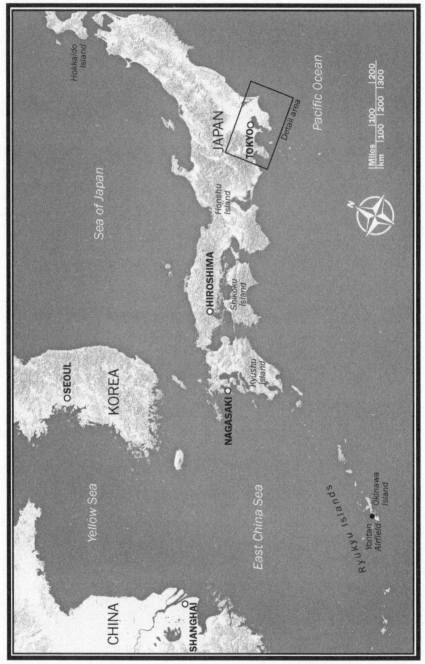

Maps by Steve Walkowiak

But they that wait upon the Lord shall renew their strength; they shall mount up with wings as eagles; they shall run and not be weary; and they shall walk, and not faint.

—Isaiah 40:31

Once you have tasted flight, you will forever walk the earth with your eyes turned skyward, for there you have been, and there you will always long to return.

—Leonardo da Vinci

PROLOGUE

JUST BEFORE SEVEN O'CLOCK on the morning of August 18, 1945, a huge, four-engined aircraft moved slowly onto the end of a 7,000-foot-long runway at Yontan airfield on the southwestern coast of the island of Okinawa. Though the machine's long, cylindrical fuselage, tall tail, and high, narrow wings gave her a certain elegance of line, on the ground she was ponderous. Loaded with fuel and men, she rocked heavily on squat tricycle landing gear as she turned her nose into the wind, then shuddered to a halt as her crew made the last preparations for takeoff.

The aircraft, a B-32 Dominator heavy bomber of the U.S. Army Air Forces' 386th Bombardment Squadron, was one of four scheduled to depart that morning on what everyone in the unit hoped would be a routine photo-reconnaissance mission over Tokyo. At that point in World War II "routine" should have been a given—Japan had accepted the Allies' terms for unconditional surrender four days earlier and President Harry S. Truman had ordered the suspension of all offensive operations against Japan on August 15. Yet four B-32s flying a photo-recon mission over Tokyo two days later had been attacked and damaged by Japanese fighters whose pilots had apparently not heard of the ceasefire ordered by Japan's Emperor Hirohito or, more ominously, had chosen to ignore it. At the early morning briefing for the August 18 mission the Dominator

1

crewmen had been told to assume they'd be flying into what might still be very hostile territory.

With final checks completed, the pilot of the lead B-32—twenty-four-year-old First Lieutenant James L. Klein—released the aircraft's brakes and smoothly advanced the throttles. The low growl of four idling Wright R-3350 radial engines quickly swelled to a gut-rumbling howl, and the Dominator—the racy nose art painted on the sides of her forward fuselage identified her as *Hobo Queen II*—rapidly picked up speed as she surged down the runway. When the bomber hit 130 mph abreast of the 4,500-foot marker Klein gently lifted the nose; the aircraft was instantly transformed from a lumbering, earth-bound behemoth into something far more graceful. Her gear coming up and flaps retracting, *Hobo Queen II* roared over the coral pit at the end of the airstrip and began a climbing 180-degree turn.

With the runway clear, the pilot of the second Dominator, twenty-seven-year-old First Lieutenant John R. Anderson, moved his bomber from the taxiway into takeoff position. The aircraft shook as Anderson did a last engine run-up and the acrid smell of burning high-octane aviation gasoline wafted through the fuselage. Seconds later, her huge paddle-bladed propellers clawing the already-humid air, the B-32 began the sprint down Yontan's runway.

As Anderson's Dominator picked up speed, four young men sat huddled on a low, cot-like settee fixed to the port side of the fuselage in the bomber's rear cabin. Two of the men were gunners; once the Dominator was airborne they'd take their places, one in the tail turret and the other in the rearmost of the B-32's two top turrets. The other two men—twenty-nine-year-old Staff Sergeant Joseph Lacharite and twenty-year-old Sergeant Anthony Marchione—were not members of the bomber's crew. They were assigned to the Yontan-based 20th Reconnaissance Squadron, Lacherite as an aerial photographer and Marchione as a gunner/photographer's assistant. At their feet rested a heavy canvas bag containing the K-22 camera they would use to record the images that were the ultimate purpose of the day's mission.

That mission was to photograph several Japanese military airfields sited to the east and northeast of the sprawling Tokyo metropolitan area. The reason was twofold: first, to verify that Japanese aircraft were being kept on the ground in compliance with the cease-fire terms; and second, to determine whether the fields were in good enough condition to handle the heavily laden Allied transports that would help bring in the first occupation troops. On paper the mission seemed straightforward: the four B-32s were to cross the assigned recon area at 20,000 feet and two miles apart, following parallel flight lines that ran directly east and west. When they finished "mowing the lawn," they would begin the return leg to Okinawa. The 1,900-mile round trip—roughly equivalent to a flight from Los Angeles to Seattle and back—would take eight to ten hours if all went well.

As soon as his B-32 was airborne and in her own climbing turn, Anderson headed toward Klein's Dominator, clearly visible ahead, the already bright morning sun glinting off the lead bomber's un-camouflaged aluminum skin. The two other aircraft soon joined up, and in loose echelon formation the four B-32s began a gradual climb toward their cruising altitude and pointed their noses toward Tokyo.

AT THAT SAME MOMENT, some 900 miles to the northeast of Yontan, Emperor Hirohito and his senior advisers were most probably wondering if another Japanese city—perhaps even Tokyo itself—would soon disappear beneath a roiling mushroom cloud.

Hirohito had been under no illusion that his August 15 radio address announcing the decision to surrender would be immediately accepted by all senior members of the government and the military, yet even he was shocked by the events that unfolded in the hours and days following the broadcast. The announcement had sparked an army-led coup intended to reverse the emperor's surrender order, and naval and air units at various points around the country were still in open revolt, vowing to fight on to the last man. Should such pointless and ultimately futile military action convince the Allies that Hirohito was unable to enforce his surrender decision or, worse, that his government's agreement to the Allied ultimatum was simply a delaying tactic meant to give Japan more time to organize its defense against an Allied invasion, the consequences for Hirohito's much-diminished empire could well be catastrophic.

AMONG THOSE DIEHARDS ABOUT whom Hirohito should have been most worried were several of the finest fighter pilots in the Imperial Japanese Navy. On the morning of August 18 the men—members of the elite Kokutai (Air Group) based at Yokosuka, just twenty-four miles south of the emperor's Tokyo palace—had agreed to commit mutiny for the second time in as many days.

The Yokosuka Kokutai's primary purpose by this point in the war was the development and testing of naval aircraft, which meant that among its members were some of the most experienced, talented, and successful pilots in what was left of Japan's naval air service. As a result, the unit was also tasked with aiding in the air defense of the greater Tokyo–Yokohama region. Over the preceding months the Yokosuka Kokutai pilots had joined in the fierce defense of the east-central part of their homeland against the hordes of American B-29 Superfortress bombers and Allied land- and carrier-based strike aircraft that had been systematically reducing the military facilities, harbors, industrial centers, and key cities of eastern Honshu to smoking rubble.

The willingness of the Yokosuka Kokutai pilots to launch themselves continually at the overwhelming numbers of enemy aircraft appearing daily, and nightly, over their nation implies a level of patriotic dedication verging on fanaticism—and Hirohito's August 15 announcement of his decision to surrender to the Allies did little to dampen that nationalistic and professional fervor. Despite official orders from Imperial Japanese Navy headquarters to cease attacks on Allied aircraft, many of the Yokosuka Kokutai pilots felt—as did other army and navy aviators elsewhere in Japan—that the nation's airspace should remain inviolate until a formal surrender document had actually been signed. That belief had led several Yokosuka pilots to attack the B-32s engaged on the August 17 mission, and the passage of twenty-four hours had done nothing to cool their martial zeal. They were ready once again to disobey direct orders and punish any Allied airmen who came within range.

ALTHOUGH THEY COULD NOT have known of the political turmoil in Tokyo or the mood of the Yokosuka Kokutai pilots, the men aboard the Dominators winging ever closer to the coast of Honshu on August 18 were only too aware of the mission's potential for disaster. Most had seen enough combat in the past months to have an inherent, visceral distrust of their enemy, an emotion validated in their minds by details revealed at the morning's preflight briefing of the Japanese fighter attacks on the B-32s involved in the previous day's mission. Adding to the airmen's underlying unease was the fact that their own defenses had been reduced by half; about five hours after that morning's takeoff from Yontan two of the Dominators had aborted the mission due to mechanical problems and returned to Okinawa. Adding insult to injury, both Klein's aircraft and *Hobo Queen II* were dealing with balky turrets and inoperable guns.

Sadly, the mission would ultimately play itself out in ways that would exceed even the most pessimistic crewmember's fears. Before the day ended there would be one last desperate air combat between Americans and Japanese. That combat would come perilously close to reigniting a war that seemed all but over and a young man would quietly bleed to death in the bright, clear skies above Tokyo, in the process gaining the dubious distinction of being the last American killed in air combat in World War II.

CHAPTER 1

SON AND GUNNER

THE AMERICAN AIRMAN WHO would suffer most from the decision to send B-32s back over Tokyo despite the August 17 fighter attacks was born almost exactly twenty years earlier—on August 12, 1925—in Pottstown, Pennsylvania.

Anthony James Marchione, or Tony, as he was always known to family and friends, was in many ways the embodiment of the millions of young Americans who left their homes and families to serve in the nation's armed forces in World War II. Indeed, Tony's personal history—a loving, all-American son of immigrant parents who grew up in a small town, dreaming of a career as a musician until war drew him far from home—might make him seem almost like a caricature of the clean-cut, self-effacing, and resolutely brave servicemen portrayed in the scores of rousingly patriotic movies made during the early 1940s.

Yet, by all accounts Tony Marchione was exactly the fine, up-standing young man that he appeared to be. And much of the credit for that rightly goes to his parents, who themselves traveled far from their childhood homes to make a new life in the New World.

ITALY IN THE EARLY twentieth century was a land of widespread economic inequality, with the northern parts of the country vastly better off in most respects than the central and southern regions.

7

The nation's population was growing rapidly, and many people emigrated to avoid what they saw as a future of crushing poverty. Among those who made the momentous decision to leave their ancestral homes for the promise of a better life abroad were two young people from the Abruzzo region on Italy's Adriatic coast: Raffaelle Marchione and Emelia Ciancaglini. Though born in the same week of June 1897 and in villages only nine miles apart—he in San Buono and she in Scerni—the young man and woman who would become Tony Marchione's parents never knew each other in Italy.[1]

Raffaelle was the first to arrive in America, sailing into New York harbor on September 30, 1913, aboard the SS *Ancona*. He was just sixteen, and spent his first few years living with his older brother, Nicola, who had already established himself in the sprawling Little Italy section of New York City. America's 1917 entry into World War I prompted Nicola to join the Army and Ralph, as he was now known, followed his brother into that service in January 1918. Assigned to the Army Medical Department, Ralph served in France before being honorably discharged in October 1919. After leaving the Army the young man settled in Pottstown, where he lived with a cousin while apprenticing as a shoemaker.

It may well have been in a shoe-repair shop that Ralph first met Emelia. The young woman had arrived at the port of Philadelphia in May 1921 on the SS *Taormina*, and was met by an aunt and uncle who lived in Pottstown. It was while staying with them that she first encountered Ralph. The two obviously hit it off, for they were married in the city's St. Aloysius Roman Catholic church on June 25, 1922. The newlyweds settled in the heavily Italian south end of Pottstown, and Ralph continued to work for other people until he was able to open an independent shop in the mid-1930s. By that time the couple had three children—Tony; Theresa (Terry), born in 1927; and Geraldine (Gerry), born in 1932.

At about the same time that Ralph opened his own shop—Peoples' Shoe Repair on High Street—he and Emelia bought a modest three-level rowhouse at 558 King Street in central Pottstown. The rhythms of life in the Marchione household were dictated by work—six days a week in the shop for Ralph, every day in the home for Emelia—and school for Tony and his sisters. The elder Marchiones were devout Roman Catholics; though they sent their children to public schools, they ensured that Tony and the girls went to catechism at St. Aloysius on Saturday mornings and to Mass on Sundays. The family didn't have a car when the children were young, so parents and children walked wherever they needed to go.

The 1930s were economically challenging for most American families, and the Marchiones—like many others—lived frugally. Ralph had a backyard garden in which he grew tomatoes and peppers, and when the season was right Emelia would can the produce for later use. In addition to her long hours cooking and cleaning, Tony's mother also made a few extra dollars by knitting socks at home for a local company. She turned the heels by hand, and was paid for every pair she completed. Despite her workload and family responsibilities, Emelia maintained what her children later remembered as a generally cheerful disposition, singing Italian songs at the top of her lungs while she worked. Nor were songs the only Italian heard in the home—unlike Ralph, whose time in the Army and work in the shop had allowed him to become fluent in English, Emelia was far more comfortable in her native tongue and generally spoke Italian to both her husband and her children.

As the only son and oldest child in a traditional Italian-American family, Tony was doted on by his parents. This could have been a recipe for disaster, in that many children in similar situations grow up self-centered and spoiled, but Tony was devoted to Ralph and Emelia and by all accounts did all he could to ease their hard lives. He would often scrub the floors in the home so that his mother wouldn't have to do it, and from the age of fourteen he worked after school at a local bakery to earn the family a little extra money. He occasionally brought home leftover desserts, a trait that endeared him to his sisters.

Fortunately for their hardworking parents—and likely because of the loving and nurturing atmosphere Ralph and Emelia created in the home—Tony and his sisters got along well together. Eighteen months older than Terry and five years older than Gerry, Tony was an easygoing and supportive brother. Although he took his family responsibilities seriously, he was always ready with a smile or a joke and would often pull out his trumpet to play Terry and Gerry new tunes he'd heard on the radio.

Music was a huge part of Tony's life. He'd started taking trumpet lessons while in elementary school, and by the time he entered Pottstown Senior High School as a sophomore in 1940 he was so accomplished with his horn that in addition to playing in the school orchestra he was asked to join the swing band made up almost entirely of juniors and seniors.[2] The group played at school dances and during halftime at football games. Tony and a few of the others also got the occasional paid "gig" at local churches and, in the summer, at Pottstown's community swimming pool.

It was as a high school junior that Tony discovered another creative outlet. An average student in most subjects, he excelled in drafting and mechanical drawing. Having designed a built-in bookshelf for the family home as part of a school assignment, Tony went on to a considerably more ambitious project: he drew up the complete plans for opening up an enclosed stairway in the King Street house by taking out most of a non-load-bearing wall and replacing it with a mahogany handrail and white balusters.

Tony's skill with the drafting pen apparently grew from some innate creative ability, for he was also something of an artist. He occasionally worked with watercolors but his preferred medium was simple graphite. His pencil sketches of people, objects, and landscapes decorated his school workbooks and were pinned to the walls of his bedroom. The understanding of scale and perspective that he'd acquired in his drafting classes stood him in good stead in his drawing, as it did when he became interested in photography during his senior year. Tony characteristically immersed himself in all aspects of the art form, including the technical: he was fascinated by cameras and their mechanical components.

Tony graduated from high school in June 1943, some two months shy of his eighteenth birthday. While he had hopes of ultimately becoming a professional musician, he knew—as did every young and healthy male leaving high school that summer—that his personal plans would have to wait. The United States had been at war for sixteen months and Tony was certain to be drafted after he turned eighteen. Rather than attempt to launch himself into further schooling or a career that would certainly be interrupted before it had truly begun, Tony took a full-time job at the Pottstown factory of the Doehler-Jarvis Corporation. The metal-castings manufacturer produced shell casings and other military matériel, and offered decent wages for workers willing to undertake twelve-hour shifts.

Tony stayed on the assembly line as summer turned to fall, waiting for the letter that would change his life. But as he waited he also considered his options. He knew that as a draftee he would have no say in the type of duty, or even the branch of service, to which he'd be assigned. Although he was happy to serve his country, he had no great desire to undertake that service as an infantryman or sailor, and he knew that the only way of avoiding either of those possibilities was to enlist before his draft notice arrived. He'd always been fascinated by airplanes and the technical aspects of aviation, so on November 20, 1943, he did what must have seemed the logical thing: he joined the U.S. Army Air Forces.

RALPH AND EMELIA MARCHIONE were understandably devastated by their only son's decision to enlist, but they understood his motivations. His sisters were proud and supportive, and when it came time for Tony to report for induction the whole family saw him off at the Pottstown railway station.

Tony's first stop was New Cumberland Army Air Field, some sixty miles west of Pottstown and just south of Harrisburg. It was a brief stay, however, for after only a few days of initial processing—which included a basic physical, a host of inoculations, and the assignment of Army serial number 33834700—he and several hundred other young men left the snow-covered post aboard a train bound for a much warmer location, Miami Beach, Florida. Their ultimate destination was officially known as USAAF Technical Training Command Basic Training Center Number 4, and upon his arrival Tony was assigned to Flight X-202 of the 409th Training Group. Over the following four months he and his fellow trainees were introduced to the Army way of doing things, from how to march in formation to how to field strip and fire the standard M1 Garand rifle. This first taste of military life was probably as jarring and as challenging for Tony as it is for most everyone who goes through basic training, but the few records that survive from this period in his life indicate that the young man from Pottstown adapted quickly and did well.

Tony may have harbored hopes of becoming a pilot, but for reasons that are now lost to history the USAAF apparently had other plans for him. Upon completion of his training in Miami Beach he was transferred to the 569th Signal Aircraft Warning Battalion at Drew Army Air Field near Tampa. As its designation indicates, the 569th's mission was to locate and identify enemy aircraft in combat zones using mobile ground-based radar systems. The unit had been established just a few months before Tony joined it, and the logical assumption is that he had been tapped for training as either a radar operator or some sort of technician. The surviving records don't clearly indicate the nature of his assignment with the 569th, yet we can be certain that Tony wasn't pleased with it. For some reason—most probably because watching aircraft on a radar screen was not his idea of aviation—just weeks after arriving at Drew Field Tony volunteered for a job that would definitely allow him to fly: he signed up to be an aerial gunner.

As America's participation in World War II progressed, the Army Air Forces fielded thousands of light, medium, and heavy bombers of various types, and all of them carried defensive machine guns. These weapons were mounted in power-operated, manned turrets (except on the B-29, which used remotely operated turrets) and on flexible, hand-held mounts. The AAF had opened its first flexible gunnery school in 1941 at Las Vegas Army Airfield, and by 1944 it and six other installations were turning out a collective average of 3,000 gunners a month. Because gun turrets were of necessity small and cramped spaces, enlisted gunners could be no more than six feet tall and weigh no more than 180 pounds. Prospective gunners also had to possess excellent eye-hand coordination and have a high level of mechanical aptitude in order to care for their guns and the turret systems.[3] At five feet six inches and 125 pounds, Tony Marchione certainly met the physical requirements, and we can assume that his scores on the standard mechanical-aptitude tests were equally sufficient because he was accepted for instruction and transferred to the 38th Flexible Gunnery Training Group at Tyndall Army Airfield in Panama City, Florida.

Tyndall's location on the Florida panhandle made it an ideal aerial gunnery training installation, in that the Gulf of Mexico afforded vast stretches of open water that could be used as machine-gun ranges. The first class of students began training in February 1942, and by the time of Tony's arrival in mid-1944 the process for producing qualified and capable aerial gunners had evolved into a six-week, 290-hour mix of academic and practical instruction.

Every day that the prospective gunners spent at Tyndall, except Sundays, began in the same way—with an hour of physical training meant to ensure that the young men were fit enough to handle the rigors of aerial combat. Early on in their training they were also tested for their ability to work at high altitudes, an evaluation that was carried out in Tyndall's low-pressure chamber. The men filed into the air-tight enclosure in small groups, put on demand-flow oxygen masks,[4] and then sat, unmoving, until the pressure within the chamber replicated the conditions they would experience at 35,000 to 38,000 feet. They were then told to take off their masks in order to familiarize themselves with the first signs of hypoxia, or oxygen starvation; within minutes they would be unable to perform even simple tasks, and instructors often had to help them put their masks back on. Any man who had obvious difficulty dealing with the altitude—whether it was severe sinus, ear, or vision problems, or an inability to come to grips with the sensations involved—was immediately dropped from the gunner-training program and transferred to other, nonflying duties.

Those men who passed the altitude tests—including Tony Marchione—went on to learn the nuts and bolts of their new profession, beginning with in-depth study of what would soon be the primary tool of their trade: the Browning M2 .50-caliber heavy machine gun. Over the course of forty-one hours of classroom instruction the trainees studied every aspect of the M2's design and construction, memorizing the nomenclature, location, and function of every one of the machine gun's parts. They learned the different types of ammunition the weapon could fire—including ball, tracer, armor-piercing, and incendiary—and how to clean and maintain the eighty-three-pound gun. Most important, the would-be gunners repeatedly practiced how to tear the weapon down and reassemble it, a process known as "stripping." There were two methods the men had to master. The first, detail stripping, involved the disassembly of every removable piece of the weapon and would normally be done only when the ".50-cal" was to be thoroughly cleaned. In the second method, field stripping, the trainees removed only the parts required to discover the source of a given malfunction.[5] Given that the latter operation might have to be done in the dark and at altitudes that would require the gunner to wear cold-weather gear, the trainees had to learn to field strip and reassemble the M2 while wearing a blindfold and heavy flying gloves.[6]

Though learning the mechanics of the machine gun was important, of course, being able to put the weapon to effective use against the enemy was ultimately the only reason for a gunner's presence on an aircraft. Tony and his fellow trainees at Tyndall were therefore taught the science of air-to-air gunnery in a series of cumulative steps, beginning with classroom instruction in the physics of projectiles. This covered such topics as how a bullet's trajectory is affected by gravity and air density, by the speed and orientation of the aircraft from which it is fired, and by the relative speed and position of the target aircraft. The trainees learned how to estimate a target's speed, range, and direction of flight, and learned to hit a target by using the techniques of deflection shooting—the way in which the gunner must "lead" the target by firing at a point ahead of, below, or above it, depending on circumstances. To aid them in the sighting process the gunners-to-be also learned how to use and maintain a variety of optical and mechanical gunsights.

All of this theoretical instruction was put into practice on Tyndall's ground gunnery ranges. After being introduced to and mastering stationary skeet shooting with shotguns (in order to hone their eye-hand coordination), the trainees progressed to shooting at clay pigeons launched from the backs of moving trucks. They then moved on to firing BB guns at carnival-type moving target enclosures, and used electronic "guns" to fire at motion picture images of attacking aircraft projected on a screen. During the third week of training they graduated from "peashooters" to the real thing, firing .50-caliber machine guns first at standing paper targets, then at aircraft-shaped targets moving across the width of the range atop poles attached to pulleys or vehicles. During this phase they fired both from flexible mounts and from a variety of aircraft gun turrets mounted on wooden platforms—turrets that they also had to learn to maintain and repair. In their last week at Tyndall Tony and the other trainee gunners finally got to take to the air, firing from the rear seats of AT-6 Texan dual-place trainers at target sleeves pulled—usually at a safe distance—behind other aircraft. Then, after passing a series of comprehensive examinations that evaluated not only their weapon knowledge and skill but also such other vital abilities as aircraft recognition and combat first aid, the trainees became full-fledged MOS (Military Occupational Skill) 611 aerial gunners, their new incarnation denoted by the silver wings awarded to each man at the graduation ceremony.

That ceremony was a hugely important waypoint in Tony's young life, of course, and he marked it by buying a postcard he intended to send to his parents. Purchased at Tyndall's small post exchange, the card carried a bit of rhyme that expressed the pride and esprit de corps that Tony and his fellow newly minted gunners felt. Titled "A Gunner's Vow," it read:

> *I wished to be a pilot,*
> *And you along with me.*
> *But if we all were pilots*
> *Where would the Air Force be?*
> *It takes GUTS to be a GUNNER,*
> *To sit out in the tail*
> *When the Messerschmitts are coming*

> *And the slugs begin to wail.*
> *The pilot's just a chauffeur,*
> *It's his job to fly the plane,*
> *But it's WE who do the fighting,*
> *Though we may not get the fame.*
> *If we all must be Gunners*
> *Then let us make this bet:*
> *We'll be the best damn Gunners*
> *That have left this station yet.*

As it turned out, Tony was able to deliver the card in person, for he was granted "leave en route" to his next assignment and was able to spend a few days at home in Pottstown. He was welcomed joyously by his parents and sisters, and spent most of the precious few days with his family. He taught Gerry the Army Air Forces song and how to jitterbug, the latter a skill he'd apparently picked up during his off-duty hours at Tyndall. His leave ended all too quickly, and at the end of the week Ralph left sixteen-year-old Terry in charge of the shoe shop and he and Emelia boarded the local train to Philadelphia with Tony. At the city's main terminal they bade farewell to their son, who then boarded a train bound for a place none of the Marchiones had ever been: Arizona.

Like all newly minted aerial gunners, Tony's next assignment was to a combat crew training school where he would integrate his skills with those of other airmen before they all shipped out for overseas duty. In his case the school was located at Davis-Monthan Army Air Field, just outside Tucson. Run by the 233rd Army Air Forces Base Unit, part of the 16th Bombardment Operational Training Wing, the 223rd was dedicated exclusively to forming and training ten-man replacement crews for the Consolidated B-24 Liberator bomber. The pilot, copilot, navigator, and bombardier were officers whereas the others—the flight engineer/top turret gunner; the nose, tail, and ball (belly) turret gunners; and two waist gunners—were enlisted men. All members of the crew had already qualified in their respective skills, and it was during the ninety-day combat crew training that they learned to work and fight as a team.

Upon his arrival at Davis-Monthan Field Tony was assigned to a crew headed by lanky, twenty-three-year-old Second Lieutenant Robert W. Essig. The Iowa-born pilot had played semipro baseball before entering the service, and his approach to both flying and leadership was professional and competent, but relaxed. Tony eventually wrote home to his parents that Essig was "the best doggone pilot in the country" and a "top-notch leader," and that "every member of the crew would stick by him till the very end." Tony also wrote glowingly about three crewmates with whom he became fast friends, fellow gunners Raymond Zech, Rudolph Nudo, and Frank Pallone.[7]

It was a good thing that the men of Essig's crew bonded so well and so quickly, because the training they underwent at Davis-Monthan was intense. Given the nature of the air war in both the European and Pacific theaters, much of that training focused on high-altitude, long-distance formation flying, initially in groups of two to four aircraft and later in twelve-plane "squadron box" formations. The B-24s flew practice missions that lasted eight to ten hours, during which they would drop live bombs on target ranges and undertake formation evasive action against simulated enemy air attack. These flights also offered Tony and the other gunners the opportunity to coordinate their responses to incoming fighters—usually portrayed by war-weary P-40 Warhawks—by alerting each other to the "enemy" plane's changing position as it zoomed into and through the B-24 formation.

All of the training that Bob Essig and his men underwent at Davis-Monthan was intended to turn them into a first-rate B-24 bomber crew that could undertake combat missions immediately upon arrival in an overseas theater. Throughout their training Essig and his men had been told that they would ultimately be assigned to a bomb group of Major General Nathan F. Twining's Italy-based Fifteenth Air Force, a possibility that was especially pleasing to Tony, Rudy Nudo, and Frank Pallone, all of whom still had relatives in the "old country." But on December 16, 1944, a few days after the crew completed training at Davis-Monthan and while they were awaiting orders for overseas movement to Italy, the plans changed abruptly.[8] As Tony later described it:

It was getting late in the morning and the sun was getting hotter by the minute. The enlisted men of the crew were just getting out of their sacks after a late-morning nap. We didn't have anything to do now since we were waiting for our final orders to ship out. We all knew that our training here in the U.S. had been completed and that we were headed overseas for the big fight . . . we just wanted to get in the fight, for the sooner we got there the sooner this damn war would be over, according to us. One thing each one of us was sweating out was whether we were going to get a furlough to see our families and girl friends before we left.

Just then Bob [Essig] comes walking in our barracks dressed to kill. He had his pinks [officer's dress uniform] on and they were as neat as could be, with creases in his pants as sharp as a knife.

"Well fellows, I have some bad news for you." As he said this he looked as if he had just lost his best friend. "A special order has just been handed to me stating that five crews have been chosen for advanced training. They want each one of those five crews to report to Will Rogers Field to become a photo-reconnaissance crew. We happen to be one of those five. As to the length of our training, no one knows. . . . There's nothing we can do about it. We have until the 25th to report there. Yes, Christmas Day we must be there ready to start school."[9]

This last-minute change of plans was understandably upsetting for Tony and the other members of his crew. They had just completed three months of training to drop bombs on the enemy, not to take his picture. And while they were pleased to learn that they would have nine free days before they had to report to Will Rogers Field in Oklahoma City, they were more than a little dismayed that they wouldn't be able to actually spend Christmas with their loved ones. Moreover, the young airmen would not be traveling home on official government orders—those would only cover their move from Davis-Monthan directly to their new duty station—so if they chose to go home during the furlough period they would not get any sort of railway priority. In Tony's case it could therefore take up to three days to make the train journey from Tucson to Pottstown, and at least two days to get from Pennsylvania to Will Rogers.

It must have seemed like a journey worth making, despite the brevity of the visit, for Tony did take a train home. He and the family celebrated an early Christmas—not realizing, of course, that it would be the last one they would all spend together—and after only a few days in Pottstown Tony hopped a westbound Pullman headed for Oklahoma City. It wasn't an especially enjoyable trip; the young aerial gunner got "bumped" from the train at least once so that his seat could be given to a serviceman traveling on permanent-change-of-station orders. Tony nevertheless reported to Will Rogers Field on time, and ate his Christmas dinner in a mess hall with Nudo, Pallone, and several hundred other GIs.

Essig's crew—minus the bombardier, who wouldn't be needed in the new role—was assigned to Will Rogers' Combat Crew Training Station-Photo-Reconnaissance and began instruction on December 27 as Crew 86. Although the aircraft they flew during their time in Oklahoma outwardly resembled the machine they had flown at Davis-Monthan, it differed in several significant ways. Designated the F-7A, the recon version of the standard B-24J retained its full defensive armament but carried no bombs. The aircraft's forward bomb bay was fitted with long-range fuel tanks and its aft bomb bay was sealed shut to create a workspace for an aerial photographer. This section was provided with a heater, not for the comfort of the crew but to maintain a constant temperature for the two vertical cameras mounted to shoot through small windows cut into the sealed bay doors. A three-camera "trimetrogon" system intended to capture overlapping images was installed in the former bombardier's position in the nose, and was also fixed to shoot through small windows in the aircraft's lower fuselage.

Though already a trained heavy bomber crew by the time they arrived at Will Rogers, the different requirements of photo-reconnaissance work meant that Essig and his men had to further sharpen some of their existing skills. Because photo-recon aircraft almost always flew alone, rather than in large formations, the navigator had to be particularly accurate in his calculations. Likewise,

Essig and his copilot, Second Lieutenant John Ziegler, had to be extremely good at instrument flying, both to get the airplane to and from the target area and to keep it on a precise course during the photo run, no matter how bad the conditions might be. The fact that the aircraft would not have the protection afforded by the mutually supportive fires of a combat box formation meant that the gunners would have to be that much better at locating, identifying, and successfully engaging hostile aircraft. In addition to that vital task, Tony Marchione, Ray Zech, Rudy Nudo, and Frank Pallone were also trained as photographer assistants, learning such new skills as how to attach the cameras to their mounts and how to load and change film magazines. Although the actual operation of the cameras would be the responsibility of the aerial photographer—who would join the crew upon its arrival in the combat zone—Tony was particularly interested in the cameras and their capabilities.

Essig and his crew spent nearly three months at Will Rogers Field, and their "final exam" was a complex photo-mapping mission that took them from Oklahoma to Colorado and back. Their "target" was the area around Denver's Lowry Army Airfield—the primary training station for AAF aerial photographers—which they "shot" from an altitude of 20,000 feet. Having successfully completed that mission and all of their assigned course work, Essig and his men were rated as "fully prepared" for their work as a photo-recon crew. In late March they received orders to report to Hunter Army Airfield in Georgia, a processing center for replacement crews bound for overseas units.

Despite the rigorous training at Will Rogers that had obviously kept Tony extremely busy, he apparently found time for romance, as evidenced by a poem he wrote during the train trip from Oklahoma to Georgia.

> *While riding along in this weary train,*
> *thoughts of memories run through my brain.*
> *A thought, a poem, it's not very much,*
> *just to remind me of your sweet touch.*
> *When we were together I never could talk,*

but always wanted to go for a walk.
You've put a new world in my mind,
and that's the world I want to find.
The stars that shine in these dark skies,
remind me of your large, blue eyes.
Your little manners are very sweet,
your little, soft voice cannot be beat.
There's a little too much to tell you, Jo,
a lot more things that we all know.
Just how you walk and fix your hose,
The way you smile and turn your nose.[10]

These few, earnest lines provide us a rare glimpse into Tony Marchione's emotional life. By this point he was, of course, a trained Army Air Forces aerial gunner bound for the war that he felt it was his duty to help fight. But he was also a young man of just nineteen, and it is quite apparent that the girl he speaks of—her full name is lost to history, as is the story of how they met—had touched his life in a real and meaningful way. Thoughts of the "girl he left behind" and of the promise that a future with her might hold have sustained many a young man as he went off to war; we can assume that thoughts of the young woman named Jo buoyed Tony as he set out on a journey from which he knew he might not return.

WHEN BOB ESSIG AND his men arrived at Hunter Field they were still under the impression that they were headed for the Mediterranean or, perhaps, England. They were soon disabused of that notion, however, for they were assigned as a replacement crew for the 20th Combat Mapping Squadron, a unit then stationed "somewhere in the Southwest Pacific," most often a euphemism for Australia or the Philippines.

After only a few days in Georgia the young aviators were back on a train, this time headed west to Utah's Kearns Army Air Base. Located some seven miles southwest of Salt Lake City, the installation had been a B-24 training center until mid-1943, when most of its aircraft were transferred to other stations. By the time Tony and his fellow crewmembers arrived in early April 1945 Kearns's main tenant organization was the Army Air Forces Overseas Replacement Depot (West), which handled the processing and onward movement of personnel destined for the Pacific and Far East. Essig and his men remained at the rather austere base for just over two weeks, during which time they received yet another physical exam followed by inoculations meant to protect them against a bewildering array of tropical illnesses. They were also told to completely update their next-of-kin information and confirm the beneficiaries for their GI life insurance.

Surviving records do not indicate how Tony and his fellow aviators made the journey from Utah to the Pacific, though the standard method was by troopship or converted ocean liner from one of the two main West Coast ports of embarkation, Seattle or San Francisco. Vessels bound for the Southwest Pacific and Far East normally called at Pearl Harbor to refuel—without allowing the embarked troops ashore—then traveled on to Sydney, Australia. Upon arrival there the replacement aircrews assigned to the Far East or India would board another ship bound for their ultimate destination; in contrast, by early 1945 the men headed for New Guinea, the Philippines, or adjacent island areas would most often be transported by train to northern Queensland to board C-47 Skytrain troop carriers for the final leg of their long trans-Pacific journey. For Bob Essig's crew that journey ended at Clark Field on Luzon, where they joined the 20th Combat Mapping Squadron by the middle of May.

Organized at Colorado Springs Army Air Base in July 1942, the 20th had deployed to the Southwest Pacific in December 1943 as part of the 6th Photographic Group and initially operated from Nadzab, New Guinea, flying F-7As. Early combat operations revealed several flaws in that initial photo-recon variant of the B-24, however, most notably that the center, vertical camera in the trimetrogon installation in the nose was inadequately protected against jarring and had to be carefully realigned before each flight. Moreover, the presence of the bow turret, and the gunner's need to move to and from it, made for such crowded conditions in the nose compartment that changing the three camera film magazines was extremely difficult.

The 20th Combat Mapping Squadron noted these shortcomings in a detailed report—as did several other units operating the F-7A—and by July 1944 the unit began receiving the upgraded F-7B. This variant grouped the trimetrogon system in the rear bomb bay with the other cameras, a change that greatly increased the success rate of photo-recon and aerial mapping missions, and within a few months virtually all of the squadron's F-7s were B models.

In April 1945 the 20th received the first of an eventual five F-7Bs equipped with the AN/APS-15 ground-mapping radar system, widely referred to as H2X and "Mickey," which had been developed from the British H2S set as a way to allow accurate bombing through cloud cover and at night. The retractable dome enclosing the radar's antenna replaced the F-7B's ball turret, and a radar repeater in the aircraft's camera bay allowed crews to take photographs of the images of ground locations. The ultimate purpose of this arrangement was to allow the images to be passed on to H2X-equipped bomber units to help them better identify those targets when they appeared on their radar screens, though in practice the 20th Combat Mapping Squadron used its Mickey systems mainly to locate and map targets at night or in bad weather.

It is likely that Bob Essig and his crew had received at least some H2X training while at Will Rogers Field, because they were tapped to fly their first "Mickey" mission soon after joining the squadron. The purpose of the flight was to photo map more than a dozen Japanese positions in and around the Balete Pass in central Luzon, about sixty-five miles northeast of Clark Field. Highway 5, the two-lane road that snaked over the 3,000-foot-high pass, was the only route between Central Luzon and the strategically important Cagayan Valley. The pass had therefore been the scene of continuous, bitter fighting since U.S. and Filipino forces had launched the battle for Luzon the previous January.

Essig and his crew, augmented by aerial photographer Staff Sergeant Hunter, took off on the morning of June 1 in F-7B 44-41943. The short distance to the target area did not make the flight any less challenging, for the presence of significant enemy anti-aircraft defenses around the pass dictated frequent changes of course and altitude in order to secure the required images without getting shot up in the process. And although few Japanese fighters were still active over Luzon by that point in the war, Tony Marchione and his fellow gunners had to maintain their vigilance throughout the multi-hour flight. There was no enemy opposition, fortunately, and Tony's first combat mission ended with the aircraft's safe return to Clark Field just before sundown.[11]

Essig's crew was not assigned a specific aircraft, and the area-familiarization and radar-training missions they undertook over the following weeks were flown in various F-7Bs. But flying was not the only thing Tony and his crewmates did at Clark Field. The men were all assigned what the military calls "collateral duties," which for an officer might entail serving as squadron morale or recreation officer or managing the inventory of a deceased airman's possessions before they were sent to his next of kin. The nonflying tasks for Tony and his fellow gunners included such things as working in the machine-gun maintenance shed and standing airplane guard duty. This latter task, as its name implies, required enlisted men from all of the squadron's crews to undertake rotating four-hour shifts at night guarding the flight line to prevent sabotage or the theft of equipment.

On June 15 the broadening of the unit's mission from combat mapping to photographic and radar reconnaissance resulted in a change of designation. From that point on the unit was known by the admittedly accurate but decidedly unwieldy title 20th Reconnaissance Squadron, Long Range, Photo-RCM (for "radar countermeasures"), or 20th Recon Squadron, for short.

Four days after the designation change Bob Essig and his crew flew their second H2X combat sortie. The mission was to be far more challenging than the Balete Pass operation, in that the target areas were on the Chinese coast. Both were port cities: Swatow, 174 miles northeast of Hong Kong, and Amoy, another 125 miles farther up the Taiwan Strait.[12] The mission objective—to capture pictures and H2X images of the port facilities and their air defenses—would require a 1,500-mile round-trip flight. The aircraft assigned was the same F-7B used on the Balete Pass flight, and a Staff Sergeant Frasher was tapped as the aerial photographer for the mission.

Bob Essig lifted the F-7B off from Clark Field just after dawn and set a course to the northwest. The first leg of the flight took the aircraft out over the western edge of Lingayen Gulf, just east of Santiago Island. From that point there was nothing but water for some 600 miles, and there was little for Tony and his fellow gunners to do but continually scan the surrounding skies for any sign of enemy fighters. There were none, and the only evidence of hostile action was some inaccurate anti-aircraft fire far below the F-7B as it made landfall just south of the first target, the port at Swatow. Complete cloud cover over the area made it impossible for Frasher to take any photos, but the crew was able to get some usable H2X images. After completing a series of runs over the port facilities Essig turned the F-7B back toward the sea, and once about twenty miles offshore turned to the northeast for the 120-mile leg to Amoy. The weather was no better over the second target, however, and after Frasher captured some H2X imagery Essig banked the aircraft for home. The F-7B landed safely at Clark Field ten hours and thirty minutes after taking off.

Less than a week after Essig and his crew returned from their second combat mission U.S. forces completed the capture of Okinawa. Within days of that hard-won and costly victory the 20th Recon, like the B-32–equipped 386th Bomb Squadron, received a warning order for a permanent change of station to Yontan Airfield. Before that move took place, however, Tony Marchione and his crewmates would undertake one last mission from Clark Field—one that would prove to be the most difficult yet.

The flight on July 9 was undertaken in another H2X-equipped aircraft, F-7B 44-42028, and differed significantly from the two previous combat flights. The target was the Japanese airdrome at Koshun, Formosa—the same field that the 386th's Dominators had bombed on their third combat-test mission less than a month earlier—and Essig and his crew would be flying the 20th Recon Squadron's first night-photography sortie over enemy territory. The nature of the mission required a few special modifications to the aircraft. The first was the installation of a K-19B night-reconnaissance camera, fitted vertically in the F-7B's aft compartment. The 9-by-9-inch format camera was fitted with a photocell unit that would trip the shutter when an artificial light source illuminated the target. That light source was the fifty-one-pound AN-M46 flash bomb; to carry and drop ten of them, the F-7B's forward bomb bay was unsealed and bomb shackles were reinstalled on one side.

The Army Air Forces had first used night aerial photography in combat during the 1943 Allied invasion of Sicily, and by July 1945 the techniques were well established. The AN-M46 was dropped like a conventional bomb from an altitude of 10,000 to 12,000 feet and a mechanical time fuze detonated it at 3,000 feet. The resultant 700-million-candlepower flash lasted barely a second, but allowed the K-19B to capture an image of an area roughly two miles long by four-and-a-half miles wide. Although the system worked well, there were definite drawbacks from the point of view of the dropping aircraft's crew. The flash bomb was notoriously fragile, and the slightest jarring—such as that caused by turbulence in flight or the nearby explosion of an anti-aircraft round—could render it inoperable. More seriously, the time fuzes were known to be unreliable, and it was not uncommon for the flash bomb to detonate as soon as it left the bomb bay, with all the obvious consequences. And, finally, the fuzes could not be reset in flight, which meant that if the dropping aircraft needed to make repeated passes over the target it had to do so at a fairly constant altitude, making it a sitting duck for ground gunners.

Bob Essig and the men of his crew were undoubtedly aware of these issues, as were the two aerial photographers assigned to the mission, Staff Sergeants Hannagan and Kelsey. There were no problems during the loading of the flash bombs, however, and the F-7B lifted off from Clark Field on schedule just before sundown. The flight to Formosa was also routine, but as the aircraft started its first photo run things started to go sour. Unusually accurate anti-aircraft fire bracketed the F-7B, and when it came time to drop the first AN-M26 the plane's bomb-release system malfunctioned. Four of the flash bombs tumbled from the bomb bay on their own, without arming, dropping harmlessly into the night.

As Tony later described the events in a letter to a friend, the navigator and flight engineer volunteered to drop the remaining six flash bombs by hand.[13] This was a particularly harrowing process. To disconnect the devices from their shackles and pull the arming wires from the fuzes before casting the flash bombs into the night, the men had to stand on the narrow catwalk that bisected the open bomb bay, with no safety line securing them and exposed to the cold wind and the buffeting caused by the ack-ack bursts. And they had to do that more than once, given that the F-7B made repeated runs over the target for nearly an hour, frequently illuminated by Japanese search-lights. Nor did things improve much after Essig turned the aircraft for home. Just after leaving the target area the number one (left out-board) engine caught fire—whether as the result of enemy action or a mechanical malfunction is unclear—and Essig had to shut the engine down and feather the propeller. The F-7B made the remain-der of the journey back to Clark Field on three engines, and landed safely after eight hours and twenty minutes of total flight time.[14]

The men of Essig's crew made it through the difficult mission without injury, but on July 13 Tony Marchione ended up in the Clark Field base hospital with what he described to a friend at home in Pottstown as "a slight case" of hepatitis.

> There's an epidemic of it here on Luzon—it's nothing serious. It's just that you lose your appetite and you're quite sick in your stomach, but that only lasts for a week, and then you're well, but they keep you in [the hospital] for 30 days regardless so they can keep you on a diet. Right now I feel as great as ever, but not a chance of getting out for another two weeks. Not too bad [though], getting plenty of rest and we can go swimming.

Swimming and quiet rest were apparently not the only way Tony and his fellow patients were allowed to pass the time, for they were able to attend a USO show featuring "The Ol' Professor of Swing," band leader Kay Kyser. It was obviously a performance that thrilled the young would-be swing trumpeter:

> [He] put on a great show the other night, wow! . . . He didn't have his band with him, due to his radio show

in the States—think he said Phil Harris or Phil Baker is taking his place during his [USO] tour. He got up a GI band and they were really solid! He did bring 4 of the most beautiful girls along—they had everything, wow! You know Kay is about the best showman of all the big band leaders—he doesn't need a band because he's the whole show.

Then, good son that he was, Tony asked his friend to keep the news of the illness to himself:

Oh, listen, don't mention to anyone that I'm in the hospital, because if you do it's very possible [the news will] get around to my folks and you know how mothers are. They worry over nothing, and especially my mother. Okay? I'll let them know as soon as I get out.[15]

In the letter Tony also wrote something that his friend might well have misunderstood, saying that he wished "to hell" that he could get out of the hospital so he could "put in some combat time." This wasn't false bravado, it was simple pragmatism. Just days after Germany's unconditional surrender in early May 1945 the U.S. War Department implemented a point system to govern the return to the United States and demobilization of Army personnel in Europe. "Rotation points," as they were informally called, were awarded for time in service, years deployed overseas, awards received, total flight hours and combat flight hours, among other things. Those men with at least eighty-five points were the first to be sent home for demobilization, and most U.S. military personnel in the Pacific Theater assumed (rightly, as it turned out), that the same system would be instituted following Japan's surrender. Tony's desire for more combat time was therefore likely no more than a wish to earn as many points as possible as quickly as possible in order to speed his return to Pottstown once the fighting ended.

It was a desire that was soon to have tragic consequences.

THOUGH TONY'S STAY IN the Clark Field base hospital was originally supposed to last thirty days, he was released four days early—on August 9—so he could join his crewmates for the move to Okinawa. The 20th Recon Squadron's headquarters staff and several F-7s had departed for Yontan on August 3, with the remainder of the squadron scheduled to leave Clark Field on August 11. The afternoon before that, however, the base radio station received word of Japan's conditional acceptance of the terms of the Potsdam Declaration. The word spread quickly, and even though it wasn't actual surrender, everyone at Clark—and throughout the Pacific Theater, for that matter—saw the news as a great reason to celebrate. As Tony wrote to another hometown friend:

> We didn't believe it at first, but when [celebratory] flares and ack-ack started to fill the skies and searchlights circled the skies we knew this was it. The GIs went wild. Wow! What a celebration we had. The officers had a barrel of whisky. Can you imagine, feller, a barrel (55 gallons). So the squadron had one big time. We all had to turn our [pistols] in first, tho'. Ya know when the men get tight anything can happen. I didn't drink much because I didn't want to get sick again.[16]

Not overindulging in the whisky was probably a very smart move on Tony's part, for he and the remaining 20th Recon Squadron aircrews and key staff personnel took off from Clark Field on the morning of the eleventh bound for Yontan. For those still suffering from the previous day's merrymaking, the 900-mile flight to Okinawa would certainly have been an unpleasant and painfully long journey.

Though the men of the 20th got right to work once they landed at Yontan, Bob Essig gave Tony permission to take a few hours off on the afternoon of August 12 to observe a milestone—his twentieth birthday. His pals Nudo and Pallone had managed to preserve a bit of the whisky that had flowed on August 10, and the three young

Italian-Americans apparently passed a few enjoyable hours whoop-
ing it up in the tent they shared just off the Yontan flight line.

From that same tent on August 15 Tony wrote to a friend about
his impressions of Okinawa, calling it "beautiful" and "the closest
country I've seen here in the Pacific that reminds me of the U.S."
He also provided a glimpse of how austere life was on the as-yet
uncompleted Yontan base:

> First few days we were here we ate nothing but Spam,
> bully beef & dehydrated foods & it was miserable.
> Today we had fresh pork and potatoes. Boy, that
> really was a treat after those darn rations. . . . Since our
> showers aren't completed as yet we have to walk nearly
> a mile to a creek to bathe—down a mountainside too.
> Also do our own laundry till the squadron laundry is
> operating.

The big news in that August 15 letter, of course, was that the
"happy day has arrived." Tony wrote that Japan's unconditional acceptance that very day of the Allied surrender terms and the ceasefire that had gone into effect throughout the Pacific Theater were
wonderful, but added that he didn't think his chances of getting
back to the States "are very good for a while yet. Think we'll have
to stay over & do some peace time mapping—much to my dislike,
darn it!"

Tony was also aware that the end of hostilities would have other
professional consequences: "Don't think I'll make that rocker [a
fourth stripe indicating promotion to staff sergeant] now that the
war is over. My guess is that ratings will be frozen, but I don't give a
darn. All I want is to be a PFC & I don't mean in the Army."[17] It was
almost certainly Tony's heartfelt desire to be a civilian sooner rather
than later that led him to make what would ultimately turn out to
be the worst decision of his young life.

Following its arrival on Okinawa the 20th Recon Squadron was
tapped to provide personnel for any B-32 mission that had a reconnaissance aspect. Men from Tony's squadron were aboard the

Dominators that conducted the shipping sweeps over the East China Sea and the Korea Strait on August 13–14, and on *The Lady is Fresh* and *Hobo Queen II*, when they were recalled late on the fifteenth. Though the 20th continued to be responsible for providing the necessary personnel for any B-32 reconnaissance flights conducted after the ceasefire announcement, the squadron commander decided to allow men to volunteer to assist the photographers assigned to the mission. Because any flight over Japan would be counted as a combat mission until the actual signing of the surrender document, those who volunteered to take part in the B-32 flights would accrue additional rotation points while not actually running the risk of getting shot at. Moreover, volunteers would have the opportunity to see Japan from the air well before their comrades would step ashore for occupation duty.

As a qualified aerial photographer assistant, Tony Marchione could legitimately boost his rotation points by taking part in a B-32 mission. It must have seemed like an ideal way to increase his chances of a quick return to the United States: he would get combat points for riding along on what promised to be a long but delightfully boring flight. But Tony wasn't a fool; he waited until the August 16 mission over Tokyo went off without any enemy interference before adding his name to the roster of 20th Recon Squadron men offering to take part in a Dominator mission.

On the morning of August 17, well before the four B-32s ran into the hornet's nest over Tokyo, Tony wrote a cheerful, almost whimsical letter to his sister Gerry. Datelined "Somewhere on the Ryukyu Islands," the missive bore no indication that he had any reason to regret his decision. Indeed, after mentioning that censorship of mail would soon be lifted he added that "in the next few days we'll be able to write whatever we please—won't that be great?"

It would be the last letter Tony Marchione ever wrote.

CHAPTER 2

THE SECOND-STRING
SUPER BOMBER

By THE TIME TONY MARCHIONE sat down at a makeshift desk in his tent at Yontan on August 17 to write to his youngest sister, America's participation in the Allied war in the Pacific had lasted three years, eight months, and ten days.[1]

That war had initially not gone well for the United States and its allies, of course. The devastating Japanese attack on Pearl Harbor and other installations on the Hawaiian island of Oahu on December 7, 1941, had been followed by what at the time seemed to be an unending string of defeats throughout Southeast Asia and the western Pacific—the Philippines, French Indochina, British Malaya, and the Netherlands East Indies had all fallen to Japan's seemingly invincible air, sea, and land forces. Even when the tide began to turn in the Allies' favor following the June 1942 Battle of Midway, the road to Tokyo promised to be long, difficult, and bloody.

One of the greatest challenges the Allies faced in the war against Japan was the sheer expanse of what military planners now refer to as the "overall battlespace." For World War II's Pacific Theater was truly vast: it spanned multiple time zones *and* the International Date Line, encompassed some three million square miles of the planet's surface, and even in 1941 was home to more than half of the world's population.

These geographic realities ensured that the Pacific war would of necessity be a maritime struggle; however, since the early 1930s American war planners had clearly understood that military airpower would also play a major role in any conflict with Japan. Unfortunately, at the time of the Pearl Harbor attack the vast majority of U.S. Navy, Marine Corps, and Army aircraft in the Pacific were obsolescent or simply outclassed by the Japanese types they were up against, and American pilots had to make do with what they had until newer and more capable machines became available.

Among the organizations most affected by the initial shortage of suitable aircraft was Major General George C. Kenney's Australia-based U.S. Fifth Air Force. The gruff and plain-spoken Army aviator had arrived in the Land Down Under in July 1942 to take command of the Southwest Pacific Area's Allied Air Forces, an organization that the fifty-two-year-old Kenney quickly determined was "the goddamndest mess you ever saw."[2] With the support of General Douglas MacArthur—who had been given command of the Southwest Pacific Area (SWPA) after his arrival in Australia from the besieged Philippines in March 1942—Kenney had reorganized Allied Air Forces into Fifth Air Force. To further enhance the new organization's operational capabilities, Kenney subdivided it into V Bomber Command and V Fighter Command, with both units receiving procurement, supply, and repair support from Fifth Air Service Command.[3]

Simply activating these organizations did not make them immediately capable of effectively carrying the war to the enemy, however. In the early days of operations from Australia and, later, from New Guinea, Fifth Air Force and its subordinate units faced significant challenges. Kenney initially had to make do with a motley collection of tired and well-worn aircraft—among them early model B-17 Flying Fortress heavy bombers; A-20 Havoc, B-25 Mitchell, and B-26 Marauder medium bombers; P-39 Aircobra and P-40 Warhawk fighters; and a grab bag of transport types. Indeed, the operational and environmental challenges Fifth Air Force faced in its earliest days initially made its designation as the Allies' main offensive air arm in SWPA more an aspiration than a reality.

As the war in the Pacific progressed, however, Kenney and the "Flying Buccaneers" of Fifth Air Force received newer and more capable aircraft, replacing their original B-17 bombers with longer-ranged B-24s, and fielding P-38 Lightning and P-47 Thunderbolt fighters in lieu of the increasingly outmoded P-39s and P-40s. All of these aircraft types were put to good use supporting the Allied advance northward from Australia, in New Guinea in 1943 and 1944 and the Philippines in 1944 and 1945.

In June 1945—a month after the liberation of the Philippines— Kenney was named commander of Far East Air Forces (FEAF); as such, he not only retained control of Fifth Air Force (now commanded by his former deputy, Major General Ennis C. Whitehead), he gained both the U.S. Thirteenth Air Force and the formerly Hawaii-based Seventh Air Force.[4] Operating from Luzon, Fifth Air Force ranged widely along the coasts of French Indochina, mainland China and over Formosa, as well as undertaking long-distance anti-shipping missions throughout the South China Sea. But Kenney had even bigger things in mind for the entire Far East Air Forces.

The primary goals of the United States' "island-hopping" strategy in the Pacific included securing forward bases from which armadas of new Boeing B-29 Superfortress very heavy bombers could intensify the direct bombardment of the Japanese Home Islands, an assault that began in mid-June 1944 when, from austere bases in China, B-29s of the Twentieth Air Force launched the first U.S. air attack on Japan since the April 1942 Doolittle raid.[5]

While serving as a staff officer at the then–Army Air Corps Materiel Division at Wright Field, Ohio, from 1939 to 1942, George Kenney had been part of the team that developed and refined the design and performance requirements for the Very Long Range bomber program. Boeing's B-29 was one of the aircraft produced as a result of that program, and its very long range, heavy bomb load, and sophisticated self-defense systems made it immensely attractive to every U.S. Army Air Forces combat commander in the Pacific and Far East. As one historian later expressed it, Kenney "seems to have entertained some belief that [because of his time at the Materiel Division] he enjoyed a personal priority in plans for [the B-29's] use."[6] Whether he held that opinion or not, Kenney, like Douglas MacArthur, firmly believed that the B-29 was ideally suited for operations in the Southwest Pacific, and he continuously and aggressively lobbied for the big bombers to be assigned to him.

Unfortunately, Army Air Forces chief General Henry H. "Hap" Arnold believed that the B-29s would be most effective if they flew from the Mariana Islands rather than the Philippines, and when the logistical difficulties of supporting Superfortress operations from bases in China became overwhelming, Arnold ordered the big bombers moved to fields on the newly captured islands of Saipan, Guam, and Tinian. Kenney, never one to give up a fight easily, continued his adamant lobbying for the B-29s far beyond the point of prudence, in the process angering Arnold so much that he seriously considered relieving the FEAF commander and replacing him with someone less troublesome.

In early March 1945, with the battle for the Philippines essentially over, Kenney decided to travel to Washington. His mission was twofold: first, he wanted to smooth relations with Arnold, who was still recovering from a heart attack he'd suffered several weeks earlier. Second, Kenney wanted to personally examine a bomber that he'd heard might be a decent stand-in for the B-29s he so coveted, but was apparently never going to get. The possible replacement aircraft—the machine with which Kenney hoped to make a significant contribution to the aerial bombardment of Japan so long foreseen in American war planning for the Pacific—was the B-32 Dominator, and Kenney's introduction to it would ultimately have tragic consequences for Tony Marchione.

WHEN GEORGE KENNEY ARRIVED in Washington, D.C., on March 14, 1945, he was a worried man. Before leaving the Philippines he had heard from a trusted aide newly returned from the States that Army Air Forces headquarters was buzzing with rumors regarding Hap Arnold's imminent relief of Kenney because of the latter's constant—and far too vocal—campaigning to receive B-29s.

Understandably concerned that he might be removed from his command before the war in the Pacific was won, Kenney was determined to see Arnold at the earliest opportunity.

An immediate audience with the Army Air Forces chief wasn't forthcoming, however, because Arnold was still recuperating in Florida. Kenney instead made the rounds at the Pentagon, participating on MacArthur's behalf in several high-level meetings pertaining to Operation Downfall, the planned Allied two-phase invasion of the Japanese Home Islands. Kenney also checked in with Lieutenant General Barney M. Giles, chief of the Air Staff and the Army Air Forces' deputy commander. The two men had known each other for years, and Giles was characteristically blunt: Kenney wasn't going to get B-29s, ever, and for the good of his career he needed to drop his continuing effort to obtain the Superfortress for FEAF. Finally convinced of the futility of his campaign for B-29s, Kenney—like any good staff officer confronted with a superior's negative response—trotted out his fallback plan. As Kenney later recalled: "I asked about the B-32, a Consolidated Aircraft bomber that had been built as an ace in the hole in case the B-29 had not turned out successfully. Giles said they were building about 200 of the B-32s but the assignment would be up to Hap Arnold."[7]

Anxious both to save his job and to gain priority access to the B-32, Kenney quickly made an appointment to meet with Arnold in Florida. Though the senior officer was leery of a face-to-face encounter with a subordinate who could be extremely irritating even when halfway around the world, Arnold consented to the meeting, which occurred in Miami on March 17. Kenney was apparently on his best behavior, and after the two men had "buried the hatchet" and sat down to lunch, the Far East Air Forces commander carefully brought up the second reason for his trip south from Washington:

> I told [Arnold] how things were going in the Pacific and broached the subject of assigning me enough B-32s to equip one of my heavy groups. If he would give me the plane I would give it a real test so that he could make a decision whether to go on with production or abandon it. He finally promised to send them out

to me, beginning in June, when about 20 would have been delivered from the factory.[8]

Undoubtedly relieved that he wouldn't have to listen to any
more of Kenney's pleas for B-29s and apparently feeling expan-
sive, Arnold picked up the telephone and ordered that two B-32s be
flown to Bolling Field outside Washington. He directed Kenney to
go back north and look the aircraft over. If after inspecting the B-32s
he still wanted the type for the Southwest Pacific, Arnold said, he
would provide enough for two bombardment groups—some ninety
aircraft under then-current tables of organization.[9]

Kenney was back in Washington by March 20, and that afternoon
he walked out onto the Bolling Field flight line to examine the aircraft
he hoped would change both the composition of his command and
the nature of the air war it was conducting against Japan. One of the
B-32s had been flown up from Florida's Eglin Field, and the other had
come in from Wright Field in Ohio. Although the squat, single-tailed
B-32 was perhaps not as elegant as the Superfortress for which Kenney had long carried a torch, he liked what he saw. And his initially
positive reaction was reinforced when he took one of the Dominator's
controls during a forty-minute flight over the snow-covered Maryland and Virginia countryside. Impressed by the bomber's flight
characteristics and its potential ability to carry ten tons of bombs from
Clark Field on Luzon to southern Japan, Kenney was a confirmed fan
of the B-32 by the time the aircraft thumped back down onto Bolling's
runway. He immediately called Giles at the Pentagon and told him
that Far East Air Forces would take Arnold up on his offer to send
Dominators to the Southwest Pacific.[10]

Unfortunately, Kenney's enthusiasm for the B-32 and the possibilities it appeared to offer FEAF helped convince him to overlook
an inconvenient reality: the reason Dominators were available when
B-29s were not was simply that, in the competition to produce a long-
range American superbomber, the B-32 had come in a distant second.

BY THE EARLY 1930s it had become an article of faith for U.S.
Army Air Corps planners that an American victory in any future

war—especially one fought against Japan in the Pacific and Far East—would largely depend on the nation's ability to project its airpower over vast distances.[11] And, given the prevailing doctrine at the time, the projection of airpower specifically referred to strategic bombardment; the ability to defeat an enemy almost solely through the systematic aerial destruction of his industrial centers and military infrastructure. Throughout the decade the Air Corps Materiel Division at Wright Field continually refined the performance and capability requirements for large, long-range aircraft capable of carrying significant bomb loads to distant targets. The Boeing B-17 and the Consolidated B-24—and, to a greater extent, the innovative but ultimately impractical Boeing XB-15 and Douglas XB-19—were important steps toward developing what the Air Corps called the Very Long Range (VLR), or, occasionally, the Very Heavy, bomber.[12]

Yet by the end of the decade no suitable VLR bomber had reached the production stage. The XB-15 and XB-19 had not evolved past the experimental stage and the B-17 and B-24, though excellent aircraft in many respects, simply could not be economically upgraded enough to meet the VLR requirements. The Air Corps needed longer-ranged machines capable of bombing from altitudes between 5,000 and 30,000 feet and of being fitted with enough machine guns to defend themselves adequately during the journey to and from their distant targets.

The September 1939 outbreak of war in Europe provided just the shock needed to transform the VLR project from theory into practice. On November 10 Air Corps chief Arnold asked the War Department for permission to initiate the development of a long-range, four-engine heavy bomber that would surpass in all respects the then-current models of the B-17 and B-24. His request was granted with what passed for speediness in Washington, and on January 29, 1940, the nation's top aircraft manufacturers began receiving "Request for Data R-40B," the document that laid out the Army's specifications for the new bomber.

The requirements were ambitious: the aircraft would have to carry 2,000 pounds of bombs some 5,300 miles at 400 miles per hour, would have to be mechanically reliable under virtually all weather and operational conditions, and—in keeping with the Air Corps' dedication to the concept of high-altitude precision bombing— would have to be pressurized. On April 8, 1940, Boeing, Lockheed, Douglas, and Consolidated-Vultee submitted preliminary design studies. An Air Corps evaluation board designated the proposed aircraft in order of preference as, respectively, the XB-29, XB-30, XB-31, and XB-32,[13] and signed contracts with each firm to provide preliminary engineering data. Lockheed and Douglas subsequently withdrew from the competition, leaving the XB-29 and XB-32 as the only viable contenders.

San Diego–based Consolidated's entry was known within the company as the Model 33. The design featured a shoulder-mounted high-lift/low-drag Davis wing with a span of 135 feet, twin end-plate fin and rudder assemblies, an eighty-three-foot-long cylindrical fuselage, tricycle landing gear, and dual "roll-up" bomb bays. Each of the XB-32's four planned turbo-supercharged Wright R-3350–5 Cyclone engines would produce 2,200 horsepower and the two inboard power plants would be fitted with reversible-pitch propellers.[14] The new aircraft would be pressurized, and its defensive armament would be housed in remotely operated and retractable gun turrets. All these new features were expected to give the XB-32 a gross weight of just over 100,000 pounds.

The Air Corps approved Consolidated's design proposal on September 6, 1940, and ultimately awarded the firm a contract for three prototype aircraft, with the first to be delivered within eighteen months of the contract date and the second and third at ninety-day intervals after the initial example. Wind-tunnel testing of a scale model of the XB-32 indicated that the aircraft's directional stability would be insufficient, so Consolidated's wooden XB-32 mockups were modified to reflect minor changes intended to correct the issue—but kept their twin tails. Army inspectors approved the revised control surface mockups in early January 1941 and the power plant mockups in April, and in June the Army ordered thirteen YB-32 service test machines in addition to the XB-32s.

The flight testing of the XB-32s was a long and difficult process. From the time the XB-32 first flew, on September 7, 1942, the aircraft was plagued by problems with its various subsystems and continued to have stability issues stemming from the twin-tail arrangement. The second prototype crashed, killing Consolidated's senior test pilot, and the flight-test program got so far behind schedule that it seriously jeopardized the Army Air Force's long-range contingency plan for America's eventual entry into the war. Completed by the Air War Plans Division in August 1941 and designated AWPD/1, the plan laid out a program of precision strategic bombing of Nazi Germany and required 6,834 bombers organized into ninety-eight groups, sixty-eight of which were to be "Very Heavy" groups built around B-29s and B-32s. Because the XB-29 was also encountering delays, it was imperative that the Consolidated aircraft reach full-scale production as soon as possible if AWPD/1 were to proceed on schedule.

Timely production of the B-32 was never in the cards, however. Myriad mechanical problems continued to dog the aircraft, and in February 1943 the Army cancelled the order for the thirteen YB-32s. By that time the B-29 had largely overcome its own teething troubles and some influential Army Air Forces officers were beginning to advocate the outright cancellation of the B-32 in favor of the Boeing bomber. Consolidated wasn't ready to throw in the towel, though, and went to great lengths to modify the aircraft's design in response to service recommendations. These changes included replacing the remotely operated defensive weapon system with ten .50-caliber machine guns mounted two each in five manned turrets; eliminating pressurization; improving the power plants and flight-control systems; and, perhaps most important, replacing the trouble-plagued twin tails by a single vertical stabilizer.

The virtual redesign of the XB-32, coupled with the continuing need to meet the requirements of AWPD/1, ultimately led the Army Air Forces to place orders for some 1,200 B-32 bombers, including TB-32 trainer versions. This number was intended to allow the Eighth and Fifteenth Air Forces in the Mediterranean and England, respectively, to convert their B-17 and B-24 heavy bomb groups to B-32s, though by the spring of 1944 it was all too obvious that continuing delays in testing the aircraft coming off Consolidated's

Fort Worth, Texas, line[15] would make it impossible to achieve that goal. Indeed, the Army Air Forces directive concerning the comprehensive testing of production B-32s wasn't even issued until mid-August 1944, the same month that the aircraft's name was officially changed from the original "Terminator" to "Dominator."[16] That directive called for a 200-flying-hour test program to be conducted by three different Army Air Forces agencies spread across five states, as well as for an overseas combat test. But, again, production delays derailed the best-laid plans, and by mid-December 1944 the entire Dominator program was on the verge of cancellation.

The B-32 won a stay of execution almost solely because of an evaluation of the aircraft undertaken by Brigadier General Donald Wilson, the chief of the Army Air Forces' Proving Ground Command and, perhaps not coincidentally, George Kenney's former chief of staff at SWPA's Allied Air Forces and Fifth Air Force. Although his report acknowledged the Dominator's troubled gestation and continuing difficulties, Wilson pointed out that it would be financially and militarily irresponsible to kill off the B-32 before it had been thoroughly tested. He therefore recommended that both the service test program and the training of B-32 crews proceed, and suggested that the Dominator might yet evolve into a capable and dependable bomber. Hap Arnold, likely still hoping to supplant some of his overworked B-17s and B-24s with B-32s, accepted Wilson's recommendations and ordered the testing and crew-training programs to proceed.

Conducted between June and September 1945, the B-32 service test program confirmed that the Dominator had several less-than-sterling qualities. Among them were high interior noise levels that were wearying for the crew, especially on the flight deck; many instruments and controls were poorly positioned; the electrically operated manned gun turrets were prone to jamming during rapid traverse; and, most alarming, serious design flaws in the engine nacelles contributed to an unusually high number of power plant fires. But the B-32 also proved to have good points—it was surprisingly nimble for an aircraft of its size, with especially impressive directional control at low speeds; its gun turrets provided better than adequate protection (when they worked); it was relatively easy to maintain; and, of particular importance, it was a solid and stable bombing platform.

Although these data would certainly help Consolidated's engineers improve the performance and capability of later Dominator variants—should there be any—Kenney's lunch with Arnold in Florida had already ensured that the B-32 would undertake its most challenging evaluation even before the service tests began. On March 27 Arnold disregarded the advice of several of his most senior advisers—many of whom argued that to put any further effort into the troubled aircraft would be a prodigious waste of time, money, and manpower—and authorized a Dominator combat test.

Despite its reputation as the Army Air Forces' problem-child superbomber, the B-32 was going to war.

A FOUR-STAR GENERAL'S DIRECT and unequivocal order tends to have a galvanizing effect on subordinate officers, even those who may for whatever reason disagree with their commander's reasoning or intent. So it was that Arnold's desire that the B-32 undergo a comprehensive combat test was swiftly translated into action. Military personnel from several Army Air Forces agencies and civilian representatives from Consolidated were assembled into a thirty-two-member test detachment led by Colonel Frank R. Cook of the Air Technical Service Command (ATSC).

The highly experienced thirty-five-year-old was a good choice to head up the combat test, which had been given the purposely obscure designation Special Project 98269-S but which was widely referred to as the "Cook Project." During his time with ATSC Cook had flown every bomber type in the Army Air Forces and was something of a proponent of the B-32, believing it to be both easier to fly and more docile on takeoff and landing than the B-29. He also judged the Dominator's locally controlled turrets to be a better defensive arrangement than the Superfortress's remotely operated system. Cook believed that the combat test was the one way in which the B-32 could prove itself a worthy stablemate of the B-29, and he was anxious to get his men and aircraft to the Philippines for testing.[17]

That journey originated in Fort Worth. Cook and his assigned personnel gathered at Consolidated's Texas production facility on May 1 for processing and to pick up the three Dominators selected for the combat test: aircraft 42-108529, 42-108531, and 42-108532. In addition to their serial numbers, two of the big bombers bore the sort of semi-risqué nose art popular with aviators apparently since the dawn of manned flight—a buxom blond in a two-piece, striped bathing suit identified 529 as *The Lady is Fresh*, while 532 bore an equally well-endowed and similarly scantily clad young woman with a kerchief tied to a stick and the name *Hobo Queen II*. A main-gear collapse on landing after a pre-deployment test flight led to 531's replacement by 42-108528, a factory-based B-32 that had seen hard test use and that harbored chronic mechanical issues as a result.

The first leg of the flight to the Philippines—a 1,400-mile hop across the desert Southwest to Mather Army Air Field in Sacramento, California—began as scheduled on May 12, but only for *The Lady is Fresh* and *Hobo Queen II*. Mechanical problems kept 528 in Texas for two additional days, and when all three B-32s were preparing to leave Mather on May 16 further problems delayed 528 yet again. Nor did the troubled aircraft's performance improve as time went on; it was at least two days behind the other Dominators as they made their way to Luzon via Hawaii's Hickam Field, the recently lengthened Japanese-built runway on Kwajalein Atoll, and Harmon Field on Guam.

Despite the challenges presented by the trans-Pacific ferry flight, all three B-32s had gathered at Clark Field, some forty miles northwest of Manila, by May 25. There they were met by a party of dignitaries that included Whitehead, who had replaced Kenney as Fifth Air Force commander; Colonel Merritt Burnside, the B-32 project officer for V Bomber Command; Lieutenant Colonel Selmon W. Wells, the twenty-nine-year-old leader of the 312th Bombardment Group; and Captain Ferdinand L. Svore, commander of the 312th's 386th Bombardment Squadron. The 386th had been tapped as the parent unit for the three Dominators, and Svore was to join Cook and Wells in the triumvirate that would lead B-32 operations during the combat test.

That evaluation was to consist of eleven missions flown in varying weather conditions, with differing ordnance and against as wide a variety of targets as possible. The test was scheduled for completion by July 11, and its successful conclusion would trigger the 386th's complete conversion to B-32s. Wells's other three squadrons—the 387th, 388th, and 389th—would ultimately follow suit, eventually making the 312th the first of three planned Dominator-equipped combat groups in the Pacific.

Wells's unit seems, at first glance, to be a rather odd choice for conversion into a B-32 group. Activated in Kentucky in March 1942 with single-engine dive bombers, the 312th had received the twin-engine Douglas A-20 Havoc light bomber soon after arriving in New Guinea in December 1943. The nimble Havocs flew almost daily low-level parafrag and strafing missions against Japanese airfields, railroads, harbors, ships, troop concentrations, artillery positions, and targets of opportunity, and carried out similar missions after moving to the Philippines in the fall of 1944.[18] It was a highly specialized form of attack aviation, and one whose skill-set differed radically from that required for four-engine heavy bombers like the B-32.

Yet the 312th's selection as the likely first Dominator group was not as illogical as it first appears. Although the A-20 had done yeoman service supporting the hard-slogging Allied advance from Australia northward through New Guinea and into the Philippines, Army Air Forces planners foresaw a lessening need for relatively short-range light bombers as the air war against Japan moved into its final phase—the sustained strategic bombing of the Home Islands. Rather than have the B-32 combat test interrupt the ongoing operations of one of FEAF's long-range B-24 groups, Arnold determined that it made operational sense instead to take an A-20 unit offline. He did, however, decree that in order to help speed the 386th's transition to the larger aircraft, Svore would additionally be provided with experienced Luzon-based B-24 pilots for whom the conversion to the four-engine B-32 would presumably be smoother and less time-consuming. Nearby Liberator units would also be tasked to provide the other specialized crewmembers that the B-32s would need and that the A-20-equipped 312th could not provide—navigators, bombardiers, gunners, and electronic warfare officers to operate the Dominator's sophisticated radar and counter-measures systems.

As it happened, the B-32's combat debut was to take place even before the 386th's conversion had formally begun.

THE TIMELINE FOR THE B-32 combat test was nothing if not ambitious, and in order to stay on track for the program's scheduled July 1 completion the triumvirate of Cook, Wells, and Svore scheduled the first mission for May 29, just days after the three Dominators had all finally assembled at Clark Field and before their planned move to the 312th's home base in Floridablanca, forty miles northwest of Manila. Because the trouble-plagued 528 was the only aircraft that had arrived in the Philippines with a complete ten-man combat crew, two B-24 crews—minus pilots and copilots—were dragooned from a Clark-based Liberator unit.

The first mission was purposely planned to be a shakedown cruise for the Dominators rather than the type of very long range, high-altitude strike for which the aircraft had been designed. Each of the three B-32s was loaded with nine 1,000-pound general purpose bombs,[19] 3,000 gallons of fuel, and thirteen men—ten crew and three observers. The target, as briefed by the 386th's intelligence officer, Captain William Barnes, was a Japanese supply depot at Antatet, in Luzon's Cagayan Valley. Although the enemy position was not expected to be defended by anti-aircraft weapons, it would offer a different sort of challenge, Barnes said: it was within 2,000 yards of an area held by friendly Filipino guerrillas.[20]

The three Dominators were ready to go by 10:30 A.M. local time, but problems with the manifold pressure on two engines forced 528 to abort. The other two aircraft carried on as briefed, *Hobo Queen II* in the lead with Cook as pilot in command and Wells along as an observer. After forming up above Clark Field the B-32s set out on the 190-mile trip to the target, arriving over the Cagayan Valley some forty-five minutes later. The bombers circled Antatet to positively identify the Japanese depot, then each made a run at 10,000 feet.

With perfect visibility and absolutely no enemy anti-aircraft fire or interceptors to worry about, both B-32s were able to blanket the target and, after taking post-strike bomb-damage assessment photos, they returned to Clark Field without incident.

The Dominator's introduction to combat had been essentially a "milk run," but Cook and Wells knew that the remaining ten test missions might well be far more challenging and there was a good chance that enemy action might begin to kill or injure B-32 crewmembers. Given that a pool of at least twelve full crews would be needed to meet immediate and projected operational demands and replace any casualties, converting aviators from the 386th Bomb Squadron and nearby B-24 units onto the B-32 was a distinct priority. Indeed, the importance of the conversion training was reiterated by Brigadier General Jared V. Crabb of V Bomber Command, who in a June 1 memo to Wells underlined the importance of "instructing flying and ground personnel on the operation and maintenance of the B-32 airplane."[21]

Given the need to expand the B-32 personnel pool as quickly as possible, Cook and Wells got the conversion-training effort started almost immediately following the May 30 move of the three B-32s and their support personnel from Clark Field to the 312th's home field at Floridablanca. Classes were established for each crew position, with Cook and the military and civilian members of his test detachment serving as instructors.

Although men with less flight time or combat experience would require more in-depth training, for the higher-hour aviators the conversion process could be amazingly brief. The experience of "Tony" Svore, the twenty-eight-year-old 386th commander, was apparently typical. Originally commissioned as an infantry officer, Svore had gone through flight school as a lieutenant and by the time he first saw a Dominator he was a veteran of some eighty-eight combat missions in A-20s. His introduction to the B-32 consisted of reading the pilot's manual from cover to cover, taking a single introductory flight, and then shooting two landings as Cook looked on from the copilot's seat. After the second landing the test detachment chief officially designated Svore as a qualified B-32 squadron commander and instructor pilot. The brevity of his training didn't particularly bother Svore; he later remarked that after two and a half combat tours he'd become a little calloused about flying. "It's difficult to imagine how we did things in those days," he said. "Our point of view was, 'if you can fly it, you can fly it.'"[22]

But the A-20 pilots tapped to convert from the diminutive and nimble Havoc to the massive, four-engine B-32 faced other issues besides just mastering the differences in size, capability, performance, and tactical employment. Wells, Svore, and the other 312th pilots would also have to adjust to being responsible for a significantly larger crew—in the Pacific theater the A-20s operated with only a pilot and a top-turret gunner, whereas the B-32 carried between ten and thirteen men, depending on the nature of the mission.

Nor were the pilots the only ones for whom the B-32's arrival would cause significant adjustments. Armorers used to the not-inconsiderable effort required to load 2,000 pounds of bombs onto an A-20 would have up to ten times that weight of explosives to deal with when "bombing up" the Dominator. Technicians accustomed to dealing with just two relatively straightforward radial engines would be responsible for maintaining four larger and far more complex turbo-supercharged power plants, and the B-32's electronic subsystems were far more technologically sophisticated than anything carried by the A-20. Even the 312th's intelligence officers would have to quickly refine existing skills. Long used to planning the sorts of low-level, tactical interdiction and ground-support strikes for which the A-20 was so well suited, the men of the 312th's intelligence shop would end up being sent to a nearby B-24 unit on Luzon to learn how to plan for high-altitude, long-range heavy bomber missions.[23]

Important though they might have been, the issues that surfaced during the establishment and conduct of the conversion training were not allowed to hinder the conduct of the all-important combat test. The success or failure of the remaining ten missions would literally decide the Dominator's fate, and each would present its own challenges.

Mission 2

Flown by *Hobo Queen II* and *The Lady is Fresh* on June 12 (528 was unavailable because of a needed engine change), the second combat-test mission originated from Floridablanca and was intended to knock out a Japanese-held runway near Basco on Batan, an island in the South China Sea about halfway between Luzon and Formosa.[24]

The two Dominators lifted off at 9:30 that morning and headed northwest toward Luzon's Lingayen Gulf, then turned northeast and followed the coastline for about 140 miles. Once past the most northerly tip of Luzon the B-32s began a steady climb as they set out over the open South China Sea, arriving over Basco just after 11:30 at an altitude of 16,000 feet. The complete absence of enemy opposition allowed each aircraft to make two fairly leisurely single-ship runs over the target, dropping twenty 500-pound bombs on each pass. The explosives rendered the runway completely unusable, and the B-32s returned to Floridablanca the same way they'd come.

After the bombers landed, ground crewmen discovered what they at first thought was a bullet hole in the vertical stabilizer of *The Lady is Fresh*. Closer examination showed the damage had been caused by a bomb fragment the B-32 had picked up on the previous day's training mission. The time needed to repair her wounded tail would prevent the Dominator from participating in the following day's strike.[25]

Mission 3

The third mission, flown on June 13, racked up two firsts for the Dominator combat test: it was the big bombers' initial visit to Formosa,[26] and it marked 528's offensive debut. That trouble-prone aircraft was able to join *Hobo Queen II* for the raid on Koshun airfield, a Japanese auxiliary strip located 480 miles due north of Floridablanca on Formosa's extreme southwest coast.[27] The field was a frequent target of strikes by FEAF B-24s and B-25s and U.S. Navy carrier-based aircraft. For their strike, the two B-32s each carried twelve 1,000-pound bombs.

The Dominators were also hauling quite a few people when they took off at 8:00 A.M. local time. In addition to the usual ten crew-members, each bomber carried four conversion-course trainees and an observer. In the event, the flight turned out to be a perfect sortie for both the crews and the crewmembers-to-be—there was no enemy opposition, and despite significant cloud cover both B-32s made textbook single-ship runs over the already battered airfield, further cratering the taxiways and main runway. The entire six-and-a-half-hour round-trip flight was uneventful, except for the fact that 528 also seemed to have her usual band of gremlins[28] aboard: three of her 1,000-pounders refused to drop on the target and had to be coaxed out of the bomb bay over the South China Sea on the way back to Floridablanca.[29]

Mission 4

One purpose of the Dominator combat test was, of course, to determine if the B-32 could accurately deliver under actual field conditions the full range of ordnance it had been deemed capable of carrying. Having already dropped 500- and 1,000-pounders, on the fourth combat mission the participating aircraft—*The Lady is Fresh* and *Hobo Queen II*—were each loaded with eight 2,000-pound bombs.

Again carrying trainees and an observer in addition to their normal crews, the aircraft took off from Floridablanca at 8:00 A.M. on June 15 and three hours later unloaded their lethal cargoes on a sugar mill complex outside Taito, a town on Formosa's southeast coast.[30] Each aircraft bombed individually through scattered cloud cover from 15,000 feet, with mixed results. This mission is primarily notable for being the first time that a B-32 came under enemy fire: the second aircraft to bomb was the target of some twenty rounds of poorly aimed "ack-ack" (anti-aircraft fire), all of which burst at the Dominator's altitude but significantly behind the aircraft. Both machines returned to Luzon unscathed.[31]

Mission 5

In what must have seemed like a minor miracle to the 386th Bomb Squadron's maintenance personnel, all three B-32s were able to take part in the fifth mission of the combat test.

Although a good omen for the future of the Dominators, the strike flown on June 16 proved disastrous for the Japanese garrison and residents of Taito town, who the day before had watched as the nearby sugar mill was largely reduced to rubble. The agent of that looming disaster was the 500-pound AN-M17A1 incendiary cluster bomb, forty of which were loaded aboard each of the B-32s. The device consisted of 110 individual four-pound M50 incendiaries containing a mixture of thermite and magnesium, all bound together by thin metal straps and fitted with a rudimentary nose cone and tail fins. An adjustable time fuze set before the planes took off regulated the distance each cluster would fall before a strand of explosive cord would detonate—usually at about 5,000 feet above the intended target area—severing the straps and allowing the individual incendiaries to fall free. The cluster weapon could be devastating against urban areas built largely of wood, as the men aboard the Formosa-bound Dominators were about to demonstrate.

Having taken off from Luzon at the usual 8:00 A.M., *The Lady is Fresh*, *Hobo Queen II*, and 528 arrived over Taito town at about 10:30. Flying in a loose arrowhead formation, the three B-32s dropped their ordnance from 19,000 feet through minimal cloud cover. The American aviators didn't have to wait long to see the effects of their attack. Within minutes, as the narrative mission report recorded, Taito

was an inferno of smoke and flames that completely enveloped the center of the town. An accommodating breeze spread the fires northward to cover the sections of town that the bombs had missed. Smoke was rising up to 4,000 feet by the time the planes left the target. Two hours later the 43rd Bomb Group passed by Taito, and reported that the fires were still burning intensely, and smoke was trailing 25 miles away.

The Dominators' incendiary attack on the Formosa town closely resembled—albeit with slight differences and on a much smaller scale—the firebombing raids being conducted over Japan by Marianas-based B-29s of the Twentieth Air Force's XXI Bomber Command, and the narrative mission report noted that the B-32 crews "were enthusiastic over the results of this Taito [version of the] 'Tokyo Treatment.'" Other than a few bursts of inaccurate ack-ack, the attackers encountered no resistance, and all three Dominators returned safely to Floridablanca.[32]

Mission 6

The first five missions of the Dominator combat test had allowed Cook, Wells, and the others involved in the program to evaluate fairly accurately the B-32's performance in several key areas, including bombing accuracy from both medium and high altitudes. The sixth test mission would address three important capabilities that had not yet been explored.

The first was the Dominator's ability to undertake successful long-range, long-endurance combat missions. Though the two components sound similar and are, of course, interrelated, they differ in that range is a measure of how *far* the aircraft can fly and endurance is a measure of how *long* the crew can continue to function effectively. Put another way, an aircraft's range is based on its mechanical reliability and fuel consumption—if well-maintained and correctly operated the machine should be capable of flying as far as it was designed to. However, if adverse conditions inside the aircraft—excessive noise or vibration, poorly configured systems, and so on—cause undue fatigue or stress for an otherwise healthy crew, the flight's duration can be significantly shorter than it should be.

The second thus-far unevaluated capability the sixth mission would address was the Dominator's suitability to operate offensively at night. The first five strikes had all been conducted in daylight with navigation to and from the targets largely undertaken using visual references. Moreover, the bombing on those strikes had all been done solely with the Norden M-9 optical bombsight, a device that despite its technical sophistication would be considerably less accurate at night unless operated in conjunction with the B-32's AN/APQ-13 radar bombing and navigation set. The latter system—which had not yet been used on an operational Dominator combat test sortie—would allow the B-32s to locate and attack targets at night.

The third evaluation of the sixth combat mission was of the Dominator's capability for low-altitude bombing, or LAB, as it was inevitably referred to. The B-32s had proven their ability to bomb targets successfully from altitudes between 10,000 and 19,000 feet, but the ability to undertake low-level attacks against ships would add to the Dominator's potential value in the Pacific Theater.

The most efficient combat scenario in which to evaluate the B-32's capabilities in all three areas, planners decided, was a long-range, night shipping-interdiction mission. *Hobo Queen II* was tasked to fly the sortie, which would first take her and her crew northwest from Luzon toward the Luichow Peninsula, the southernmost part of China's Kwantung Province, then southwest toward the port city of Haikow on Hainan Island, then almost directly south toward the coast of French Indochina[33] before returning to Floridablanca. The Japanese were known to use fleets of small merchant vessels, often escorted by warships, to move troops and materiel among the coastal ports of the eastern South China Sea and within the Gulf of Tonkin. Mission planners believed there was a better than even chance *Hobo Queen II* would find a target for the nine 500-pound bombs nestled in her bomb bay.

Taking off from Floridablanca just after 7 P.M. on June 18, the B-32 reached the assigned search area some four hours later. *Hobo Queen II* prowled the area at altitudes of 4,000 to 6,000 feet, but when her radar picked up no suitable waterborne targets her crew elected to bomb Haikow. For reasons now lost to history, the bomb run—conducted just before 3 A.M. local time—was performed visually rather than with the help of the AN/APQ-13 and at 8,500 feet. Bombs were seen to impact west of the town's center, but owing to the darkness no bomb-damage assessment was possible. *Hobo Queen II* soon turned for home, and was safely back in the Philippines almost exactly twelve hours after taking off.

Although the sixth mission did not allow an evaluation of the B-32's low-altitude or radar-bombing capabilities, it did show the Dominator to be mechanically capable of long-range operations and proved that during extended flights the aircraft was not especially wearying for her crew. In addition, the mission demonstrated that the B-32's radio communications suite worked very well at long ranges and was apparently not susceptible to jamming by the Japanese.

The last was a capability that would ultimately help put Dominators over Tokyo.

Mission 7

On June 19 all three B-32s were sent against railway bridges spanning the Beinan River on Formosa, the intention being to disrupt Japanese efforts to move men and equipment along the island's east coast. The attack would be part of a much larger Far East Air Forces effort that would also see seven squadrons of B-24s hitting the extensive port facilities at Kiirun, three squadrons of B-25s attacking the railway marshaling yards at Shoka, and thirty-six P-38 Lightning fighters strafing and rocketing the bridge leading to the yards.[34] For their part in the day's activities the Dominators were loaded with 1,000-pound bombs—twelve on *The Lady is Fresh* and nine each on *Hobo Queen II* and 528[35]—with the fuzes set for .01-second delay. An electrical problem kept 528 on the ground for thirty-five minutes after the other aircraft took off, but the three Dominators ultimately joined up and made the flight to Formosa in loose formation.

The original mission briefing called for all three B-32s to strike first at the two southernmost bridges—at Paiyapai and Rokuryo—and then hit the bridge at Ikegami if they had surplus ordnance. Soon after takeoff, however, the three aircraft commanders collectively decided to alter the plan: *Hobo Queen II* and *The Lady is Fresh* would bomb the Paiyapai span, after which the latter aircraft would move on to hit the Rokuryo bridge; 528 would be solely responsible for the Ikegami structure. Though the decision to alter the briefed plan was presumably made to ensure that enough bombs hit each bridge, in the end the mission was not successful: several of the thirty 1,000-pound bombs dropped during the attack were reported as "near hits," but all three bridges remained intact and usable when the B-32s headed for home.[36]

Mission 8

The day after the inconclusive strike against the Beinan River railroad bridges the B-32s were assigned to hit a related target 130 miles to the northeast: the rail yards on Formosa's eastern coastal plain just north of the port of Suo.[37] All three Dominators were scheduled for the mission, but during the engine start-up process *Hobo Queen II* suffered a voltage surge that rendered the turbo-superchargers on all four engines temporarily inoperable. Her crew had no choice but to abort the mission, leaving *The Lady is Fresh* and 528 to carry out the strike.

The two Dominators—each carrying four 2,000-pound bombs—took off from Floridablanca just after 7 A.M., then turned north to parallel Luzon's west coast before setting out across the 160-mile-wide strait separating the Philippines and Formosa. The weather was initially good but began to deteriorate as the B-32s passed just east of the burned-out ruins of Taito, and by the time the aircraft reached the Suo area the target was completely obscured by clouds. Choosing not to radar-bomb the rail yards, the mission commander turned both aircraft south toward the secondary target—the same Paiyapai Bridge the Dominators had failed to hit the day before. Weather was also closing in there, and just before the bombardier in the lead B-32 toggled his bombs from 10,000 feet the bridge disappeared beneath heavy clouds. All four 2,000-pounders missed the bridge by considerable distances—the farthest by more than a half-mile—and the pilot of the second Dominator elected to move on to another secondary target, a group of military warehouses near the center of the small town of Tamari,[38] some thirteen miles southwest of Taito. The sky over the target was clear, and all four of the B-32's bombs scored direct hits. Huge secondary explosions rocked the warehouse complex as the Dominators circled the area, taking post-strike photos, and by the time the bombers departed the area a roiling cloud of thick black smoke had climbed 1,000 feet into the air.

Undoubtedly feeling far better about the day's bombing than they had about the previous mission's results, the crews of the two B-32s headed south. The return flight was uneventful, and the aircraft landed at Floridablanca just before 3 P.M.[39]

Mission 9

After a day off—during which B-24 pilots transitioning into the B-32 took *The Lady is Fresh* aloft on a series of short training hops and the other two Dominators underwent needed maintenance—it was back to work on June 22.

At the early morning briefing for the ninth combat-test mission the regular crews of *The Lady is Fresh* and 528 (*Hobo Queen II* was still grounded by supercharger issues) heard the somewhat disquieting news that the day's planned strike would likely be the most hazardous they'd yet flown. Located in the western Formosa town of Heito,[40] the target was a sprawling sugar refinery that had been at least partially converted for the production of butanol, an alcohol-based solvent and potential synthetic additive to aviation gasoline.

The hazard in attacking the plant came from a large anti-aircraft gun emplacement nearby, as well as from other widely dispersed weapons protecting an auxiliary military airfield and several barracks complexes. Each of these facilities had been previously attacked, most notably in a February 1945 raid by B-24s that had inadvertently killed or injured some 100 Allied prisoners of war forced by the Japanese to work in the refinery and surrounding sugar cane fields. In response to the earlier air raids, the anti-aircraft sites had recently been refurbished and at least one large-caliber gun was thought to be radar-directed. To negate that particular threat, the B-32s would drop "rope," long streamers of thin aluminum foil intended to overwhelm the Japanese gun-laying radar with false returns. *The Lady is Fresh* would attack the main anti-aircraft site with seventy-eight

260-pound fragmentation bombs, after which 528 would hit the refinery complex itself with forty 500-pounders.

The mission launched on time and the Dominators arrived
over the target to find "CAVU"—clear and visibility unlimited—
conditions. *The Lady is Fresh* made her defense-suppression run
at 15,000 feet, dropping rope as she went in. The frags began im-
pacting about 200 feet past the gun emplacement, more than close
enough to be lethal, and then marched across the adjacent barracks
complex. The second Dominator was close behind, and managed to
unload thirty of her 500-pounders on the refinery before a shackle
malfunction in her bomb bay prevented the last ten weapons from
dropping. As 528 turned off the target and salvoed[41] the hung-up
bombs, her crew saw several solid hits within the boundaries of the
sugar plant. Within minutes a plume of greasy black smoke had
risen to an altitude of 5,000 feet.

The attack was not entirely one-sided, however; the crews of
both Dominators noted intense anti-aircraft fire being directed at
them during their bombing runs. Because 528 did not use any sort
of radar countermeasure, the rounds being aimed at her were, as
the narrative mission report later dryly stated, "correct as to altitude and course with accurate tracking during the run," and several detonated close enough to bounce the aircraft around. The rope
dropped by *The Lady is Fresh,* on the other hand, prevented the Japanese gun-laying radar from maintaining an accurate plot, and the
few ack-ack rounds that jostled her were essentially "luck shots."
Neither aircraft was damaged by the enemy fire, and both returned
safely to Floridablanca.[42]

Mission 10

The penultimate Dominator combat-test mission was flown by *Hobo
Queen II* on the night of June 23–24 and was in essence a replay of
the inconclusive June 18 long-range, night shipping-interdiction
strike. The general target area was the mouth of the Canton River,
between Macau and Hong Kong, ranging as far inland as Canton.[43]
It would be another long flight, covering some 1,500 miles and

lasting upward of eleven hours. *Hobo Queen II* would be carrying nine 500-pound bombs, and the intention—as it was on June 18— was to attack enemy shipping from relatively low altitude using the radar bombing system.

Unfortunately, the results of the tenth mission mirrored those of the sixth. *Hobo Queen II's* radar only detected one vessel, and because it was outside the FEAF-designated blind-bombing zone—a measure instituted to prevent inadvertent attacks on ships of non-combatant nations entering or leaving Portuguese-owned, and thus neutral, Macau—it was not attacked. Tony Svore, the pilot in command on the mission, decided to hit the alternate target, a Japanese airfield on the near-shore island of Sanchau,[44] sixteen miles southwest of Macau. Unlike the brilliantly lit up Portuguese colony, the entire Chinese mainland was completely blacked out and, in addition, the airfield was blanketed by fog. Neither situation proved a hindrance, however, for the target was acquired and bombed from 10,000 feet using the AN-APQ-13 radar. *Hobo Queen II* dropped rope as a precaution, and was not fired on. After salvoing three hung-up bombs into the sea, Svore turned the big bomber for home.[45]

Mission 11

The *Lady is Fresh* and *Hobo Queen II* had the honor of flying the last scheduled Dominator combat-test mission, an event the trouble-plagued 528 missed because of an engine problem. The strike would take the big bombers back to Formosa, this time to hit several railway bridges near the north coast harbor complex at Kiirun. The crews were briefed that there was a high probability they would be intercepted by Japanese fighters flying from several fields in the area, and that the harbor and the bridges were protected by radar-directed anti-aircraft guns of varying calibers. The ordnance load for the mission consisted of 1,000-pound bombs: a full load of twelve in *The Lady is Fresh* and nine in *Hobo Queen II*.

The two Dominators took off from Floridablanca just after 8 A.M. on June 25 and followed the usual course northeast across the Luzon Strait until they sighted Formosa's southernmost tip. The aircraft gradually gained altitude as they followed the island's east coast northward, reaching the target area some three and a half hours after takeoff. Kiirun was almost completely obscured by clouds, but *Hobo Queen II* was able to bomb visually through a small hole in the undercast. Not able to find a similar hole, *The Lady is Fresh* instead bombed the nearby town of Giran.[46] Contrary to the warnings issued during the mission briefing, there was no enemy interference and the two B-32s had an uneventful flight back to Luzon.[47]

THE END OF THE eleven-mission Dominator combat test—two weeks earlier than scheduled and with no personnel casualties or significant damage to the B-32s—triggered the writing of three separate summary reports.

Though project commander Frank Cook's report to Brigadier General Crabb at V Bomber Command pointed out dozens of "must fix" items, Cook's overall opinion of the aircraft was generally favorable and he made a point of emphasizing how much of an improvement the B-32 was over the B-24. Lieutenant Colonel Stephen D. McElroy[48] was also cautiously positive about the Dominator in his report to Army Air Forces headquarters, saying "the B-32 airplane in its present condition is suitable for combat operations in this theater" and once corrections were made to some of its subsystems the aircraft would also be suitable for unrestricted combat operations elsewhere within Far East Air Force's area of responsibility. The third report on the results of the combat test, however, was anything but positive. In the evaluation that he forwarded to Proving Ground Command, Major Henry S. Britt—who had spent virtually all of his time on the crew of the trouble-plagued 528—stated that the Dominator "in its present condition is not a suitable combat weapon to pursue the war with Japan." Although Britt suggested dozens of key fixes that might over time make the aircraft a better bomber, the overarching tone of his report was negative and, not surprisingly, his dislike of the B-32 was palpable.[49]

The end of the official Dominator combat test did not, as Britt fervently hoped, result in the termination of B-32 flight operations. Indeed, follow-on combat missions were being planned and executed even as he, Cook, and McElroy were writing their reports. A planned raid on Formosa's Heito alcohol plant on July 4 had to be cancelled when both *Hobo Queen II* and 528 were grounded by mechanical glitches, but all three Dominators were able to participate in a July 6 strike aimed at a sugar refinery outside Takao Town, a port city on Formosa's southwest coast.[50] The fact that the three B-32s were able to undertake the mission didn't guarantee its success, however. The Dominators carried a total of thirty-three 1,000-pound bombs, but a radar-targeting error made by V Bomber Command's chief bombardier—along on the raid as a "distinguished guest"—meant that "he was able to hit Formosa with only six of the total bombs dropped. No damage was done, nothing was accomplished."[51] All twenty-seven of the other bombs missed the sugar refinery and fell harmlessly in the ocean. And on July 13 *The Lady is Fresh* was re-called from a night shipping-search mission because of unusually bad weather over much of the South China Sea.

These less-than-impressive missions did not adversely affect the B-32's future in Far East Air Forces. Some three weeks earlier, on June 23, Wells had received Movement Order 369 from Fifth Air Force headquarters directing him to begin preparations to move the 312th Group headquarters element and the 386th and 387th squadrons to Okinawa, recently secured by U.S. forces after three months of vicious combat against the defending Japanese. The assumption that both of the former A-20 squadrons were still intended to become full-fledged B-32 units was confirmed when on July 14 V Bomber Command directed the 386th to continue transition training for former A-20 and B-24 crewmen, and notified Cook and Wells that six additional B-32s would arrive from the United States during the remainder of July and in August. The members of Cook's test detachment were to remain in theater to help operate the existing aircraft and aid in the transition training. When enough trained crews were available for all nine Dominators the 386th would be officially redesignated from a "Light" to a "Very Heavy" bombardment squadron and would presumably join the aerial assault on the Japanese Home Islands.

The decision to continue B-32 combat operations was far more the result of political maneuvering in Washington than it was of military necessity in the Pacific. The B-29 groups in the theater were already doing a fine job of reducing much of Japan to smoking rubble, and adding a squadron or two of Dominators to the mix would not appreciably affect either the conduct or the outcome of the air war. Though Hap Arnold well understood this, he had other aspects of the issue to consider. The Army Air Forces commander had supported the Dominator's development despite the program's history of delays and design deficiencies and in defiance of the officially stated opinions of a considerable number of influential individuals both within the Pentagon and on Capitol Hill. He was therefore understandably loathe to discard the B-32—to do so would at best be a tacit admission of extremely poor judgment on his part and at worst might be seen as flagrant waste of vital national resources. Though the Dominator's shortcomings were well documented even before the combat test, the fact that it had actually been able to bomb enemy targets allowed Arnold to justify the time, effort, and money that had been put into the big bomber. The formal decision to add the B-32 to the American air armada that was pummeling Japan in preparation for the planned invasion had therefore already been taken well before the three summary reports of the combat test arrived in Washington.

The practical effect of that decision for the men of the 386th and 387th squadrons was a further ratcheting up of the already busy transition-training program. The late July arrival from the United States of a fourth Dominator—42-108530, ferried over by a crew commanded by Captain Byron K. Boettcher—helped ensure that Floridablanca's runway was kept active with B-32s departing on or returning from crew-familiarization flights and practice bombing missions. The continuing load-out of equipment and the progressive tear-down of the 312th's bivouac area in preparation for the pending move to Okinawa also kept people busy, though Wells attempted to reduce the frantic pace by ordering occasional afternoon "stand-downs" so his men could play softball and volleyball and drink a few beers.

On August 3 and 4 the ground echelons of the 386th and 387th squadrons and most of the group headquarters staff were transported by trucks to the sprawling port of Subic Bay, twenty miles southwest of Floridablanca. On the afternoon of the fifth, the two 328-foot-long Navy landing ships that would carry the men and their belongings to Okinawa, *LST-745* and *LST-801*, edged up onto the beach and dropped their bow ramps. Boarding began at 7 P.M. and was completed in a relatively quick twelve hours. The LSTs then moved back out into the bay, and just after daylight they steamed into the South China Sea as part of an Okinawa-bound convoy.

It is likely that many of the men embarked on the 1,000-mile, week-long voyage from Luzon to the Ryukyu Islands assumed the trip would not be a pleasant experience, given that the flat-bottomed, blunt-bowed LSTs were notoriously "lively" even in calm seas. But it is equally likely that more than a few were looking forward to a few days of relaxation, the kind that would largely come from the apparently endless games of poker and craps that seemed to spring up in those times whenever American service members were confined aboard troop transports.

As they lay in their cramped below-decks bunks, or stood on deck and gazed out at the passing sea, or found out-of-the-way places to sit quietly and write a few lines to loved ones, many of the men on that passage to Okinawa were wondering just how much longer the war in the Pacific might last. The Nazis had surrendered in Europe three months earlier; Japanese forces had been rolled back virtually everywhere and their nation was being mercilessly pounded from the air. Although most Americans in the Pacific Theater fervently hoped that the men in power in Tokyo would see that all was truly and irrevocably lost and that there was no point in continuing the fight, the fanatic tenacity with which the Japanese had thus far defended every foot of ground against the advancing Allied forces indicated that a swift conclusion to the conflict was highly unlikely. Indeed, the men of the two bomb squadrons had already been told that they would be supporting the coming invasion of the Home Islands, and some of the more pessimistic men in the unit were predicting that they *might* be home for Christmas—in 1946.

But then, on the morning of August 7, those aboard the LSTs heard the truly startling news that a single bomb, an *atomic* bomb, dropped from a B-29 the day before had obliterated the Japanese city of Hiroshima. Most of the GIs and their Navy hosts had no clue what "atomic" meant, but they all realized that the new weapon was a potential game-changer, something that could dramatically shorten the war. Men waited anxiously for news of a Japanese surrender, yet no such announcement came. The Soviet Union's August 8 declaration of war against Japan seemed to bode well, and when it was announced over the ships' loudspeakers late on August 9 that another atomic bomb been dropped on Japan, this time on Nagasaki, the general consensus among the men on both ships was that a cessation of hostilities would be announced at any moment.

But that long-awaited announcement was never made, and on August 12 the two LSTs dropped their ramps on an Okinawa beach. As the men of the 386th and 387th ground echelons came ashore they were met by Captain Woodrow Hauser, the 386th's communications officer and leader of the advance party, who directed them to board waiting trucks for the ride to their new home, the airfield at Yontan. Built by the Japanese 19th Air Sector Command in 1944 as part of a larger plan to turn Okinawa into a giant air base complex from which navy aircraft—the vast majority of them kamikazes[52]— would attack American naval units supporting the invasion, Yontan (known to the Japanese as Kita) and the nearby Kadena (Naka) airfield had been abandoned without a fight when the Japanese 32nd Army's 44th Independent Mixed Brigade withdrew from the area in April.[53] By the time the ground echelons of the 386th and 387th arrived on August 13, Yontan's bivouac area remained a sea of mud but the existing main 4,000-foot runway had been repaired, lengthened by 1,000 feet, and resurfaced by the U.S. Navy's 87th Construction Battalion. The "Seabees" had also constructed a 7,000-foot-long heavy bomber runway and were nearly finished building a second one parallel to the first. The entire complex was in almost constant use by a variety of Army, Navy, and Marine Corps squadrons.

Yontan was also already home to three of the 386th's four B-32s— *The Lady is Fresh, Hobo Queen II*, and 528—and a C-47 transport carrying the squadron and group headquarters staffs had arrived at Yontan shortly before the ground echelon personnel came ashore from the LSTs, though 42-108530 had remained at Floridablanca for some minor modifications. Moreover, the Dominators were already being prepped for combat missions; despite the widespread hope among American military personnel that the atomic bombings of Hiroshima and Nagasaki would lead to an immediate Japanese surrender, no such capitulation was forthcoming. Until Tokyo gave some official signal that it was prepared to agree to the unconditional surrender terms set out in the Allies' Potsdam Declaration, there would be no letup in the Allied campaign against Japanese forces wherever they were encountered.[54]

For the B-32 crews of the 386th Bomb Squadron the practical result of Japan's failure to capitulate in a timely manner was, simply put, business as usual. On the morning of August 13 FEAF headquarters directed that the Dominators continue "routine operations" against the enemy, but left it up to the 312th Group's intelligence and operations staffs to decide what type of sorties would be flown, and where.

The decision was made that the Dominator's fourteenth combat mission—and the first from Okinawa—would be a single-aircraft anti-shipping sweep of the East China Sea. On the night of August 13–14, 528 took off from Yontan with a load of nine 500-pound bombs, headed northwest toward Shanghai and China's wide Yangtze River delta. The bomber proved to be uncharacteristically well-behaved for most of the mission, and her crew sighted and radar-bombed a small ocean-going vessel before turning for home. However, the B-32's gremlins woke up as she was on final approach to Yontan—the aircraft's right outboard engine caught fire, almost certainly because of either an oil leak or an exhaust stack problem, both of which had been continuing issues for all three of the combat-test aircraft. Though the Dominator landed safely, the fire destroyed the engine nacelle and all its associated systems, and 528 was out of commission for several days.[55]

The second mission from Yontan was flown by *The Lady is Fresh* and *Hobo Queen II*, also on the night of August 13–14. The flight was to be a combined night fighter-shipping search, with the primary objective being to locate, intercept, and destroy Japanese aircraft believed to be ferrying senior military officers across the Korea Strait, the 120-mile stretch of ocean separating the Japanese island of Kyushu from the southeastern coast of Korea. Both B-32s were fitted with bomb-bay fuel tanks, which restricted their bomb loads to nine 500-pounders each. The aircraft took off from Yontan an hour apart and both set out directly to the north. As the first B-32 neared Fukuejima, the southernmost of Japan's Goto Islands, it veered to the west and then cruised northward along the Korean coastline from Cheju Do island toward Busan, but made no sightings. The other Dominator initially headed up the west coast of Japan's Tsushima Island, in the center of the Korea Strait, then turned southwest and just after dawn located and bombed a 75-foot sloop about ten miles due south of Yeosu, Korea. No direct hits were scored out of nine bombs dropped, but several near misses caused the vessel's crew to abandon ship. Thirty minutes later and twelve miles to the northeast the B-32 located a 150-foot-long, four-masted sailing ship, which the Dominator peppered with 4,000 rounds from its .50-caliber machine guns. Although the vessel remained afloat it was in decidedly less seaworthy condition by the time the B-32 departed for the return flight to Okinawa. Both Dominators landed safely on the morning of the fourteenth.[56]

The results of the night's missions were not spectacular in terms of damage done to the Japanese Empire, but they did underscore the Dominator's ability to undertake long-distance, low-level sorties (minus, of course, the occasional engine fire). That capability was to be utilized in the next mission launched from Okinawa, a two-plane night reconnaissance sortie to southern Korean and western Honshu. Though the flight was primarily intended to monitor and, if possible, interdict Japanese aerial activity over the same part of the Korea Strait that had been the focus of the previous anti-shipping mission, both *The Lady is Fresh* and *Hobo Queen II* were loaded with the usual number of 500-pound bombs in case they came across suitable maritime targets.

The Dominators rolled down the Yontan runway just before sundown on August 15, then formed up and headed north at about 4,000 feet. Their crews settled in for the long transit flight to the patrol area, some of the men opening the simple box lunches provided for them and pouring the first of what promised to be many cups of strong coffee from thermoses each man stashed near his position. But less than three hours into the flight the radio operators aboard each plane received an identical—and potentially monumentally important— message from group headquarters back on Okinawa: the Japanese had accepted the Allied surrender terms and a theater-wide ceasefire was now in effect. The B-32s were to terminate the mission and return to base. The news spread through both Dominators in a flash, and enlisted men and officers alike whooped and slapped each other on the back—the long hard slog that began after Pearl Harbor finally seemed to be over, and they had all made it through alive.[57]

But as the two B-32s began the slow, graceful turns that would take them home, events were unfolding in Tokyo that promised to shatter the American flyers' dreams of peace.

CHAPTER 3

CRISIS IN TOKYO

ALMOST EXACTLY TWENTY HOURS before *The Lady is Fresh* and *Hobo Queen II* received the recall message that terminated their mission and so elated their crews, His Imperial Majesty Hirohito[1] stepped in front of a microphone set up in the Household Ministry building on the night-shrouded grounds of his bomb-damaged Tokyo palace. Speaking in *kanbun*, the archaic classical Japanese of the imperial court, the 124th emperor of Japan—his voice high-pitched and tremulous—read a most remarkable document as sound engineers recorded his words and court officials stood nearby, tears rolling down their cheeks.

Known as an imperial rescript, the text was Hirohito's official response to the July 26 Postdam Declaration in which the United States, Great Britain, and China outlined their terms for the unconditional surrender of Japan's armed forces.[2] Speaking in the majestic plural, the forty-four-year-old emperor addressed his people:

To Our good and loyal subjects:

After pondering deeply the general trends of the world and the actual conditions obtaining in Our empire today, We have decided to effect a settlement of the present situation by resorting to an extraordinary measure. We have ordered Our government to communicate to the Governments of the United States, Great

Britain, China and the Soviet Union that Our empire accepts the
provisions of their Joint Declaration.[3]

The emperor went on for another three-and-a-half minutes. Although
he never used the word *surrender* and the overall tone—especially
in Hirohito's obfuscation of his own role in initially supporting the
war—was more than a little disingenuous and self-serving, his pronouncement was no less historic. Here was a Japanese emperor acceding to the wishes of foreign governments and telling his people,
albeit indirectly, that their nation had lost the war and that he, and
they, could "pave the way for a grand peace for all the genera-
tions to come" by "enduring the unendurable and suffering what is
insufferable."[4]

And yet Hirohito's people would not hear his historic address
for another twelve hours. The imperial rescript was being recorded
for delayed broadcast and would not go on the air until after the
government of Prime Minister Kantaro Suzuki had officially notified the Allies of Tokyo's conditional acceptance of the Potsdam ultimatum and had, in turn, been assured that the notification had
been received. There had thus far been no response to the cables
sent to the Allied capitals via Japan's embassies in neutral nations,
so the emperor had more than enough time to read two additional
"takes" of the rescript to correct slight errors and lower the pitch of
his voice. Those recordings completed, Hirohito walked stiffly from
the room. Minutes later, just after midnight on the sultry, windless,
and very early morning of August 15, he climbed into the car that
had earlier brought him across the palace grounds and was driven
back to his private quarters.[5]

The diminutive monarch's recorded rescript would soon announce to his subjects—however obliquely—that the nation had
been totally defeated and would suffer prolonged occupation by
foreign troops for the first time in its history, yet he was at peace
with his decision that the war had to end. A figurehead emperor
throughout the conflict, Hirohito had routinely rubber-stamped
the decisions made by the six-member Supreme Council for the Direction of the War, but over the preceding months he had come to

believe that the only way to preserve Japan as a sovereign nation—and, of course, to protect the hereditary monarchy—was to end the war as quickly as possible. He had initially agreed with those of his advisers who advocated a negotiated peace with the Allies, but the atomic bombings of Hiroshima on August 6 and Nagasaki three days later had convinced him that immediate surrender—even if it meant acceding to the onerous conditions set forth in the Potsdam Declaration—was the only way to save his nation and its people from the "prompt and utter destruction" the Allies threatened to visit on Japan should the nation continue to resist.[6]

Indeed, so certain was Hirohito of the immediate need to terminate the war that four days before recording the rescript for broadcast he had taken an uncharacteristically bold step: he'd actually agreed to impose his will upon the fractious Supreme Council. That body's members were Prime Minister Suzuki, Foreign Minister Shigenori Togo, Army and War Minister General Korechika Anami, Navy Minister Admiral Mitsumasa Yonai, Chief of the Army General Staff General Yoshijiro Umezu, and Chief of the Naval General Staff Admiral Soemu Toyoda. Referred to collectively as the "Big Six," the men were equally divided when it came to the idea of surrender. The "doves," Suzuki, Togo, and Yonai, all believed fervently that immediate capitulation was the only way to prevent more atomic bombings and ensure the continuation of Japan's monarchy. The "hawks," Anami, Umezu, and Toyoda, were fiercely adamant that the nation could and should fight on tenaciously, inflicting such grievous casualties on the Allied forces expected to invade the Home Islands that Washington and London would agree to negotiate an end to the war on terms more favorable to Japan. The terms the hawks hoped to force the Allies to accept included Japan's right to disarm herself, Japanese control of any war-crimes trials, and absolutely no Allied occupation of the Home Islands.[7]

On the afternoon of Thursday, August 9, the division of opinion between doves and hawks had caused the Supreme Council to adjourn an emergency meeting without deciding on how to respond to the Potsdam Declaration. Suzuki then took the question to his full cabinet. Because several members of that larger body shared the hawkish point of view, the outcome of the meeting was predictably inconclusive—no decision about the question of surrender had been reached by the time the cabinet meeting ended about two hours before midnight. Tradition demanded that the Japanese government—in this case, the members of the Big Six and the cabinet—had to agree unanimously on a policy before seeking the emperor's formal permission to enact that policy, so the impasse essentially guaranteed that Japan would be incapable of responding to the Allied demands. That lack of response, in turn, could very well bring the Potsdam Declaration's threat of "prompt and utter destruction" into horrendous reality.

In a last-ditch effort to avert catastrophe, Suzuki and Togo agreed on a bold and unprecedented plan. They would ask Hirohito to step down from the lofty heights of total impartiality to which tradition and Japan's constitution relegated him and intervene personally to break the deadlock between doves and hawks. They would, in short, call upon the emperor to personally decree that the immediate acceptance of the Allied terms set forth in the Potsdam Declaration was his divine will and the only way to save the nation. Though as a constitutional monarch he actually had no such power to dictate policy, the traditional and mystic reverence for the person of the emperor—believed by his people to be the direct lineal descendant of Amaterasu, the Sun Goddess of Shintoism—ensured that his deadlocked government would hear and obey his will. Or so Suzuki and Togo hoped.

The two men had put their plan in motion by summoning the chief cabinet secretary, Hisatune Sakomizu, and asking him to convince Admiral Toyoda and General Umezu to put their names to a petition that would allow Suzuki to convene a meeting of the Big Six in the emperor's presence. The military chiefs of staff were to be told that the measure was simply a way to ensure that such a meeting could be called quickly if made necessary by fast-changing events; the two senior commanders accepted that explanation and signed the petition. Suzuki and Togo then hurried to the palace for an audience with Hirohoto, during which they explained the deadlock in the council and their point of view that any further delay in accepting the terms set forth in the Potsdam Declaration would be catastrophic for the nation. The emperor heard them out and agreed with their logic, and then directed them to convene the Big Six immediately.

A few minutes before midnight on August 9 the emperor, the members of the Supreme Council, and several staff assistants and court officials had gathered in the cramped and humid imperial bomb shelter. Suzuki read out the Potsdam demands in their entirety, explained the nature of the impasse within the Big Six and the corresponding disagreement within the larger cabinet, and then gave various men in the room the opportunity to voice their opinions. Finally, at just after 2 A.M. on August 10, Hirohito rose and in a low but steady voice expressed his opinion that there was no reason to prolong a war that was so obviously already lost. He reflected on the suffering of his people and the devastation visited on his empire, then ended his remarks by saying he sanctioned Foreign Minister Togo's proposal to accept the terms of the Potsdam Declaration as presented, with the sole condition being that the national polity[8]—Japan's sovereignty as vested in the position and influence of the emperor—not be diminished in any way.[9]

When Hirohito finished speaking Suzuki quickly adjourned the meeting, for there was much left to do. The emperor's pronouncement had apparently quelled the dissent within the Big Six, but the only government entity with the constitutional authority to ratify the surrender was the cabinet. All of the Supreme Council members therefore immediately left the bomb shelter for the prime minister's official residence, where the follow-on cabinet meeting was to be held. By four in the morning that body had hammered out the wording of the conditional surrender message to be sent to the Allies via the Japanese embassies in Sweden and Switzerland, and upon transmission of those cables Hirohito had finally taken to his bed, believing that his intervention had eliminated discord within his government and would result in a swift and orderly transition from war to peace.

Unfortunately, he was wrong on both accounts.

DESPITE THE DEFEATS IT had endured and enormous losses in men and matériel it had suffered thus far in the war, in August 1945 the

Japanese army arguably remained the single strongest and most structurally coherent organization in the country.

The army was also permeated by the principles of *Bushido*, the ancient "way of the samurai" that during the first decades of the twentieth century had been cynically distorted by Japanese militarists into a virulently nationalistic code that demanded unquestioning loyalty from soldiers of all ranks and emphasized that surrender to one's enemies was so dishonorable that suicide—both personal and national—was vastly preferable. Although the Japanese navy was also steeped in the traditions of *Bushido*, it was the army that styled itself the protector of both the monarchy and the nation's sacred honor. As a result, the service's members had repeatedly shown an almost cavalier willingness to take the law into their own hands when they believed that "mere politicians" were acting against the interests of the military, the emperor, or the nation. In February 1936, for example, some 1,200 members of the army's Tokyo-based First Guards Division—one of three similar formations that on a rotating basis undertook the protection of the emperor, his family, and the imperial palace—had risen against the government because they objected to a proposed transfer of their unit to Manchuria. Before the three-day revolt was crushed by loyal units, the rebels had assassinated Lord Keeper of the Privy Seal Makoto Saito, Finance Minister Korekiyo Takahashi, and several senior officers, and had badly wounded the emperor's grand chamberlain.[10]

Nine years later that grand chamberlain, now Prime Minister Suzuki, was only too aware that in seeking to break the deadlock between doves and hawks in the Big Six and cabinet he and Togo were quite probably putting their lives on the line. And he was right: news of the emperor's intervention during the August 9–10 meeting, and of the government's subsequent decision to conditionally accept the demands set forth in the Potsdam Declaration, had spread like wildfire through the senior levels of the army, emanating from no less a source than Army and War Minister Anami. Scant hours after Hirohito retired to his bed in the early morning hours of August 10 the squat general had called senior War Ministry staffers together to tell them of the night's developments. Anami's announcement was met with stunned disbelief that quickly turned to outrage as the gathered officers realized the full import of his words—most believed to the depth of their souls that surrender would not only mean the utter disgrace and degradation of the nation, they knew without a shred of doubt that it would also result in the complete and ignominious dissolution of the army.

As a chorus of angry voices swelled around him Anami firmly reminded his listeners that they were all soldiers and that they must not deviate from strict military discipline. In the crisis facing Japan, he told them, one man's uncontrolled actions could bring ruin upon the entire nation. When a younger officer stood up and directly asked Anami if he himself supported the surrender, the general slammed his swagger stick onto the top of a table and stonily replied that anyone who chose to disobey his orders would have do so over his dead body.[11]

Anami's exhortation notwithstanding, he himself had grave reservations about the decision to surrender. Several of the officers in the crowded room knew of their commander's doubts. One of them, Lieutenant Colonel Masao Inaba, decided in his capacity as Anami's speechwriter to draft a statement on the general's behalf that urged overseas army units to continue combat operations against Allied forces until the proposed surrender actually occurred. The finished statement was read and approved by several senior officers, though not by Anami. He had left for the Foreign Ministry building to help draft an official but purposely vague cabinet statement to be broadcast to the Japanese people that afternoon announcing, essentially, that momentous news regarding the conduct of the war would soon be forthcoming.

Before Anami returned to his office, and before he had the opportunity to read "his" statement, the text was picked up by Lieutenant Colonel Masahiko Takeshita, a staff officer who also happened to be Anami's brother-in-law. Takeshita conveyed the message to the same central Tokyo radio station that was scheduled to broadcast the cabinet statement. When Hiroshi Shimomura, the director of the government's official information bureau, heard about the unexpected "army proclamation" bearing Anami's name he immediately telephoned the general, who said he knew nothing of it but added that he was under increasing pressure from restive junior officers to disavow the decision to surrender. Fearing that Anami would be assassinated if the proclamation were not broadcast, Shimomura directed that it be read in conjunction with the cabinet statement.

So it was that when those Japanese who still had working radios tuned in to the regular afternoon news broadcast on August 10 they heard two wildly conflicting communiqués. The first, issued in Anami's name and titled "Instructions to the Troops," stated in part:

> We have but one choice: we must fight on until we win the sacred war to preserve our national polity. We must fight on, even if we have to chew grass and eat earth and live in the fields—for in our death there is a chance for our country's survival. The hero Kusunoki [a fourteenth-century samurai] pledged to live and die seven times in order to save Japan from disaster. We can do no less.[12]

The far-less-stirring cabinet statement simply announced that the Allies had attacked Japan with a new type of weapon, and concluded, rather too optimistically, that

> our fighting forces will no doubt be able to repulse the enemy's attack, but we must recognize that we are facing a situation that is as bad as it can be. The government will do all it can to defend the homeland and preserve the honor of the country, but it expects that Japan's 100 million will also rise to the occasion, overcoming whatever obstacles may lie in the path of the preservation of our national polity.[13]

Rigorous censorship had prevented the vast majority of the Japanese people from learning just how badly the war had been going, and many were understandably confused by the apparently contradictory statements beamed into their homes and shops that afternoon. That confusion spread ever further throughout the nation the following day, when Japan's major newspapers printed the texts of both communiqués.

Confusion was not an issue for many mid-level staff officers in the War Ministry and other key units in Tokyo, however. On the morning of August 11 some fifteen men gathered secretly in the bomb shelter beneath the ministry building to discuss ways they might negate the government's "dishonorable" peace overtures to the Allies and ensure that the war continued at least to a point that would allow Japan to secure a negotiated settlement. The conspirators included Takeshita, Anami's brother-in-law; Inaba, the writer of the "Instructions to the Troops" that was broadcast the night before in the war minister's name; and a particularly fanatical army major named Kenji Hatanaka. The men who filed into the stuffy and quickly smoke-filled shelter did not intend to depose Hirohito; on the contrary, they were devoted to the emperor and his essential role in the "national polity," believed that he had been "misguided" and "tricked" by Suzuki and other doves within the government, and felt that in "protecting" Hirohito—even against his will, if it became absolutely necessary—they were acting in the best interests of the monarchy, the nation, and their own sacred honor.

The conspirators' repeated references to "sacred honor" did not keep them from agreeing to undertake some distinctly dishonorable actions in the emperor's name. In order for their plot to succeed, they decided several people would have to die, and quickly: Suzuki, Togo, and Marquis Koichi Kido, the current Lord Keeper of the Privy Seal and a key supporter of the "doves," were to be assassinated at the earliest opportunity. Other key senior officers—including Lieutenant General Takeshi Mori, commander of the 1st Imperial Guards Division, and General Shizuichi Tanaka, whose 12th Area Army (also referred to as the Eastern District Army) controlled the greater Tokyo region—would be offered the opportunity to join the rebellion, but were to be killed if they refused. Takeshita told the plotters that he was certain he could win Anami's support for the coup, assuring them that the war minister secretly shared their beliefs and would agree wholeheartedly with their aims. Having decided on the substance of their action, the plotters turned to its timing. The coup had to be carried out before Japan received the Allied response to its surrender offer, they agreed, so as to

prevent the "defeatist" Suzuki government from having the opportunity to disgrace the nation by accepting whatever counteroffer
the Allies might make. With this last detail seen to, the conspirators
dispersed.[14]

The coup plan hatched in the War Ministry bomb shelter had
barely been put into motion when news of a response to Japan's
conditional acceptance of the Potsdam Declaration terms arrived in
Tokyo, though not via official channels. At forty-five minutes after
midnight on the very early morning of August 12 a radio-monitoring
station outside Tokyo picked up an Associated Press news flash,
broadcast by a shortwave station in San Francisco, carrying the full
text of the Allied answer to Japan's offer to accept the Potsdam terms.
The reply, drafted by American Secretary of State James F. Byrnes,
was immediately transmitted to the Foreign Office, where it landed
like a third atomic bomb. Rather than accept the Japanese condition
that nothing in the surrender agreement should prejudice "the pre-
rogatives of His Majesty as a sovereign ruler," the Allies replied em-
phatically that "from the moment of surrender the authority of the
Emperor and the Japanese Government to rule the state shall be subject to the Supreme Commander of the Allied Powers, who will take
such steps as he deems proper to effectuate the surrender terms."[15]

In a single, concise sentence the Allied response effectively destroyed Japanese hopes of preserving the "national polity." The
emperor—the hereditary god-sovereign of the nation—and his ministers were to be stripped of their power and influence and reduced
to mere subordinates of some as-yet-unidentified Allied military
officer. This was a crushing blow, but worse was to come with re-
gard to the tradition that Japan's sovereignty stemmed solely from
the hereditary emperor: "The ultimate form of government of Japan
shall, in accordance with the Potsdam Declaration, be established by
the freely expressed will of the Japanese people."[16] Heaping insult
upon already grievous injury, as the Foreign Ministry staffers read
it, the Allies were declaring that not only would the emperor lose
the mantle of mystical, sacred, and inviolable sovereignty that had
for centuries surrounded his Chrysanthemum Throne, his subjects

were actually to be given the right to decide for themselves what form their government should take.

The Allied response was shocking to those in the Foreign Ministry and among the members of the emperor's inner circle, once the news had reached the palace, but it was within the Japanese military that the pronouncement ignited the hottest flames of rage. Many senior commanders had harbored hopes of a negotiated settlement that would somehow allow Japan itself to decide where and when the nation's armed forces would lay down their arms; a settlement that would also prevent any foreign occupation of the Home Islands. Yet the Allied *diktat* clearly stated that the emperor "shall issue his commands to all the Japanese military, naval and air authorities and to all the forces under their control wherever located to cease active operations and to surrender their arms." And, further, that "the armed forces of the Allied Powers will remain in Japan until the purposes set forth in the Potsdam Declaration are achieved."[17]

As might be expected, these last two components of the Allied reply prompted an immediate reaction from the army and navy chiefs of staff. At 8:20 on the morning of Sunday, August 12, General Umezu and Admiral Toyoda—almost certainly in response to the frenzied pleadings of their firebrand subordinates and without requesting authorization from Anami and Yonai, their respective superiors—made an unscheduled joint appearance at the imperial palace and requested an immediate audience with Hirohito. Once closeted with the emperor and his chief military aide, General Shigeru Hasunuma, the two men made lengthy presentations in which they declared the Allied reply to be absolutely unacceptable. The men argued that Japan should continue the fight no matter the consequences, both to preserve the honor of the nation's military forces and to win better terms from the Allies. Hirohito listened attentively, then informed the two senior officers that he could make no decision on their presentation because he could not act based upon the intercepted news flash from San Francisco; he had to await the formal text of the Allied reply, which would be forthcoming from Secretary of State Byrnes through normal diplomatic channels.

Hirohito's statement was more than a little disingenuous. Despite the unexpectedly uncompromising tone of the Allies' response to Japan's surrender overture, the emperor remained determined to bring the war to an end as soon as possible. He repeated this determination to Togo during a scheduled 2 P.M. audience, and found that his foreign minister was in total agreement that the Allied terms had to be accepted, though they foreshadowed fundamental and irrevocable changes within the highest levels of Japan's ruling civilian and military elites. It was now up to Togo to sell the military's senior leaders and, more important, the full cabinet on the absolute necessity of issuing an immediate, positive response to the Allies.

That would prove to be a herculean task, however. The tenor and content of the Allied reply had reopened the vast chasm between the hawks and the doves within both the Big Six and the cabinet, despite the emperor's August 10 sanctioning of an immediate end to hostilities. Moreover, even as Togo was leaving for the prime minister's home to attend the special afternoon cabinet meeting at which he would repeat Hirohito's edict and ask for unanimous agreement to accept the Allied terms, the officers bent on a coup d'état were attempting to pull the still-reluctant War Minister Anami into their cabal. Seven of the conspirators hurried into the general's office after his return from the palace and as he was preparing to leave for the cabinet meeting. With Takeshita acting as spokesman, they begged him to join their rebellion. Buckling on his sword, Anami told Takeshita to call on him at home that evening, then rushed out to his waiting staff car for the short ride to Suzuki's residence.

The cabinet meeting began promptly at 3 P.M., but that was perhaps the only thing that went according to Togo's plan. Suzuki read a translation of the Allied reply to Japan's conditional surrender offer, stressing more than once that it was the "unofficial" version taken from the intercepted radio broadcast. Then Togo rose. After admitting that the Allied terms were not perfect, especially in the restrictions they placed on the emperor's powers and his place in Japanese society, Togo argued eloquently and at some length that they must nevertheless be accepted, and quickly, to ensure the nation's very survival.

Hardly had Togo retaken his seat when Anami stood and launched into the by-now familiar litany of reasons why acceptance of the Allied terms would be the greatest and most catastrophic error in Japanese history. The "national polity" would be destroyed, the military would be humiliated, and the homeland would be desecrated for eternity through its occupation by foreign troops. To Togo's consternation the war minister's reasoning seemed to resonate with many of the cabinet members, and even Suzuki himself seemed swayed by Anami's words. Realizing that any immediate vote might well go against him, Togo announced that because the official version of the Allied message had not yet arrived through diplomatic channels the cabinet should postpone any further discussion—and any final decision—until after the communiqué had been received and authenticated. Somewhat to his surprise the majority of those in attendance agreed, and Suzuki adjourned the fractious session nearly four hours after it began.

Worn out by the long and contentious meeting, Togo shuffled into an anteroom of the prime minister's residence and telephoned his deputy, Shunichi Matsumoto, to report on the gathering. When the foreign minister expressed his fear that the untimely arrival of the official Allied response that night might prompt an emergency cabinet session that could well result in a vote to continue the war, Matsumoto suggested a simple yet elegant solution: he would direct the staff of the Foreign Ministry's communications office to hold any official message arriving from Secretary Byrnes for the remainder of that Sunday until the following morning. The time and date stamp indicating when the Allied cable arrived would thus read Monday, August 13. If nothing else, the administrative ruse would give Togo additional time to muster his forces and, conceivably, again enlist the emperor's aid in bringing about Japan's immediate surrender.

Matsumoto had put his plan into action just in time: Byrnes's official cable arrived at the Foreign Ministry at 6:40 that Sunday evening and was immediately stamped as having been received at 7:30 Monday morning.

Concealing the cable's arrival from virtually everyone in the government did prevent the emergency cabinet meeting that Togo feared would result in a vote to continue the war; however, it did not keep the anti-surrender factions from working to advance their own agenda. Late on the night of August 12 two key members of the coup plot—Lieutenant Colonel Masataka Ida and the fanatic Major Hatanaka—called on War Minister Anami at his family home in the Tokyo suburb of Mitaka. They passionately repeated all the reasons why they believed acceptance of the Potsdam Declaration terms would mean the complete and utter destruction of Japan and its centuries-old institutions, then pleaded with Anami to do all he could to prevent the Suzuki government from caving in to Togo and the peace faction. Although the war minister himself favored rejection of the Byrnes ultimatum once the official version of it arrived, he was hesitant to throw in his lot with the conspirators without first determining which other senior officers were willing to support a coup. Because any revolt would fail completely without the army's support, the first man Anami had to quiz regarding his position on surrender was General Umezu.

Steeped as he was in his nation's cultural and societal traditions, the war minster sought to confirm the chief of staff's views indirectly. Before dawn on the morning of August 13 Anami therefore dispatched his military secretary, Colonel Saburo Hayashi, to Umezu's home bearing a verbal message. The war minister, Hayashi was to say, was considering asking Field Marshal Shunroku Hata, commander of the Hiroshima-based Second General Army, to make a personal appeal to Hirohito that the emperor reject the Allied terms and continue the fight. Whether Anamai was aware that Hata was, in fact, in favor of ending the war quickly is unclear. And it may not have been important anyway, for telling Umezu about the proposed overture to Hata was simply a covert test; if the chief of staff supported the idea, then Anami would know he could most probably be trusted to lend the army's support to the coup. The gruff chief of staff had made it very clear during meetings of the Big Six and cabinet that he also believed that Japan should fight on, so Anami was fairly certain his response would be a positive one from the conspirators' point of view.

It was, therefore, a huge shock when Hayashi returned to Anami's home just after sunrise with Umezu's answer. Though the army chief of staff found the Allied surrender terms to be repugnant, he had sorrowfully—and apparently rather suddenly—come to the conclusion that continuing the war was pointless. Given that the Americans seemed entirely willing to keep dropping atomic bombs on Japan's major cities—and one had to assume, he pointed out, that Tokyo was quite likely next on the target list—attempting to continue the war would most probably only result in millions more dead Japanese and the conversion of the Home Islands into a continuous landscape of radioactive rubble.

Umezu's stunning response was undoubtedly on Anami's mind when he climbed into his staff car just hours later, at around 7:00 on Monday morning. A meeting of the Big Six had been set for 9 A.M., and before attending it the war minister wanted to converse privately with Lord Privy Seal Kido, a key supporter of the emperor's decision to accept the surrender terms. Indeed, so widely known were Kido's pro-peace views that he'd been receiving death threats from diehard military officers, and for his own protection he had moved from his suburban home into the imperial household building on the palace grounds. Anami had known the emperor's counselor for nearly two decades, and although the two men were not close friends, the war minister was apparently convinced that he could win Kido over to his point of view through a forceful but respectful recitation of the calamities that would befall the nation should Hirohito insist on accepting the Allied surrender terms.

Yet when Anami was finished with his presentation—during which he assured his "honored friend" that Japan's military forces would absolutely refuse to lay down their arms and would gladly die fighting alongside the entire civilian population in a final, decisive battle against the invaders—Kido remained unmoved. The emperor, he pointed out, did not himself object to the harsh realities of the Allied terms and had already announced his acceptance of them to the members of his government and to the Allies. If Hirohito were to suddenly change his mind and call for continued war, he would look like a liar and a fool and, more important, the Allies would almost certainly employ their terrible new bombs in attacks throughout the Home Islands. The Japanese people would hold the emperor personally responsible for the resulting devastation, Kido said, and would likely turn on him and the entire imperial system. Was that an outcome the war minister really wanted? It wasn't, of course, and as he rose to leave, Anami said, almost as though he were pursuing the continuation of the war only as a way to appease the diehards in his own organization, "You don't know what it's like in the Ministry."[18]

Whatever Anami's true feelings might have been about continuing the war, he walked into the 9 A.M. Big Six meeting in the prime minister's bomb shelter still advocating rejection of the Byrnes ultimatum. Admiral Toyoda, the navy chief of staff, continued to support the war minister's point of view. And, strangely, so did the army's General Umezu, despite his earlier declaration to Hayashi that he privately supported acceptance of the Allied terms. His public solidarity with the "hawks" might well have been simply an expression of service solidarity or personal loyalty to Anami—or perhaps of mere self-preservation—but the practical effect of Umezu's stance was that the Supreme Council for the Direction of the War remained deadlocked. Moreover, when he and Toyoda were called out of the meeting so that Hirohito could personally ask them not to order any offensive military action that might prompt an overwhelming Allied response, Umezu responded by saying that both services would refrain from provocative, offensive moves but that they would also be authorized to defend themselves if fired upon.

Just days later, Umezu's almost offhand statement would have dire consequences for members of the 386th Bomb Squadron.[19]

THE BIG SIX ADJOURNED their meeting in the early afternoon of August 13, then reconvened as part of a full cabinet meeting that began at 4 P.M. Three hours of argument and counterargument did not break the previously existing logjam regarding the Allied surrender ultimatum. When Suzuki asked the ministers for their positions three remained opposed, twelve favored immediate acceptance, and one was still undecided. The prime minister then announced that the continuing lack of unanimity left him no choice but to ask Hirohito for a second imperial decision.

As the ministers filed out of the bomb shelter, Anami took Suzuki aside and asked him to wait two days before seeking the emperor's intervention. The prime minister refused, saying "our opportunity is now—we must seize it at once." After Anami walked away an army medical officer named Kobayashi, who had heard the exchange, approached Suzuki and asked why it was impossible to wait just a few more days before responding to the Allies.

The prime minister looked at the doctor and, as though speaking to a slow-witted child, said, "if we don't act now, the Russians will penetrate not only Manchuria and Korea but northern Japan as well. If that happens our country is finished. We must act now, while our chief adversary is still the United States."

"General Anami will kill himself," Kobayashi responded.

Suzuki nodded gravely, looked the physician in the eye and said, "yes, that will be very regrettable."[20]

The man of whom they were speaking was not quite ready to fall on his ceremonial sword, however. After the deadlocked cabinet meeting Anami returned to his official residence, where at 8 P.M. a group of ten young army officers arrived to secure his authorization for the coup they planned to launch the following morning. Among the men seeking Anami's blessing was the firebrand Hatanaka, who told the war minister that the peace factions in the Big Six and cabinet had decided to kill Anami if he continued to resist the emperor's decision to accept the Allied surrender terms. The young officer's ploy to gain the war minister's approval of the coup was apparently fairly transparent, for Anami simply laughed. He then went on to say that the plan the conspirators had presented—which involved the imprisonment and possible execution of Suzuki, Kido, Togo, and others, as well as the proclamation of martial law throughout the country—was not detailed enough. Despite their pleas that he give them a yes or no answer immediately, Anami sent the plotters away with the promise to consider their plan further and give them his decision soon.

The remainder of the night passed quickly for the war minister, who quite probably spent the hours until dawn contemplating what a coup—whether successful or not—would mean for the nation and for himself. Just after sunrise on August 14 Anami breakfasted with Western District Army commander Field Marshal Hata, who had driven straight from Hiroshima and gave the war minister a no-holds-barred account of conditions in the first city to feel the horri-fying effects of a nuclear explosion. What impact the aging soldier's account had on Anami we do not know, though the historical re-cord does show that just before the two men parted the war minister asked Hata to share his insights about the effect of the atomic bomb-ing with the emperor. With the field marshal's unflinching report almost certainly still on his mind, Anami stepped into his staff car just after 7 A.M. for the drive to his War Ministry office.[21]

At roughly the same time, Lord Privy Seal Kido was walking into a hastily arranged meeting with Hirohito. The purpose of the audience was to inform the emperor that since late the previous day American B-29 bombers had been dropping leaflets across the country—leaflets that told the Japanese people not only about the surrender terms put forth in the Potsdam Declaration, but also about the imperial government's August 10 conditional acceptance of those terms. The American tactic was profoundly dangerous for both Japan and its emperor, Kido told his sovereign, because it could very well spark widespread public revolt and would likely set off the military coup d'état that most senior government officials feared. Soon after Suzuki arrived to join the discussion, Hirohito declared that he would order all members of the Big Six and the cabinet to attend an emergency imperial conference at which he, as emperor and titular commander in chief of the nation's armed forces, would instruct the attendees to accept the terms set forth in Secretary Byrnes's cable. Moreover, Hirohito said, he would com-mand them to draft an imperial rescript that would be broadcast to the nation. And finally, the emperor directed that the imperial conference be convened at 10:30 that very morning so as to give any coup plotters within the military less time to put their plans into action.[22]

Immediately upon hearing of the emergency conference, Anami urged the emperor to first receive a delegation of senior military officers, a group that would include the war minister himself, Field Marshal Sugiyama, the navy's Fleet Admiral Osami Nagano, and Field Marshal Hata. Anami apparently assumed that the latter officer, much-decorated and widely respected, would argue in favor of continuing the war despite the Americans' use of the new bomb. The war minister must therefore have been deeply surprised when the elderly Hata, with tears rolling down his cheeks, described in gruesome detail the destruction and suffering in Hiroshima. The field marshal then peered closely at each man in the room and pronounced what was effectively the death knell for the hawks' hopes of prolonging the war. Speaking in his capacity as commander of the Japanese forces slated to defend Kyushu in the event of an Allied invasion, he said he did not believe such an assault could be stopped and therefore agreed with the emperor's decision to accept the terms set forth in the Byrnes cable.[23]

Having thereby dropped his own bombshell, the field marshal sat to await Hirohito's response. After a moment's reflection, the emperor quietly said that there was no way Japan could halt either the oncoming Soviet forces or the Americans' further use of their new bomb, and he therefore asked the gathered senior officers to support him in his quest to end the war immediately. Having issued what was tantamount to an imperial command, Hirohito rose and slowly walked from the room, pausing only for a moment to mutter that he would see them all shortly in the bomb shelter.

When Hirohito entered that chamber, the same one in which the fateful August 10 imperial conference had been held, some twenty men stood and bowed in silent deference. The room was very warm and more than a little humid, and those in attendance—the Big Six, cabinet members, palace officials, and the emperor himself—were soon bathed in sweat. Dressed in a simple military uniform, Hirohito sat down behind a small desk at the head of the room, and nodded to Suzuki to begin what all those present knew was to be a momentous meeting that would quite literally change the course of Japanese history.

The aged prime minister rose to his feet and carefully recounted, yet again, the terms outlined in Secretary of State Byrnes's official response to Japan's conditional surrender offer. Suzuki then called upon Anami, Umezu, and Toyoda to recite their by now all-too-familiar list of reasons why the Byrnes note was unacceptable. The three military men spoke passionately, though one suspects that by this time both Anami and Umezu were simply going through the motions for appearances' sake. When the chamber was once again quiet, the eyes of all present turned toward Hirohito. As tears welled in his eyes, the emperor said:

> I have listened carefully to all the arguments opposing Japan's acceptance of the Allied reply as it stands. My own opinion, how-ever, has not changed. I shall now restate it. I have examined the conditions prevailing in Japan and in the rest of the world, and I believe that a continuation of the war offers nothing but con-tinued destruction. I have studied the terms of the Allied reply, and I have come to the conclusion that they represent a virtually complete acknowledgement of our position as we outlined it in the note dispatched a few days ago. In short, I consider the reply to be acceptable.

Pausing briefly to take a deep, shuddering breath and to draw a handkerchief across his eyes, Hirohito assured his listeners that he believed the Byrnes cable was evidence of the Allies' good intentions to maintain "the national structure," referring, if rather obliquely, to the continuation of the monarchy. The emperor then looked point-edly at Anami and Toyoda, and added that he fully understood how difficult it would be for the officers and men of the nation's armed forces to be disarmed and to see their beloved country occupied. Af-ter expressing his own deep sorrow for the hardships and suffering his subjects had experienced, Hirohito concluded:

> As the people of Japan are unaware of the present situation, I know they will be deeply shocked when they hear of our deci-sion. If it is thought appropriate that I explain the matter to them

personally, I am willing to go before the microphone. . . . I am willing to go wherever necessary to explain our decision. I desire the cabinet to prepare as soon as possible an imperial rescript announcing the termination of the war.[24]

Once again having clearly expressed his imperial will, Hirohito rose and walked slowly out of the room with tears streaming down his cheeks. Many of those to whom he had spoken then broke down completely, sobbing for their emperor, their nation, and—because many were almost certain to be charged with war crimes by the Allied occupiers—quite probably for themselves. Then, despite their deep emotion, they got on with the work Hirohito had charged them to do. The cabinet members convened almost immediately after their sovereign left the bomb shelter. They drafted and then ratified the nation's unconditional acceptance of all the terms set forth in the Byrnes cable, and ordered the response to be transmitted immediately to Washington via Japan's embassies in Sweden and Switzerland.

Within hours the emperor would be in the Household Ministry building, recording the imperial rescript message. But even before he stepped before the microphone the coup d'état he and so many others feared was already under way.

FROM THE TIME OF their first, clandestine meeting in the War Ministry bomb shelter on August 11, the coup plotters had worked diligently—if covertly—to lay the groundwork for the revolt they fervently believed would save both the nation and the armed forces. Takeshita, Hatanaka, and the rest had begun reaching out to fellow officers, both in Tokyo and at key army and navy installations throughout the country, attempting to determine which men could be counted on to support them and which might have to be "neutralized." They had also extended feelers to certain members of the Kempeitai, the nation's dreaded, military-run secret police. When the revolt began, the plotters reasoned, Japan's equivalent of Nazi Germany's Gestapo would be needed to help secure the Imperial Palace and the Tokyo headquarters of NHK, the national radio broadcast service. And, once the coup had succeeded, Kempeitai agents would arrest those whom the revolt's leaders designated as "defeatists."

The plotters had decided to launch the coup at 10 A.M. on August 14, but War Minister Anami's continued evasions about whether he would join the revolt forced a postponement. Takeshita tried to intercept Anami before the day's imperial conference in order to ascertain the grizzled general's position once and for all, but he arrived minutes after his brother-in-law had walked down into the imperial bomb shelter. When Anami finally reappeared, Takeshita could tell from the look on his face that a momentous decision had been made. Pulling the war minister aside, the younger man begged for him to order the mobilization of troops to "maintain security" within the city—a very thinly veiled plea that Anami support the coup. Then, repeating a rumor that was circulating within the War Ministry, Takeshita said that army Chief of Staff Umezu had thrown in his lot with the plotters.

The statement—which was untrue—did not sway Anami.

"The emperor has made his decision," the war minister said wearily, "there is nothing I can do. As a Japanese soldier I must obey my emperor."[25]

Takeshita finally had the definitive answer he had been seeking, though it was not the one for which he had been hoping. Knowing from the look on Anami's face that his mind was made up and his decision would not change, the younger officer turned and walked slowly back to his waiting staff car. Before he headed back to the War Ministry to share the news with his fellow conspirators, Takeshita sat for several minutes pondering what he now knew to be a simple truth: without his brother-in-law's active support, the coup was doomed to certain failure. What then, he wondered, was the point in going ahead with it?

As Takeshita sat thinking, Anami was himself already on the way back to the ministry building. Just after 3 P.M. he walked into his outer office to find a dozen subordinates waiting none too patiently, desperate to know the outcome of the imperial conference. Keenly aware that the young officers wanted to hear that the nation would fight on and that the enemy would never be allowed to set foot on Japan's sacred soil, the war minister took a deep breath and then broke their hearts: the emperor, he said, was firm in his desire to end the war, and would announce Japan's acceptance of the Allied surrender terms to all his subjects in an imperial rescript to be broadcast the following day. So there would be no misunderstanding about his own position, Anami then further stunned the gathered officers by saying that he, like all other Japanese soldiers, was honor-bound to accept that decision and bend to the imperial will. With a final glance around the suddenly silent room, the war minister turned, walked into his office, and firmly closed the door.

Though Anami had intended that his pronouncement would dampen the fires of revolt among his subordinates, it had exactly the opposite effect on Major Hatanaka and several of the other men standing in the now deathly silent room. Already furious that the morning launch of the planned coup had been postponed, they knew that the revolt would have to be put in motion before the broadcast of the imperial rescript if there was to be any hope of success. After a quick hallway conference, the men split up and rushed from the building.

Not of high enough rank to merit a staff car, Hatanaka jumped on his bicycle and tore off through the rubble-clogged streets of Tokyo. He made first for the headquarters of the Eastern District Army, where somewhat to his surprise General Tanaka refused to join any revolt. Hatanaka then pedaled as quickly as he could through the oppressive summer heat to the Imperial Guards Division command post. Two of the unit's officers—majors Sadakichi Ishihara and Hidemasa Koga—were members of the conspiracy and Hatanaka likely communicated to them the importance of quickly seizing control of the imperial palace and either preventing the recording of the rescript or, failing that, keeping the completed recording from being broadcast. Late that same afternoon trucks bearing a battalion of troops from the 1st Guards Division's 2nd Regiment rumbled through the gates of the Imperial Palace. This was unusual in that the sprawling compound was normally guarded by a single battalion, and one was already on duty. Moreover, the new arrivals were personally led by the regimental commander, Colonel Toyo-jiro Haga.[26]

After returning to the War Ministry Hatanaka huddled briefly with co-conspirator Lieutenant Colonel Jiro Shiizaki, then sought out Lieutenant Colonel Masataka Ida of the ministry's Military Affairs Section. Like several officers who had been present when Anami had earlier announced his support for Hirohito's decision to surrender, Ida had decided to kill himself and Hatanaka found him calmly preparing to commit *seppuku*.[27] Believing that Ida's position would allow him to issue orders that would support the coup, the firebrand major argued that a successful revolt would protect the emperor from the "traitors" that surrounded him and also prevent Japan's surrender—thereby preserving both the national polity and the army. Assisting in the coup, Hatanka argued, was therefore a far more glorious path than Ida's plan to preserve his own personal honor through suicide. The young major's logic was at least partially convincing, for though Ida did not agree outright to lend his support to the coup, he said he would postpone his suicide and await further developments.

He didn't have to wait long. Some three hours later, at about 10 P.M., Hatanaka returned to Ida's ministry office, accompanied by Shiizaki. The two younger officers excitedly told Ida that the coup now had the support of key officers in the Imperial Guards Division; all that was needed to ensure the revolt's success was for the division commander, General Mori, to join the plot. Hatanaka said that he and Shiizake were on their way to enlist the general's support, and asked Ida to accompany them. His planned suicide now on hold, the older officer agreed and the three set off for the Guards Division headquarters.

Upon their arrival the men were joined by Ishihara and Koga, and all five conspirators dashed up several flights of stairs to Mori's office. To their extreme exasperation, the general's aide told the officers to take a seat in the waiting room; Mori was closeted in his office with a Lieutenant Colonel Shiraishi, his brother-in-law and a member of Field Marshal Hata's staff, and would not be available for some time. Hatanaka and the others were thus forced to cool their heels, not knowing that less than a quarter of a mile away the technicians from NHK had just finished setting up their recording equipment and were awaiting the emperor's arrival.

More than ninety minutes ticked by before an increasingly anxious Hatanaka finally stood up and burst into Mori's office with Ida and Shiizaki close behind. Startled, the general demanded to know what the men wanted. As the young major stuttered out their request that Mori lead his division against Suzuki and the other "traitors," anger and disbelief flashed across the general's face. But then, possibly because he realized that his life and that of his brother-in-law might depend on how he reacted over the next few minutes, Mori became quite calm and agreed to listen to the conspirators' reasoning. At that point, believing that the division commander was leaning toward cooperation, Hatanaka excused himself, telling Ida he had an important engagement. It was just after midnight as the young major dashed from the room; Ida and Shiizaki stayed with Mori for another hour, finally leaving when the general said he would have to pay a brief visit to the nearby Meiji Shrine before giving them his final answer.

Hatanaka, in the meantime, had made his way to the home of Masahiko Takeshita, pounding on the door until Anami's brother-in-law ushered him inside. As the young major began recounting the evening's events Takeshita stopped him with a raised hand and calmly said he had decided not to take part in the coup. When the stunned Hatanaka asked him the reason for this apparently sudden change of heart, Takeshita replied that Anami was not with them, and without the war minister's support the revolt had absolutely no chance of success, so there was no point in even attempting it. Crestfallen, Hatanaka paced the floor, muttering to himself before finally turning to Takeshita and agreeing that the coup was most probably doomed to failure. But then, straightening up, he looked squarely at the older officer and said that he and his fellow conspirators had gained the support of the Imperial Guards Division and would carry on with the revolt despite the odds. Hatanaka bowed slightly, then walked out into the night.

By the time the young major made his way back to Mori's office it was nearly 2 A.M. on August 15 and, though Hatanaka didn't know

it, Hirohito had long since concluded the recording of the imperial
rescript. The commander of the Imperial Guards Division had not
yet left to visit the shrine, and when Hatanaka and Koga pressed
him for a decision about lending his division's support to the coup,
Mori responded that he could not, and would not, act in defiance of
the emperor's expressed will. As the general was speaking, Captain
Shigetaro Uehara, an army aviation officer and coup conspirator,
rushed into the office past Shiizaki, pushed Ida and Koga aside as
he approached Hatanaka, and asked if "the matter" was settled.

When the young major replied that it was not, Uehara looked
pointedly at Mori and, speaking to Hatanaka, said that time was
running out. The Guards Division commander, though almost certainly aware that the atmosphere in his small office had suddenly
changed for the worse, looked directly at Uehara and shouted that
he would not support the coup no matter how long the conspirators
might plead with him to do so. Without warning, Uehara drew his
sword and rushed toward Mori. When the general's brother-in-law
stepped forward to protect him, Uehara plunged his razor-sharp
blade into Shiraishi's chest, then yanked it free, reversed his hold
and with a powerful sideways blow nearly severed the man's head
from his body. Uehara then pivoted toward Mori, but before he
could strike the fatal blow Hatanaka pulled his 8mm Nambu au-
tomatic pistol from its holster and shot the general squarely in the
chest. Mori staggered sideways and collapsed atop Shiraishi's body,
and Uehara brought his blade down into the back of the general's
skull in an almost certainly unnecessary coup de grâce.

With the problem of General Mori definitively "settled" in the
most brutal way, Hatanaka and Uehara saluted the bodies and
walked calmly out of the blood-spattered office. The two officers
dispatched Ida to the Eastern District Army headquarters to convince its commander, General Shizuichi Tanaka, to support the
coup. That done, they conferred with Ishihara and Koga, who had
falsified an operations order directing the entire Guards Division
to secure the grounds of the imperial palace and the areas immediately surrounding it. The order bore Mori's signature block, and
after the others had set off for the palace Ishihara and Koga stamped

the document with the general's official seal and began distributing it to the division's field commanders. Within forty-five minutes the entire imperial closure and all its residents—including Hirohito, his family, and the majority of the "defeatist traitors" the coup's conspirators so loathed—were completely cut off from the outside world.

Yet one very powerful man—at that point potentially the *most* powerful man in Japan—was both free and at peace. After participating in the drafting of the imperial rescript at Suzuki's office, War Minister Anami had spoken briefly with the prime minister and Foreign Minister Togo, assuring both men that his stubborn opposition to the nation's acceptance of the Allied surrender conditions stemmed solely from his desire to protect the emperor and the nation from dishonor and shame. Anami had then returned to his official residence, taken a bath, and retired to his bedroom with several bottles of sake. Just after 1 A.M. his brother-in-law arrived at the house and found Anami preparing to commit *seppuku*.

That the general was about to kill himself did not surprise Takeshita. Indeed, anyone who knew Anami well was aware that he was a Japanese of the old school, a man who believed with every fiber of his being that the only way in which he could atone for his part in Japan's defeat—and, quite likely, for his opposition to the will of his emperor—was by taking his own life in the traditional samurai way. Takeshita realized that his brother-in-law was completely at peace with his decision, and rather than attempt to dissuade him the younger man decided to share the war minister's last hours. Takeshita therefore seated himself on a *tatami* mat next to Anami, and the two men settled down companionably to drink away the war minister's last night on earth.

ON THE GROUNDS OF the palace things were certainly neither as calm nor as companionable as they were at General Anami's home. Troops of the Guards Division had occupied the sprawling imperial compound and closed all of the gates leading into it. Acting in accordance with the falsified orders produced by Ishihara and Koga, soldiers had begun systematically searching the various buildings for the recordings of Hirohito's rescript. The hunt was led by Hatanaka, Uehara, and Shiizaki, who had arrived at the palace just minutes after the murder of General Mori and his brother-in-law. The conspirators were determined to find and destroy the recordings to prevent their broadcast, thereby also preventing Japan's surrender, and they knew that they were running out of time. Their assassination of the Guards Division commander would inevitably come to light sooner rather than later, and when it did the falsified orders would be immediately rescinded by officers loyal to the government. If Ida were unable to convince General Tanaka of the Eastern District Army to join the conspiracy, the revolt would have little chance of success.

In point of fact, though Hatanaka and his fellow plotters didn't know it yet, two significant failures had already doomed their coup. First, although Guards Division troops had detained Information Bureau director Shimomura, the NHK technicians, and various other officials who had been present for Hirohito's reading of the rescript, the vinyl recordings themselves had not been found, despite an exhaustive search. Because the radio technicians had clearly understood how valuable the disks were and that the anti-surrender faction would likely kill anyone possessing them in order to prevent their broadcast, the men gave the recordings to a palace chamberlain for safekeeping rather than attempting to take them directly to the NHK studio. The man had then hidden the disks in the back of a tiny, concealed cupboard in the Household Ministry building, itself a rabbit warren of small offices packed with innumerable file cabinets, and they had remained undiscovered.

Second, and more important, Lieutenant Colonel Ida had failed miserably in his attempt to enlist General Tanaka's help with carrying out the coup. Indeed, upon being told what was happening, the Eastern District Army commander ordered the by-now thoroughly dispirited Ida to return to the imperial palace and attempt to talk Hatanaka out of continuing his treasonous actions. Tanaka then directed that all regimental commanders within the Imperial Guards Division come immediately to Eastern District Army headquarters, where they were told that their earlier orders to quarantine the palace complex were false and that all of their troops on the palace grounds should immediately withdraw. Any that failed to do so, he said, would be treated as traitors and would be fired on.

The attempted coup unraveled quickly following Tanaka's refusal to throw in his lot with the conspirators. Faced with the Eastern District Army's overwhelming force—and finally convinced that they'd been misled by forged orders—the commanders of the Guards Division units that had taken control of the palace complex and other key facilities throughout Tokyo withdrew, without having found the recordings and without having captured Prime Minister Suzuki or any other leading members of the peace faction. Tanaka himself faced down the key leaders of the conspiracy—Hatanaka, Koga, Shiizaki, and Uehara—on one of the bridges leading into the palace complex and in no uncertain terms told them they had betrayed their emperor and their nation, and had brought shame upon the armed forces. Tanaka also made it very clear that there was only one way in which the traitors could atone for their actions: suicide. All four ultimately complied using either pistol or sword, thereby joining in death the far more august, and arguably less guilty, General Anami, who disemboweled himself at his home just after dawn on August 15.[28]

HIROHITO AND HIS FAMILY had remained safe throughout the attempted coup and, according to some sources, were completely unaware of the revolt until after it had ended. At noon, local time, on August 15 the emperor's recorded rescript was broadcast throughout Japan, shocking the vast majority of the emperor's subjects both with its indirect announcement of defeat and its even more frightening implication of impending foreign occupation. Thousands—indeed, perhaps tens of thousands—of Japanese reacted to the devastating news by killing themselves.

Within Japan's armed forces the broadcast of the rescript elicited decidedly mixed reactions. Though the vast majority of officers and enlisted members of the navy and army throughout Japan and across Asia and the Pacific swallowed their shame and bent themselves to their emperor's will, there were diehards in both services who fervently vowed to keep fighting. Some of these dissenters believed that the sentiments the emperor had voiced in his broadcast had been coerced and the surrender decision was thus invalid. So, therefore, were the subsequent orders issued by both army chief of staff General Umezu and his navy counterpart, Admiral Yonai, that all Japanese military forces immediately cease offensive action and prepare to lay down their arms. These "disbelievers" further argued—as had Kenji Hatanaka and his fellow conspirators—that the nation should fight on tenaciously in the emperor's name and inflict such grievous losses on the Allied invaders that they would agree to a negotiated settlement.

But there was also another category of military men who had decided that their war was not quite over. Although they had heard and believed the emperor's broadcast, these men had also determined that until the surrender had become a reality no one could be sure that the Americans would refrain from dropping more of their horrible new bombs. The men therefore determined, like the diehard fanatics but for significantly different reasons, that they would do all in their power to defend the sacred soil of Japan vigorously, right up to the moment of the nation's official capitulation.

Unfortunately for the B-32 crews of the 386th Bomb Squadron, both categories of Japan's holdouts—the diehard fanatics and the determined defenders—were well represented within the one group of Japanese military personnel that could actually transform martial zeal into potentially devastating practice long before Allied ground forces set foot on the Home Islands: the fighter pilots who defended the nation's airspace.

CHAPTER 4

CEASEFIRE, OR NOT?

WHEN CAPTAIN YASUNA KOZONO leapt behind the wheel of his staff car just after noon on August 14 he was a man in a fever, both literally and figuratively. The decorated naval aviator—known as the "Father of Japanese Night Fighters" for his pioneering efforts in that nocturnal form of aerial combat—was in the first, febrile stages of a relapse of the malaria he'd first suffered while stationed at Rabaul some two years before. But it wasn't just the disease that made him sweat and tremble as he gunned the car out of the Navy Ministry parking lot in Tokyo and headed out of the city along rubble-strewn streets. Kozono had just hours before been told of Emperor Hirohito's decision to accept the Allied surrender terms, and his face was crimson with the heat of shame.

For a man like Kozono, the idea of surrender was quite simply unthinkable. He was a career officer who lived and breathed the *Bushido* values and the traditions of the Japanese navy. He had participated in the arc of his nation's military operations from the early victories in China, Southeast Asia, and the East Indies to the seemingly endless defeats that began with the 1942 battles of the Coral Sea and Midway. He had watched as his beloved navy had been steadily reduced from a magnificent and mighty fleet to little more than a coastal defense force, its few remaining warships unable to sortie from harbor without being ruthlessly hunted down by the overwhelmingly powerful enemy that even now was preparing to land on the sacred shores of the Home Islands. Yet despite the reversals, the defeats, and the retreats, Kozono had never lost faith in his service, his nation, or his emperor. He had fought on regardless of the odds, and now—firmly convinced that Hirohito had somehow been coerced or misled by his weak-willed and traitorous advisers— Kozono was entirely prepared to keep fighting, to die gloriously in the defense of his nation, and to kill as many of the enemy as possible in the process. And unlike many other officers in Japan's armed forces, the veteran forty-three-year-old aviator still had enough men and matériel to turn his dreams of honorable and glorious resistance into something approaching reality.

FROM EARLY 1944 ONWARD the primary responsibility for the air defense of the seven prefectures that make up the greater Tokyo metropolitan area—traditionally referred to as the Kanto Plain—rested with the Japanese Army Air Forces' 10th Air Division, officially part of General Shizuichi Tanaka's Eastern District Army. At the time of its formation the organization fielded between 350 and 400 aircraft, primarily single-engine day fighters supplemented by twin-engine night fighters, though the latter were not generally equipped with radar and thus had to rely on both their own and ground-based searchlights to locate their prey.

The 10th Air Division's aircraft were organized in three lines of defense, all over land and all oriented toward the southeast. The first line was anchored in the north on Choshi, then ran parallel to the coastline for some seventy miles south through Katsuura to Shirahama, on the Boso Peninsula; the second covered the area from Kisarazu to Chiba; and the third was the city of Tokyo itself. Operating from seven main and some twenty-five secondary airfields, the defending pilots initially relied on such tactics as random airborne patrolling of given sectors or, occasionally, the blanket coverage of a particular zone by all available interceptors. Although these methods took their toll on raiding Allied aircraft—both bombers and, following the arrival off Japan of U.S. Navy surface task forces, carrier-based fighters and attack machines—the army squadrons were losing men and aircraft faster than they could be replaced. By the time the 10th Air Division gained operational independence in March 1945 under the command of Lieutenant General Kanetoshi Kondo, the number of airworthy interceptors had shrunk to fewer than 100. In order to preserve his remaining aircraft while still being able to respond to Allied attacks, Kondo introduced such innovations as cancelling the requirement to provide near-constant patrolling over such strategic facilities as harbors and factories and instead ordered his fighters to concentrate on hitting targets of opportunity. The 10th Air Division commander also sought to improve the number and quality of his early-warning radars, and also set about providing his anti-aircraft units with newer, larger-caliber, and longer-range guns.[1]

These innovations helped improve the performance of Kondo's division against Allied aircraft attacking targets in the Kanto Plain, but the sheer number of those enemy machines—coupled with the increasing number of poorly trained and inexperienced army pilots arriving to replace dead or wounded veterans—ensured that the 10th's assets continued to dwindle. Indeed, barely sixty interceptors were flyable by the time Kondo's organization was subsumed into General Masakazu Kawabe's Air General Army on April 15, 1945.

Given the battering being inflicted on the army fighter units attempting to defend the Kanto Plain, it was fortunate that the navy provided air-defense help, albeit only grudgingly and in a remarkably uncoordinated and startlingly haphazard way. Though both the army and navy were steeped in the *Bushido* traditions and staunchly supported the imperial system, their relationship had long been riven by the same sort of interservice rivalries and jealousies that remain all too common in twenty-first-century militaries. So parochial had each organization become that they separately pursued the development of aircraft, tactics, and such vital systems as airborne search and early warning radars. Although a formal agreement signed by both services in 1943 vaguely stated that defending the homeland was a joint obligation, it stipulated that the navy would be responsible for the air defense of naval bases and installations and the areas immediately adjacent to them, whereas the army would defend the national airspace as a whole.[2]

Even after the Home Islands began coming under regular Allied air attack from November 1944 onward the two services failed to integrate their real-time air-defense efforts in any meaningful way, agreeing only that navy aircraft based to the south and east of Tokyo would be responsible for engaging enemy aircraft headed toward the Kanto Plain before they penetrated the army's first defensive perimeter. Each service organized and used its own radar- and observer-based alert systems, and the only form of communication between the two regarding their respective air-defense plans and operations was a decidedly inefficient system of liaison officers who used telephones—and even couriers on motorcycles—to relay information that was often hopelessly out of date by the time it reached its intended recipient.[3]

The navy built its Kanto Plain air-defense efforts around three air stations—Kisarazu, on the east shore of Tokyo Bay in Chiba Prefecture; Oppama, adjacent to the sprawling Yokosuka naval base on the southwest shore of the bay in Kanagawa Prefecture; and Atsugi, some fifteen miles west of the bay and also in Kanagawa. Each airfield was home to both operational squadrons and specialized support or training organizations, and while each was defended by its own navy-manned anti-aircraft guns by August of 1945 all three had been heavily battered by Allied air attacks. Moreover, as part of Ketsu-Go (Decisive Operation), Japan's belatedly formulated plan to defend key areas of the Home Islands against an almost certain Allied amphibious invasion, from April 15 on the navy's remaining frontline squadrons had been told to conserve fuel, ammunition, and pilots for "the last great struggle." This meant, in effect, that the three bases would normally only launch interceptors when enemy aircraft were directly overhead or actually threatened the bases themselves.

Yasuna Kozono was well aware of the restrictions placed on the navy, both by its lack of coordination with the army and by senior commanders seeking to husband the nation's remaining military forces for the final battle. Yet he was also in a unique position to disregard those restrictions and do what he deemed necessary to prevent Japan's humiliation. For the veteran aviator was far more than a mere staff officer; he commanded what until just months before had been one of the most potent military organizations in Japan, the navy's 302nd Kokutai (Air Group) at Atsugi. Kozono's wild, malaria-hazed ride on the afternoon of August 14 had but one purpose: to force his beloved emperor to restart the war.

SITED ABOUT TWENTY-THREE miles southwest of Tokyo and eleven miles due west of Yokohama, Atsugi naval air station had originally been constructed in 1938 but, following the 302nd's arrival in March of 1944, had been expanded into the navy's largest and most elaborately protected airdrome. The field was ringed by anti-aircraft guns and its most vital facilities—command centers, fuel and ammunition storage areas, workshops, barracks, and hangers—were underground. Aircraft on air-defense alert status were housed in sophisticated hardened shelters adjacent to the runways.

The 302nd was operationally assigned to the Yokosuka Naval District and was one of three similar units organized specifically for homeland air-defense operations, the others being the 332nd in the Kure Naval District and the 352nd in the Sasebo Naval District.[4] At the time the 302nd arrived at Atsugi the unit's aircraft were among the best the navy could muster at that point in the war, comprising some twenty-four advanced Mitsubishi J2M-series land-based Raiden single-engine fighters (known to the Allies by the code name "Jack"); twenty older but still highly capable Mitsubishi A6M Zero-Sen ("Zeke") carrier fighters; and thirteen Nakajima J1N1-S Gekko ("Irving"), twelve Yokosuka P1Y1-S Ginga ("Frances"), and seven Yokosuka D4Y2-S Suisei ("Judy") night fighters.[5] These latter three types had originally been developed for other purposes—the Irving and Frances as land-based, twin-engine light bombers and the Judy as a single-engine, carrier-based dive bomber. But earlier in his career Kozono had demonstrated that they could be converted into competent bomber-killers by fitting them with Type-99 20mm cannon installed to fire obliquely from a gun bay behind the cockpit.

The Irving was fitted with four guns, two firing at a 30-degree angle upward and the other two at the same angle downward, whereas the Frances carried only the two upward-canted weapons and the Judy, just one. This armament configuration allowed the search-light- and, later, radar-equipped night fighters to eviscerate American B-24s and B-29s, often before their crews were even aware they were under attack.[6]

Kozono and his aviators put their aircraft to good use in the months following the 302nd's operational debut, by one authoritative estimate knocking down some 300 enemy aircraft by early August of 1945.[7] But it was far from a one-sided battle; increasingly frequent attacks on Atsugi by U.S. Navy carrier planes and by Iwo Jima–based U.S. Army Air Forces P-47 Thunderbolt and P-51 Mustang fighters and B-24s from Okinawa took a heavy toll of the 302nd's men and machines. By the time Kozono arrived at Atsugi at 2 P.M. on August 14 after his mad dash from Tokyo his entire unit consisted of only ten flyable Jacks, four Zekes, and two or three of the night fighters.

The paucity of aircraft available for an attack against the approaching enemy didn't seem to overly concern Kozono, for soon after roaring through Atsugi's front gate he gathered his senior staff members and ordered them to begin preparing plans for various offensive scenarios. But in a case of the flesh being significantly weaker than the spirit, Kozono was soon so deep in the throes of his malarial relapse that he had to take to his bed for several hours, finally managing to rise and stagger back to the 302nd's underground operations room—still alternately sweating and shivering—at about 8 P.M. Despite his frail condition, he stood resolutely before his deputy commander and remaining senior staffers. After apprising them of the "treasonous" events in Tokyo and informing them that the emperor's recorded rescript would be broadcast to the nation at noon the following day, he firmly announced that he was determined to fight to the end. When one of his listeners asked how they could disobey Hirohito's will and the direct and unequivocal orders of the navy's senior leaders, Kozono forcefully replied, "How can we be disobeying the Emperor's decision if what we do is for his and the country's good?"[8]

Warming to his topic despite his illness, Kozono cried out, "as long as I am commander here, the Atsugi Air Corps will never surrender! There is a supply of food underground that will permit us to hold out for two years. And I personally intend to do so. Are any of you with me?"[9]

Shouts of assent filled the small, smoke-filled room.

"Let them call us traitors," Kozono cried, his voice quivering with both passion and resolve. "It doesn't matter. Surrender is not only against our traditions, it's against our law. Japan *cannot* surrender. Are you with me?"[10]

Loud cheers echoed within the concrete-reinforced space. There was no dissent from the gathered officers, either because they were of the same diehard *Bushido*-driven temperament as their leader or because none wished to be seen as "defeatist." A drawn and shaking Kozono then retired to his quarters yet again, where he sat wearily at his desk to compose a message he intended to send to all major Imperial Japanese Navy (IJN) commands by cable. Barely able to hold the pen, Kozono wrote:

> The order to cease fire, and the order to disarm that will follow, must inevitably mean the end of our national structure and of the Emperor. To obey such orders would be equal to committing high treason. Japan is sacred and indestructible. If we unite for action, we will destroy the enemy. Of that there can be no doubt whatsoever. I hope that you will agree with me.[11]

As Kozono was completing his missive and ordering it sent to all senior IJN commanders, his officers began transforming his expressed intent into military reality. Plans were proposed, evaluated, and discarded, and by the time dawn broke on August 15 the staffers had settled on the only three tactics that seemed possible, given their limited resources. First, because American strike aircraft often arrived in the hours just after dawn, as soon as the sun was up a quartet of Jacks would take to the air to provide a combat air patrol over Atsugi. The 302nd's remaining aircraft would then bombard the Tokyo area with leaflets proclaiming that the emperor's noon speech had been coerced and calling on all "true Japanese" to reject the idea of surrender and fight on to the death. That done, the unit's pilots would go on a rotational alert status, ready to leap into the few remaining aircraft and roar aloft to do whatever they could to punish any Allied aircraft foolish or arrogant enough to transgress the skies of sacred Nippon.

As the sun rose higher over Atsugi, it quickly became apparent that the 302nd Air Group would have access to more men and aircraft than the planners had anticipated. Among the other organizations resident on the air station was a training school for kamikaze ("divine wind") pilots, men who had willingly volunteered—or, in some cases, been ordered to volunteer—to give their lives in sacred, selfless service to the nation and the emperor by crashing their bomb-carrying aircraft into enemy ships, a tactic that had worked frighteningly well during the American invasion of Okinawa. Atsugi was home to more than 1,000 young and inexperienced aviators—most had fewer than ten actual flight hours—who had been undergoing final training.[12] Having already made the choice to die for Japan, the kamikaze pilots were obviously stunned and horrified by the rumors of surrender that began circulating around the sprawling naval base in the early hours of August 15. Though not operationally part of Kozono's interceptor unit, many of the young pilots began gathering outside the entrance to the 302nd's headquarters when they heard that the legendary air group commander was determined to continue the fight against the Allies.

This must have been a heartening development for the increasingly ill Kozono, for as a senior officer he was likely aware that more than 5,300 kamikaze aircraft were at that moment hidden from Allied eyes in caves, underground storage areas, and heavily camouflaged airfields across southern Japan.[13] Though the vast majority of the machines—including the fifty or so at Atsugi—were trainers and obsolete fighters or light bombers rather than current frontline types, their sheer numbers would pose a formidable threat to any approaching Allied occupation force. The "divine wind" might also prove lethal to enemy aircraft, given that ramming a B-29 could be just as effective a way to destroy it as shooting it down. If he could rally the pilots of all the kamikazes in southern Japan to his anti-surrender cause, Kozono must have reasoned, he might well be able to scuttle the looming capitulation and force his cowardly government to fight on.

With his four-plane combat air patrol aloft Kozono moved on to the vital task of informing the citizens of Tokyo that their government was attempting to betray and dishonor them. The thousands of anti-surrender leaflets that had been printed overnight—all calling for a general uprising against the defeatists surrounding the emperor and urging "thorough resistance" against the oncoming American invaders—were loaded aboard several of the temporarily reassigned kamikaze training aircraft. These machines took off ninety minutes before the noon broadcast of the recorded imperial rescript, and their paper ordnance was therefore dropping over the capital even as Hirohito's high, tremulous voice hit the airwaves from NHK's main studio. Kozono himself listened to the broadcast sitting cross-legged on his bed at Atsugi, attempting to deal with his worsening malarial symptoms by self-medicating with cup after delicate porcelain cup of warm sake. When Hirohito's words made it all too clear that Japan was really going to do the unthinkable, the veteran naval aviator launched the second part of his plan. He ordered his remaining frontline interceptors and several of the less-decrepit kamikaze trainers aloft in search of Allied aircraft.

The Japanese pilots didn't have to look far to find the hated enemy. Though the arrival in Washington of Japan's official acceptance of the surrender terms had prompted Far East Air Forces headquarters to halt all offensive operations as of the early morning hours of August 15 (local time), at 4:15 A.M. the carriers of U.S. Vice Admiral John S. McCain's Task Force 38 had launched 103 fighters and attack aircraft on a planned sweep of the Tokyo area.[14] The American pilots were over their targets when they received the recall notice, but many had already been engaged by Japanese anti-aircraft guns and interceptors and were unable to simply reverse course and head back to their ships. In the ensuing dogfights U.S. F6F Hellcats and F4U/FG-1 Corsairs took on army and navy fighters, downing more than twenty of the Japanese aircraft over the Kanto Plain and others at sea.[15] As might be expected, however, the Americans did not escape unscathed: by the time the attackers set off for the return to their carriers, thirteen Navy and Marine Corps aircraft had been lost to fighters or ack-ack over the Kanto Plain, or just offshore. The single worst U.S. loss occurred just after the recall message was received; some twenty army Nakajima Ki-84 Hayate ("Frank") single-engine interceptors jumped six Hellcats of Navy fighter squadron 88 (VF-88) over Tokorozawa airfield, sixteen miles northwest of Tokyo. The Americans claimed nine Franks, but lost four Hellcats and their pilots.

Although it is unclear from surviving records whether the 302nd Air Group's J2M or A6M interceptors were involved in the day's many running battles over the Kanto Plain, pilots of VF-88 reported downing three Jacks within only a few miles of Atsugi. We do know, however, that several of the kamikaze trainer aircraft dispatched on the leaflet-dropping mission failed to return, either because they were shot down by the marauding Americans or because their pilots—still hoping to strike a blow against the enemy—flew off to attempt suicide attacks against the U.S warships offshore. It is entirely possible that the Judy shot down by Ensign Clarence A. Moore of USS *Belleau Wood*'s VF-31 Squadron just before 2 P.M.—the last air-to-air kill of the day and the last by a Navy pilot in World War II—was one of Kozono's night fighters or an Atsugi-based kamikaze trainer.[16]

Whatever impact the August 15 battles may have had on the 302nd's aircraft and pilots, Kozono's actions over the rest of that day indicate that he, at least, believed his organization had acquitted itself reasonably well and that its aggressive anti-surrender attitude should be replicated by other navy units. He had been sending cables to senior commanders throughout the day urging them to repudiate the emperor's surrender announcement and fight on, and was likely both heartened and humbled later that evening by the news that at least one august superior seemed to share his views: just before 6 P.M. Vice Admiral Matome Ugaki, commander of the Kyushu-based Fifth Air Fleet and the man largely responsible for launching the waves of kamikazes that so hammered American naval forces at Ulithi and Okinawa, climbed into the rear seat of a Judy and led ten other aircraft on a last-ditch suicide mission against U.S. vessels loitering just over the darkening horizon. That the admiral and his men apparently never found the enemy—no kamikaze attacks were recorded that evening—would probably not have bothered Kozono much. It would likely have been enough for the 302nd's commander that Ugaki had personally led the mission, from which neither he nor any of the others returned.

Kozono's belief that only his beloved navy had the courage and resolve to continue the fight seemed to be borne out by the fact that by the time night fell on August 15 the commanders of the majority of army aviation units in the Kanto region had finally decided to obey the order issued the day before by Lieutenant General Masao Yoshizumi, the chief of the Military Affairs Bureau in the War Ministry. Knowing that some of his aviators would be sorely tempted to keep fighting despite the emperor's decision to surrender, Yoshizumi had directed that the propellers and fuel tanks be removed from all army aircraft to prevent their unauthorized use following the ceasefire. Although many army pilots found it impossible to stand down while there were still enemy aircraft looking for a fight—witness the number of army interceptors that took part in the battles earlier that day against the U.S. carrier planes—the apparent cessation of American attacks as a result of Hirohito's acceptance of the surrender terms led most army squadrons to carry out Yoshizumi's command, resulting by midnight in the permanent grounding of nearly all of the army's remaining combat aircraft.[17]

The fact that the 302nd Air Group had not similarly responded to the ceasefire orders issued by the Navy Ministry did not go unnoticed in Tokyo, of course. Atsugi's communications center had been receiving a steady stream of urgent radio messages, cables, and telephone calls since dawn, all of which ordered Kozono and his men to stand down immediately and disable their aircraft. Though slipping deeper into the grip of his intense malarial relapse, the "Father of Japanese Night Fighters" refused to acknowledge any of the directives from higher headquarters, and a few hours after Hirohito's speech he'd ordered that all incoming communications lines be shut down. He continued to send messages out, however, dispatching couriers to nearby military installations bearing written pleas that they join the anti-surrender fight.

In seeking allies for his continuing war against the Americans, Kozono relied exclusively on the *Bushido*-infused "Japan must *never* surrender" argument that so motivated him and other diehards. But, as noted earlier, there was another type of Japanese aviator present in the Kanto region, one who understood and accepted the emperor's expressed reasons for the necessity for Japan's surrender but who had made the rational and militarily supportable decision that the nation's airspace should remain inviolate until the surrender document had actually been signed. After all, these pilots reasoned, there was no way to determine whether Allied aircraft flying over the Home Islands after the ceasefire had gone into effect would themselves actually refrain from hostile action. Perhaps the Americans would elect to drop one of their horrible new bombs on Tokyo despite the supposed cessation of hostilities, just to further punish Japan and at one stroke eliminate the emperor and all the other senior leaders whom the enemy held accountable for causing the Pacific war. Moreover, this "rationalist" argument went, Japan remained a sovereign nation—at least for the moment—and as such she had the internationally recognized right to prevent overflights of her territory by military aircraft of a technically still-belligerent nation or alliance, no matter the intent of the aerial intrusion.

Unfortunately for the B-32 crewmen who would soon find themselves over Tokyo, one of the largest groups of "rationalist" Japanese aviators was based at Oppama air station. The men, members of the famed Yokosuka Kokutai, were also among the most experienced—and thus the most potentially lethal—pilots in the Japanese navy.

First organized in April 1916, the Yokosuka Air Group—referred to by its members as the Yoko Ku[18]—was the oldest and throughout its history arguably one of the most accomplished air groups in the navy. Over the first two decades of its existence the unit was primarily a research-and-development and advanced-training organization, with its integral fighter squadron responsible for both the flight-testing of newly introduced navy aircraft and the formulation and fleet-wide dissemination of innovative aerial combat tactics. In keeping with its status and duties the Yoko Ku tended to attract the best and the brightest from among the ranks of naval aviators, and among its alumni were such luminaries as Minoru Genda, the man who helped plan the December 1941 attack on Pearl Harbor.

Despite the Yoko Ku's fame, its home base, Oppama naval air station, was nowhere near as well-equipped or prestigious as the 302nd's Atsugi. Built partially on land reclaimed from Tokyo Bay east of the entrance to Kawazana Bay a mile to the northwest of the vast naval shipyard and harbor complex at Yokosuka, the airfield dated to the late 1920s and was originally home to landplanes, seaplanes, and lighter-than-air craft. Oppama was sited among several low coastal hills across a narrow channel from the Azuma Peninsula and was known to navy pilots as a "challenging" field. Though they had been improved somewhat over the years, the base's two intersecting runways remained shorter than average and the landing approach from the west required pilots to avoid the hills while being buffeted by the near-constant winds that wafted between them. Despite, or perhaps because of, these challenges, Yoko Ku aviators were deeply attached to what was in a military sense their "ancestral home."

By February 1944 Japan's worsening strategic situation, coupled with the increasing attrition visited on the navy by Allied forces, led to the Yoko Ku's being partially relieved of its training and development duties so that half its fighter pilots could put their considerable skills to combat use. At that point the organization consisted of 108 aircraft—48 Zeke carrier fighters, 48 Kawanishi N1K1-J Shiden ("George") interceptors, and 12 Irving night fighters. About half that total complement was kept at Oppama to assist in the navy's planned air defense of the Kanto Plain, while the other half was dispatched to aid in the Japanese defense of the Marianas. Over the following months the deployed Yoko Ku aviators did what they could to help stop the American advance, attacking enemy vessels and providing air-defense cover for Japanese forces on Iwo Jima. Though the unit racked up an impressive fifty-two kills, the ferocity of the American air assault had by July resulted in the deaths of more than twenty of the Yoko Ku's top pilots and the loss of nearly two-thirds of its deployed aircraft. By the fall of 1944 the surviving unit members were sent back to Oppama, where the air group—now relieved of its training duties—was dedicated full time to the defense of the southern and eastern approaches to the Kanto Plain.

The Yoko Ku's ability to contribute meaningfully to that vital mission was greatly enhanced by the fact that, despite the battering it had taken over Iwo Jima, it still counted on its roster some of Japan's most experienced and capable naval aviators. Among them was the unit's leader, Lieutenant Commander Masanobu Ibusuki, a veteran of the attack on Pearl Harbor (flying from the carrier *Akagi*) who was renowned throughout the navy for having helped shoot down the first American warplane lost in aerial combat in World War II, a Boeing B-17C attempting to land at Honolulu's Hickam Field after a ferry flight from California.[19] Though Ibusuki never downed the five enemy aircraft traditionally required to reach "ace" status, several of his pilots had attained that honorific many times over.

Among the more colorful of Yoko Ku's aces was thirty-two-year-old Lieutenant (Junior Grade) Matsuo Hagiri, widely known throughout the navy as "Mustachio Hagiri" because of the luxuriant, and rare, handlebar that graced his upper lip. A veteran of combat above China and the Solomon Islands, Hagiri had been assigned to Ibusuki's organization in September 1943 after being severely wounded in a dogfight over Papua New Guinea. After recovering he'd become an advanced flight instructor at Oppama, passing on the skills that had allowed him to down at least thirteen enemy aircraft.

Joining Hagiri in the original instructor role was another wounded ace, twenty-five-year-old Warrant Officer Sadamu Komachi, who'd come to the Yoko Ku in the summer of 1944 with eighteen victories as well as burn scars inflicted by U.S. Navy F6F Hellcat pilot Ensign Wendell Twelves of VF-15 over Orote airfield on Guam. Komachi stood out among his fellow pilots, both because of his stature—at just over six feet tall he was literally able to look down on most of his colleagues—and because he was widely considered to be an excellent combat pilot. But the young warrant officer also had a reputation as a daredevil and hellion who was willing to bend rules and cut corners if doing so would help him further improve his already impressive technical skills or, presumably, further increase his score.

Although he shared Komachi's rank and at twenty-four was close in age, Warrant Officer Ryoji Ohara was by all accounts an altogether different type of fighter pilot. Methodical, patient, and a technician in the best sense of the term, Ohara had first seen combat over New Guinea in 1942 and since that time had downed some sixteen enemy aircraft and earned the nickname "The Killer of Rabaul." His presence at Oppama was a huge boon for the Yoko Ku because of his obvious skill in the cockpit and, apparently, because his calm and rational temperament had a moderating effect on his close friend Komachi.

Though each of these pilots and several others in the Yoko Ku helped burnish the unit's reputation as the "group of aces," it was the near-legendary exploits of one man—Lieutenant (junior grade) Saburo Sakai—that largely provided the foundation for that sobriquet. Twenty-nine years old in August 1945, the diminutive Sakai had entered the navy in 1933 as an enlisted man, initially serving on surface warships before taking the examination for pilot training. Though it took him three tries to pass the test, he excelled during flight school, showing a natural aptitude for the tactics and techniques of fighter combat. He first put his skills to the test in the late 1930s during the Second Sino-Japanese War, and by December 1941 was already an ace. Sakai participated in the Japanese assault on Clark Field in the Philippines,[20] and went on to see combat and earn promotion to officer status flying the A6M Zeke over the Netherlands East Indies and the Central Pacific. He initially joined the Yoko Ku in June 1944 and was among those pilots sent to Iwo Jima, and returned to Oppama with the survivors of that deployment. By that time Sakai had downed at least fifty enemy aircraft, but he was initially relegated to flight-instructor status owing to the many injuries he'd sustained thus far in the war—most notably damage to his eyes resulting from a 1942 encounter with the rear gunner of a U.S. Navy SBD Dauntless dive bomber. Nonetheless, he remained one of Yoko Ku's most formidable pilots.[21]

Though Oppama had been heavily battered by enemy aircraft— the airfield was officially referred to by the Allies as Target 90-7-298 and had been attacked repeatedly beginning in the fall of 1944[22]—the mere presence of men like Sakai, Hagiri, Komachi, and the rest ensured that the Yoko Ku remained a serious threat. Ordered to largely avoid combat in order to conserve fuel and ammunition for the Ketsu-Go operation, the unit's pilots—like those in other air-defense organizations throughout southern Japan—had been forced to listen in silence to increasingly shrill civilian complaints about the apparent ability of Allied aircraft to transgress the nation's airspace seemingly at will. Though most of Yoko Ku's aviators were apparently not of the diehard, *Bushido*-driven stripe, their frustration levels were high. They were among the finest fighter pilots in the Japanese military, and yet they were being told not do what they did best. It therefore undoubtedly came as a huge relief to the aviators when, within hours of the noon broadcast of Hirohito's rescript, Yoko Ku commander Ibusuki announced that despite the ceasefire and until a formal surrender had been signed he would do nothing to prevent his men from undertaking "defensive actions" over their own base.[23]

It was just the sort of decree Ibusuki's men had been waiting for, and when combined with the *Bushido*-enhanced fervor among the 302nd Air Group pilots at Atsugi it would contribute directly to the chaos that would soon engulf Tony Marchione and the men of the 386th Bomb Squadron.

PRESIDENT HARRY S. TRUMAN'S order to cease offensive action against Japanese forces—relayed to operational units worldwide late on August 14, Washington time—was followed within hours by a second presidential message announcing the appointment of

General Douglas MacArthur to the post of Supreme Commander Allied Powers, a designation that would, in essence, make him the de facto ruler of Japan once the occupation began. Before MacArthur could assume that historically unprecedented role, of course, he had to ensure that the Japanese would actually stop fighting, lay down their arms, and prepare for a formal surrender. To do that, he would have to communicate directly with Tokyo.

MacArthur first attempted that contact using the War Department communications facility in Manila. When there was no response, he tried a different tack, directing the Army Airways Communications System's Manila office to send the initial message over the frequencies used for uncoded weather information. The station, call sign WXXU, sent message Z-500 in Morse code at 9:30 A.M. Manila time, addressing it to "The Japanese Emperor, the Japanese Imperial Government, [and] The Japanese Imperial General Headquarters." After informing the recipients of his appointment, MacArthur said he was "empowered to arrange directly with the Japanese authorities for the cessation of hostilities at the earliest practicable date." The remainder of the message directed the Japanese to designate a single radio station in Tokyo that would handle all further communications— which would be undertaken *only* in English—and then, perhaps as a not-too-subtle way of informing Hirohito and his advisers of just who was now in charge, MacArthur closed with a command: "Upon receipt of this message acknowledge."[24]

That acknowledgment had not even been received when, less than thirty minutes after dispatching the first message, the communications clerks at WXXU were directed to send out another:

Pursuant to the acceptance of the terms of the surrender of the Allied Powers by the Emperor of Japan, the Japanese Imperial Government and the Japanese Imperial Headquarters, the Supreme Commander for the Allied Powers [sic] hereby directs the immediate cessation of hostilities by the Japanese forces. The Supreme Commander for the Allied Forces is to be notified at once of the effective date and hour of such cessation of hostilities, whereupon the Allied forces will be directed to cease hostilities.[25]

The message went on to direct, among other things, that the Japanese send "a competent representative" and his accompanying delegation of senior military and political advisers by air to the American field on Ie Shima, an island off Okinawa, for onward transport to Manila to discuss the details of Japan's formal surrender and its subsequent occupation by Allied forces.

Though overshadowed somewhat by the other elements of the message, the phrase "whereupon the Allied forces will be directed to cease hostilities" was later to have far more importance than MacArthur and his staff may have intended, for it implied to its recipients in Tokyo that the Allies could, and presumably would, continue their air and sea attacks on the Home Islands until *all* Japanese forces had formally surrendered. Given that millions of army troops remained under arms in Japan proper and throughout Southeast Asia and China—and that Japanese units were still engaging advancing Soviet formations in Manchuria—senior leaders in Tokyo could understandably have believed that the Allies might at any moment resume their aerial assault despite the de facto ceasefire.

No doubt partly out of a desire to avoid any further atomic bombings, the Japanese government, still led by Prime Minister Kantaro Suzuki, was quick to respond to MacArthur's initial contact. Tokyo's reply to the 9:30 A.M. message, received by WXXU in Manila barely two hours after its dispatch, provided the requested radio station information and marked the first direct contact between the Allies and Japan. What that first response from Tokyo did *not* do, however, was furnish the timetable MacArthur had demanded for the cessation of hostilities by all Japanese forces. We know that senior army and navy leaders were burning up their remaining communications links trying to notify far-flung commands of the surrender decision and secure their acknowledgment that they would cease all offensive action, but it wasn't until the evening of Thursday, August 16, that Tokyo was able to give an increasingly impatient MacArthur the information he wanted. In a message received in Manila just after 8 P.M., the Japanese stated that just hours earlier Emperor Hirohito had issued an imperial order to all armed forces units, no matter their location, to "cease hostilities immediately." In an oblique reference to the difficulties of both reaching remote units and overcoming some field commanders' resistance to the idea of surrender, the message stated that it would take from forty-eight hours (in Japan proper) to as much as twelve days elsewhere for the emperor's order to "produce full effect."[26]

It may have surprised MacArthur and some of his headquarters staffers to learn that not all elements of the Japanese armed forces were observing the ceasefire that had supposedly gone into effect the day before, but it wasn't news to certain American aviators. Earlier that Thursday, even as their newly appointed supreme commander was waiting to hear from Tokyo, several Okinawa-based airmen—including B-32 crewmen from the 386th Bomb Squadron—had personally learned that some enemy military units apparently hadn't yet decided to call it quits.

DESPITE ITS SUSPENSION OF offensive action against Japanese forces, the August 15 ceasefire order was not intended to halt all Allied air activity over the Home Islands. Indeed, three important requirements—to ascertain whether the enemy was actually beginning to abide by the terms of the ceasefire, to identify airfields and ports that could accommodate incoming occupation units, and the particularly urgent need to locate camps holding Allied prisoners so that food and medical supplies could be airdropped to them—guaranteed that Navy carrier-based and Army Air Forces land-based photographic reconnaissance aircraft would overfly Japan with increasing frequency. The latter service's machines were dedicated photo-recon variants of the twin-engine P-38 Lightning fighter (known as the F-5) and the B-24 heavy bomber (F-7), though the importance of the missions and the vast distances involved virtually guaranteed that the 386th Bomb Squadron's long-legged Dominators would be called on to assist in the reconnaissance effort.

That call came even before *The Lady is Fresh* and *Hobo Queen II* returned from their canceled night mission on August 15. A warning order from Far East Air Forces headquarters directed that two B-32s be dispatched on a recon mission as soon as possible on August 16, with the specific requirement to photograph the Japanese naval air stations at Katori and Konoike, both northeast of Tokyo, the former in Chiba Prefecture and the latter in Ibaraki.[27] Both fields were known to host kamikaze units, and it was imperative for Allied intelligence to know whether the remaining aircraft based at each installation still constituted a threat.

Though the B-32 had an internal fixture for a vertically mounted aerial camera in its central cabin, just aft of the ball turret, it was not a dedicated photo-reconnaissance platform and the 312th Bomb Group had no aerial photographers assigned to it. This issue had been dealt with just after the unit arrived on Okinawa, however, when the Yontan-based 20th Reconnaissance Squadron had been tapped to provide qualified personnel as needed. Whenever the B-32s undertook any mission that might broadly be categorized as "reconnaissance"—including the flights already conducted over the East China Sea and the Korea Strait—the Dominator's normal complement was augmented by an officer and one or two enlisted men from the 20th Recon. The officer would use the aircraft's bombsight to spot the area or object to be photographed, then trip the camera's shutter remotely. The enlisted aerial photographer and, if present, his assistant (who was also a qualified aerial gunner) rode in the central fuselage to be close to the camera in order to change its film magazine or troubleshoot any technical problems.

The general outline of the B-32s' first sojourn to the Home Islands was developed by staffers at V Bomber Command headquarters, also on Okinawa. When the plan was delivered to 312th Bomb Group intelligence officer Captain William P. Barnes and his deputy, First Lieutenant Rudolph Pugliese, just after midnight on August 15–16 they noted that despite the announced ceasefire the planned route would allow the two Dominators to avoid most known Japanese air defenses during the 2,050-mile round-trip flight.[28] After takeoff from Yontan the B-32s would head northeast for just under 1,000 miles, skirting the east coast of Chiba Prefecture to a point just off Cape Inubo. They would then turn almost directly west, complete their photo runs over the target, and reverse course to head back out to sea. Once clear of the Japanese coast the Dominators would turn southwest and start the long haul back to Okinawa. Though there were known early-warning radar sites at Shirahama on the southern tip of the Chiba Peninsula and at Choshi and Hiraiso, on the coast just east of the target airfields, Barnes and Pugliese were reasonably sure they could be avoided or "spoofed," if necessary, by the radar countermeasures sets and "rope" carried aboard the B-32s.

The two intelligence officers fleshed out the bare-bones V Bomber Command mission plan with file photos of the target airfields and maps of the areas surrounding them, all of which were pinned to the large bulletin board at the front of the 386th Bomb Squadron's briefing shack. The crewmen assigned to the flight walked quietly into the building at 4:00 A.M., and over the next forty-five minutes were given details of the mission by both Barnes and the group's operations officer. During the course of their remarks each man said that, despite the ceasefire, the flight crews should stay alert for enemy opposition and be ready for anything.

The two Dominators assigned to the day's mission were *Hobo Queen II* and *Harriet's Chariot* (42-108543), the latter being one of four B-32s that had reached Okinawa from Clark Field on August 12. Both were fitted with auxiliary bomb-bay fuel tanks for the long flight, and each carried two members of the 20th Recon Squadron in addition to its regular twelve-man crew. With preflight checks and engine run-ups completed, the two aircraft lifted off from Yontan just after 5:30 A.M. and turned their noses to the northeast.[29]

The mission was initially uneventful, the Dominators flying in loose formation with *Hobo Queen II* in the lead and her pilot, Frank Cook, as mission commander. Then, at 9:35, still over the ocean at an altitude of 16,000 feet and some 155 miles due south of Tokyo, the exhaust collector assembly in the number 2 (left inboard) engine of *Harriet's Chariot* failed. This allowed hot gases to flood the nacelle and ruptured fuel and oil lines, sparking an immediate fire that blew off one of the R-3350's exhaust ports.[30] The bomber's pilot, twenty-two-year-old B-24 combat veteran First Lieutenant Lyman Combs, immediately cut the fuel and oil flow, closed the throttle, feathered the propeller, opened the cowl flaps, and ordered his flight engineer to activate the power plant's fire extinguishers.[31] The flames quickly died, but with only three good engines there was no point in *Harriet's Chariot* continuing the mission, given that the loss of a second R-3350 would force the Dominator to ditch in the sea. After radioing his intentions to Cook in *Hobo Queen II* Combs turned his aircraft around and headed back to an eventual safe landing at Yontan.

Hardly had the damaged B-32 completed her turn toward home when the ball turret gunner aboard *Hobo Queen II* sighted an unidentified aircraft several thousand feet below the bomber on a perpendicular course. Though the machine, most probably a Japanese navy flying boat, was headed toward the coast of Honshu and posed no obvious threat, the gunner's alert over the intercom undoubtedly quickened a few pulses. Then, barely forty minutes later, more excitement: as *Hobo Queen II* came abreast of the southern tip of the Chiba Peninsula the bomber was "painted" by a Japanese Type B search radar, most likely the army-operated system at Shirahama.[32] The B-32 flew on without incident, paralleling the coast about eighty miles offshore, but her radar countermeasures operator noted "a large number" of emissions throughout the Kanto region.

Things got even more interesting as *Hobo Queen II* began her photo run. Having turned northwest and crossed the Japanese coastline at 20,000 feet just south of Kashima, the B-32 was again illuminated by a Type B radar, this one the system at Chosi. Then, without warning, a far more ominous signal filled the countermeasures operator's headphones—the steady hum that indicated a Japanese fire-control radar had locked onto the Dominator. The system provided altitude, course, and speed data to crews manning Type 10 120mm anti-aircraft guns, weapons whose 33,000-foot vertical range made them more than capable of knocking down a high-flying American bomber. Before Cook and his crew had the chance to wonder if the war was back on again, however, the radar broke lock of its own accord and the signal vanished.

The Dominator's first photo target, the airfield at Konoike, was almost completely obscured by a layer of stratus clouds between 4,000 and 6,000 feet and the 20th Recon Squadron photographer did not capture any usable images. Things were better over Katori, however, which came into the K-18A camera's viewfinder barely three minutes later. The device automatically exposed a number of frames—one every three seconds—as the B-32 passed over the heavily bombed but apparently still operational airdrome. Then, her photo run completed, *Hobo Queen II* banked sharply to port, maintaining her altitude and initiating a tight 160-degree turn back toward the coast. The course was intended to allow the big bomber to slip between the coverage arcs of the Type 2 radars at Hiraiso, north of her track, and Chosi to the south. The tactic worked, and the Dominator made it back out to sea without being "painted" by either system. Once at a point about forty miles offshore Cook turned *Hobo Queen II* to the southwest and started back for Okinawa. That last leg of the mission was uneventful except for the sighting of another aircraft at about noon—the machine was too far distant to be identified—and the B-32 landed safely at Yontan early that evening.

The August 16 mission was judged to have been largely successful, despite the difficulties encountered by *Harriet's Chariot* and the cloud cover that prevented effective photography of the airfield at Konoike. The fact that *Hobo Queen II* had not been fired on by antiaircraft artillery—despite the brief lock-on by a gun-laying radar—or attacked by fighters was taken by the aviators in the 386th and by those higher up the chain of command as a positive indication that Japanese forces were apparently willing to abide by the ceasefire. That was especially important, given that even before *Hobo Queen II* had returned from the initial B-32 reconnaissance flight over Japan Fifth Air Force headquarters had scheduled a second—and more ambitious—mission.

Unfortunately, it would not go anywhere near as well as the first.

As OUTLINED BY THE planners at V Bomber Command, the second and more ambitious recon mission would put four Dominators over the greater Tokyo area to photograph seven airfields, both to ensure that none was still conducting offensive operations and to determine which of them might be in suitable condition to accept incoming Allied aircraft when the occupation began.[33] Two of the installations—Imba and Matsudo—were long-established army bases. The airdrome at Haneda was Tokyo's prewar civilian airport, now being used as a satellite army air-defense field. The remaining four were naval air stations: Katori, which the B-32s had visited the day before; Kami-Miyagawa, an auxiliary field fifteen miles to the south, near Chosi; Tomioka, a seaplane base on the west side of Tokyo Bay, about halfway between Yokohama and Oppama air station; and Oppama itself.[34] The choice of fields to be photographed indicates that the mission planners must have been fairly confident that there would be no enemy resistance: Not only was the Kanto region dotted with hundreds of known anti-aircraft weapons ranging from 25mm to 120mm, since mid-1944 it had been protected by more aircraft than any other part of Japan. Indeed, Imba and Matsudo were both home to crack army interceptor units, the former to twenty Nakajima Ki-44 Shoki (Allied code name "Tojo") single-engine fighters of the 23rd Air Regiment and the latter to thirty-four Kawasaki Ki-45 Toryu ("Nick") twin-engine night fighters of the 53rd Air Regiment. And, of course, Fifth Air Force intelligence officers were well aware that the Yoko Ku flew from Oppama.[35]

The mission plan called for the four Dominators to fly together from Yontan to the small island of Miyaki Jima, some 870 miles northeast of Okinawa and roughly eighty-five miles due south of Yokosuka. The aircraft would then turn north toward the Kanto Plain, begin their climb to the photo altitude of 20,000 feet and gradually assume a widely spaced echelon formation that would permit them to fly parallel courses roughly two miles apart as they "mowed the lawn" on their photo runs. Each B-32 was to photograph three of twelve planned flight lines; although this would require the individual aircraft to make two course reversals over the greater Tokyo area, it would also ensure overlapping coverage of the target airdromes, cloud cover permitting. At the end of the last photo pass the Dominators would hit the coast just north of Katori, tighten their formation, and turn back to the southwest to begin the 900-mile return flight to Okinawa.

The four aircraft chosen for the mission were the hardworking *Hobo Queen II*, again with Cook as pilot; 578, flown by 312th commander Selmon Wells; *Harriet's Chariot*—her bad engine replaced overnight—with Tony Svore at the controls; and 539, piloted by

First Lieutenant Emory D. Frick, a former B-24 aviator with extensive combat experience. As on the previous day's mission, the Dominators would fly with bomb-bay fuel tanks and full loads of .50-caliber machine-gun ammunition for their gun turrets.

The latter provision was normal operating procedure; Fifth Air Force headquarters had decreed that despite the ceasefire all combat aircraft would fly armed until Japanese officials had actually signed the surrender documents. However, during the predawn briefing for the men who would be taking the B-32s to Tokyo the possibility of enemy attack was rated as "minimal"—most probably because of the lack of opposition to the previous day's mission and the news that on the evening of the sixteenth Emperor Hirohito had issued a second rescript, this one ordering all members of Japan's armed forces to lay down their arms and stop fighting. Though this would have helped ease the apprehension some of the aviators certainly must have felt about the idea of flying back and forth over the Kanto Plain, not all were convinced the flight would be a milk run. Svore, for example, believed that the Japanese would be far more likely to react violently to the B-32s' appearance above their capital than they had been to the overflight of the relatively unimportant airfield at Katori.[36]

Whatever the men assigned to the second recon mission might have felt about the possibility of enemy opposition, they did what military professionals do: they got on with the job. All four B-32s were in the air by 5:45 A.M., and the first leg of the flight went exactly as planned—there were no mechanical problems and other than being "painted" by a Type B radar upon arriving over Miyaki Jima the Dominators had not encountered any sign of Japanese interest in them. At 10:15 Cook in *Hobo Queen II* radioed the other aircraft to disperse and begin their photo runs, then turned his own aircraft toward its first assigned airfield.

Though the men aboard the B-32s didn't realize it yet, the radar station that had illuminated the American bombers had relayed the contact information to anti-aircraft batteries throughout the Kanto region. More important, as it turned out, the alert also went to the 302nd Air Group and to the Yoko Ku. At Atsugi a young lieutenant

named Muneaki Morimoto quickly secured the fever-stricken Kozono's permission to launch an interception, and within minutes
Morimoto was leading a flight of four Zekes in a full-power climb
toward the Americans' last known position.[37]

At Oppama, the first inkling the Yoko Ku pilots had that something was amiss was the shrill scream of an air-raid siren. As Saburo
Sakai later remembered, he and the unit's other pilots were caught
totally off guard. Although they'd voluntarily been standing alert
despite the emperor's August 15 rescript and his order to the armed
forces the following day to lay down their arms, the Yoko Ku aviators had been told that the Americans had pledged not to fly bombers over Japan following the ceasefire, and they therefore were not
really expecting to launch any interceptions. When the call came in
that there were, in fact, what appeared to be B-29s flying up the Boso
Peninsula, Sakai and his comrades were momentarily at a loss. The
war was supposed to be over, yet it appeared the Americans still
wanted a fight. They turned to their commander, Masanobu Ibusuki, for guidance. After a quick call to higher headquarters he ordered the engines of the alert aircraft to be started, then turned to
his pilots and said, "international law forbids us to attack the enemy
after surrender, but it is okay to get back at planes that attack us.
Come on men, go get him!"[38]

Already wearing their flight suits, ten or twelve pilots, including
Sakai and Ryoji Ohara, ran to the fueled and armed Georges and
Zekes sitting in the alert revetments. Sakai leapt into one of the latter
aircraft, pleased at the unexpected chance to fly his favorite mount
into combat one more time, and minutes later the fighters roared
aloft, clawing for altitude even as their gear and flaps retracted.

Wells and the men aboard his Dominator were the first to realize
that the Japanese intended to oppose the recon flight. Even before
578 had started her photo run a Yoko Ku George (which the Americans misidentified as the very similar-looking army Ki-44 "Tojo")
zoomed past, several hundred feet above the B-32, then rolled inverted and reversed course, coming back at the American aircraft
from the two o'clock position (off the bomber's nose, slightly to star-

board), firing as it came.[39] Wells immediately turned the Dominator directly toward the incoming fighter and the nose turret gunner opened up with his twin .50s. The pilot of the George, possibly used to attacking B-29s (which had no nose turret), was apparently startled by the volume of return fire and immediately broke off the attack.[40] Wells and his crew were not out of the woods yet, however. As 578 began her first photo run the aircraft's electronic countermeasures officer, twenty-six-year-old Second Lieutenant David S. Samuelson, warned that a fire-control radar had locked onto the B-32. He immediately began jamming the Japanese signal, but several rounds of 120mm anti-aircraft fire burst close enough to rock the aircraft as it finished its run and then turned for the coast.

Wells and his crew were not the only ones being targeted by anti-aircraft guns. At about that same time, *Hobo Queen II* was finishing the second of her flight lines, just north of Tokyo Bay. Though the B-32's countermeasures operator had not detected any Japanese radar emissions, the tail gunner suddenly called out that ack-ack bursts seemed to be creeping up on the aircraft from behind. Understandably apprehensive and likely more than a little unnerved, the gunner made his announcement rather more loudly than he probably intended, for Cook—whom the Dominator's radio operator, Staff Sergeant Robert Russell, later remembered as "real calm"— came on the intercom and said, "cut out that screaming back there. I'll get us out of this, don't worry about it."[41] Cook was as good as his word; realizing that determined Japanese resistance would make the planned mission impossible to complete, he immediately turned the B-32 south toward Tokyo Bay and put it into a slight dive to pick up speed. Though Japanese fighters ahead of and above the Dominator were sighted by one of the gunners, they did not attack, and *Hobo Queen II* was able to escape further enemy attention.

The same cannot be said for either *Harriet's Chariot* or 539, however.

Svore and his crew had started their second flight line, just west of Chiba, when one of the gunners called out incoming enemy fighters. *Harriet's Chariot* had not been fired on up to that point, but the sudden appearance of apparently hostile interceptors did not surprise the 386th's commander. He later recalled that it simply validated his belief that the Japanese would be far more likely to intercept Allied aircraft appearing over Tokyo than they would be over other, less symbolic areas. Whatever their motivation, the enemy pilots seemed determined to inflict punishment on the B-32. Six aircraft attacked *Harriet's Chariot*; they were later identified by the bomber's crew as five army Tojos and one Kawasaki Ki-61 Hien ("Tony"), though the former were actually navy Georges.[42] The first pass was made by the Tony, which started its run some 3,000 feet above and directly behind the Dominator. The fighter swooped down and pulled up astern and slightly below, and opened fire at the same time as the B-32's rear upper gunner. The fighter took several hits, began trailing smoke, then rolled inverted and dived into the clouds below. The Georges then came at *Harriet's Chariot* from different directions and altitudes, eventually concentrating their attacks on the bomber's aft end after realizing that the tail turret was malfunctioning. Though the fighters kept up their attacks for about fifteen minutes the only damage they inflicted was a small hole in the B-32's wing, and *Harriet's Chariot* was able to make it to the sea and find cover in a layer of heavy clouds.[43]

Given that Oppama was the primary photo target assigned to Emory Frick and the men aboard 539, it is not surprising that they received far more attention from the Japanese than the morning's briefing at Yontan had led them to expect. As the Dominator began the initial pass over the Yokosuka area at 20,000 feet she was the target of some fifty bursts of radar-directed 120mm anti-aircraft fire, several of which were close enough to punch holes in the nacelle of the number four engine and the inboard trailing edge of the left wing. Then, even before 539 came off the photo pass a group of fighters appeared. One of them was flown by Sakai, who was surprised to find that the quarry was not the B-29 he was expecting, but a completely different aircraft. As he was noting the Dominator's "enormous" vertical stabilizer, the other Yoko Ku pilots rolled in on her, initially from twelve o'clock high. Tracer rounds from the fighters' guns were clearly visible in the bright noontime sky as they arced in toward the bomber. So aggressive were the Japanese airmen that Frick's copilot, Second Lieutenant Joe E. Elliot, was certain they intended to ram the Dominator.[44] That didn't happen, but over the next twenty minutes the Japanese came at the B-32 from virtually every angle. The sky around 539 was so crowded, in fact, that Sakai had to abort his initial firing pass—from three o'clock high—when another fighter pulled in front of him.

As soon as the attack started Frick had begun a sweeping turn to the south, toward the entrance to Tokyo Bay. His gunners kept up a steady defensive fire throughout the maneuver, observing hits on at least two of the fighters, both of which they later claimed as "probably destroyed." As he completed the turn Frick put the B-32 into a slight dive and jammed all four throttles to their stops. Sakai, at this point waiting his chance for another pass, saw the Dominator accelerate so quickly that he wondered whether the bomber was equipped with some sort of auxiliary rocket engine. He and his wingman—most probably Ryoji Ohara—kept up the chase nevertheless, as did one or two of the other fighters, lobbing rounds at the B-32 as it pulled away from them. One by one the Japanese pilots gave up and turned back toward Oppama, with Sakai and his partner hanging on until the Dominator reached Miyake-jima. Then, fearing they might run into U.S. Navy carrier fighters, the two pilots broke off their pursuit and turned back toward Yokosuka.

The departure of the last Japanese fighters was undoubtedly greeted by a sigh of relief from the men aboard 539. Though none of them had been injured in the aerial melee, their B-32 was somewhat the worse for wear—20mm cannon rounds and 12.7mm machine-gun bullets had holed both wings and the rudder trim tab. The damage was not serious enough to prevent the Dominator's return to Okinawa, however, and as Frick took up a course for Yontan the men aboard 539 settled in for the long flight and the first of many discussions about the day's events. Similar conversations were undoubtedly taking place aboard the other three B-32s, each of which was making its own way back to Okinawa.

THE B-32 CREWMEN WERE not the only people talking about what had happened over Tokyo, of course. Terse radio accounts of the

Japanese attacks radioed back to Yontan by Cook, Wells, and Svore had also sparked intense concern among senior officers at V Bomber Command and FEAF headquarters. Although the interception of the Dominators was the most serious breach of the ceasefire, it was not the only one that had taken place over Japan that day. A Consolidated F-7 Liberator on a recon mission to Yokohama had also been fired on by anti-aircraft batteries, as had two F-5 Lightnings over Kyushu.[45]

The high level of command interest in what had happened to the B-32s was clearly evident when the aircraft finally landed at Yontan at about 5 P.M. The Dominators were immediately surrounded by dozens of senior officers—and reporters both civilian and military—all clamoring to know what had happened over Tokyo. As soon as the men stepped from their aircraft they were whisked off to the standard post-flight debriefing, where for the next few hours they were grilled about their actions and those of the Japanese. The aviators were understandably proud that they'd been able to give better than they'd received—the Dominators' gunners claimed a total of four "probable" kills of Japanese fighters for no losses or injuries on their own side—but they were also angry. In their minds the Japanese had once again shown themselves to be treacherous and deceitful, their apparent disregard for the ceasefire just another example of Tokyo's perfidy.[46]

For the senior V Bomber Command and FEAF officers the issues presented by the attacks that day were potentially far larger, however. The fact that these events occurred just two days before Japanese envoys were scheduled to fly to Manila as MacArthur had directed was understandably troubling for the men who'd been tasked to plan and implement the aerial portions of the occupation. Was it all just a misunderstanding? After all, in his initial messages to the Japanese MacArthur had indicated that no bombers would fly over Japan, but he'd said nothing of reconnaissance flights. Had the Japanese fired on the F-7 and B-32s because they were assumed to be bombers that might have some secret, hostile intent? Were the Japanese attacks simply the acts of diehards and renegades, they must have wondered, or did they foreshadow something far more sinister on the part of Japan's leaders?

After reviewing all the information presented by the returning Dominator crewmen and evaluating the most current intelligence reports, the men from V Bomber Command and FEAF apparently decided that the day's events were some sort of aberration, for they made what appears in hindsight to be an otherwise inexplicable decision. Despite what had happened to the four B-32s that day, they decided to dispatch four more Dominators to the Japanese capital the following morning.

It was a decision that would cost one young American his life.

CHAPTER 5

___

A DESPERATE FIGHT

THE JAPANESE FIGHTER ATTACKS on the Dominators involved in the August 17 mission over the Kanto region confused and angered the American airmen involved in the engagement. More important, the interception of the B-32s caused senior leaders all the way up the chain of command to wonder whether the incident had been an anomaly or was the first sign of Japan's decision to repudiate its earlier agreement to accept the Allied surrender terms and continue the war. But there was another, more immediate concern: the appearance of the Japanese fighters had forced the Dominators to cut short their aerial-photography mission, and news of the attack had also caused the cancellation or recall of other reconnaissance flights over the Home Islands. Far East Air Forces headquarters still needed to know which Japanese airfields would be usable for incoming occupation troops, and that meant that reconnaissance aircraft would have to be sent back over the Tokyo area despite what had happened on August 17.

In determining that additional recon flights were necessary, the V Bomber Command planners decided on a multi-mission approach. Aircraft from several units were tapped to participate, including both the 20th Recon and the 386th Bomb Squadron. The former would send four F-7s over the area south and west of Tokyo, while the latter would put a quartet of Dominators back over the northeastern part of the Kanto region. Though the decision to send B-32s back to Japan on August 18 may have been a nod to the Dominator's demonstrated abilities as a stable, long-range camera platform that could defend itself when necessary, it was more probably simple expedience—the big bombers were available, capable of performing the task, and not otherwise engaged.

The mission plan called for four B-32s to photograph airdromes to the east of greater Tokyo in Chiba Prefecture. These included several of the bases that had not been imaged on the seventeenth because of the fighter attacks, as well as the army fields at Shimoshizu and Kioroshi. The B-32s were to cover a roughly rectangular area of some 600 square miles, flying two miles apart and "mowing the lawn" at 20,000 feet. Planners estimated that it would take the four machines approximately an hour to complete their photo runs—if they were allowed to complete their task without interference.

Whether the Japanese would oppose the B-32s and other reconnaissance aircraft was, at that point, an open question. As strange as it may seem, there had apparently been no attempt to communicate with the Japanese regarding the August 17 attack, either by FEAF or by MacArthur's staff in Manila. It is always possible that someone of exalted rank in one of the headquarters determined that the fighter interception of the B-32s had been the last hurrah of a small band of renegade pilots who had since been brought to heel, but even the idea that no one attempted to verify that assumption before sending multiple crews back into what was quite possibly still the lion's den is staggering.

Moreover, the number of Japanese interceptors involved in the initial incident and the fact that the nature of the photo-recon mission had required the individual B-32s to fly too far apart to offer each other mutually supportive defensive fire logically argued that the August 18 missions by the Dominators and the 20th Recon aircraft should be escorted by friendly fighters. Iwo Jima–based P-51 Mustangs and P-47 Thunderbolts of VII Fighter Command were more than capable of rendezvousing with the B-32s and F-7s off the Japanese coast and accompanying them during the photo runs, yet no such escort was to be provided.

It is certainly possible, of course, that the mission planners decided not to send fighters along on August 18 out of an excess of caution. They may have reasoned that the arrival over Japan of large, four-engine bomber-type aircraft escorted by fighters would be more likely to prompt an aggressive response than it would be to prevent one. After all, during the previous two years the appearance over Tokyo of exactly the same sort of mixed bomber-fighter formations had heralded imminent death and destruction, and the Japanese might well assume that in retaliation for the August 17 attacks on the B-32s the Americans had decided to renew at least limited air assaults on the Home Islands.

However, it is far more likely that the decision not to send escorting fighters was based on a simple, operational reality: the August 15 theater-wide ceasefire had resulted in a dramatic and fairly rapid scaling back of the elaborate air-sea rescue network that had been put in place to assist airmen who, for whatever reason, were not able to make it back to their island bases after missions to Japan. By the last few months of hostilities that network had grown to include American and Allied submarines and surface vessels stationed off the Japanese coast as "plane guards" specifically to locate and retrieve downed pilots, as well as scores of "Dumbo" aircraft—B-17s, B-24s, and B-29s equipped with air-droppable life rafts—that orbited at set locations in order to respond quickly to a ditching or bailout. The rescue effort had been particularly valuable to the aircrews of VII Fighter Command, whose single-engine aircraft had been far less likely than larger machines to make it home safely if they encountered mechanical difficulties or had been significantly damaged by enemy action. The planners' decision not to dispatch fighter escorts as part of the August 18 recon missions may therefore have been forced on them. Given the rapid scaleback of offensive air operations following the ceasefire, it would have been nearly impossible to put adequate air-sea rescue coverage together in time to support the August 18 effort, particularly because many of the rescue units were preparing their aircraft to support the coming occupation airlift. Without that coverage to and from Japan the "Little Friends," as the Mustangs and Thunderbolts were called by those they escorted, would have been facing extraordinary and unacceptable risks even if they never encountered Japanese fighters.

There is another, though admittedly very improbable, explanation for why the reconnaissance aircraft tapped to overfly the Tokyo area on August 18 did so without a protective fighter escort. As the 386th Bomb Squadron's assistant intelligence officer, Rudy Pugliese, later postulated, the mission planners might intentionally have sent the B-32s and F-7s to the Kanto region on their own as a test of Japan's willingness to actually follow through with the surrender. While the overflights certainly had a legitimate and vital intelligence purpose—in that the photos the aircraft would bring back would be used in planning the arrival of Allied occupation forces— Pugliese believed the missions might also have been a rather cold-blooded "fidelity test." According to this scenario, if the Japanese did not interfere in any way with the unescorted American aircraft it would be a solid indication that the August 17 attacks had been the last desperate act of diehards rather than an indication that Japan's announced resolve to surrender was ebbing away.[1] Although this seems a highly unlikely possibility—not many senior officers would risk eight very expensive airplanes and their crews just to determine if the Japanese were still willing to shoot at them—stranger things have certainly happened in wartime.

Whatever the reason, the B-32s and F-7s that would be dispatched from Yontan to the Kanto region on August 18 would make the trip unescorted, with only their gunners to defend them should the Japanese prove "unfaithful."

BY THE MORNING OF August 18 the 386th Bomb Squadron officially "owned" seven B-32s, with two more still making the long trans-Pacific journey from the United States. Of those aircraft actually present at Yontan, three were grounded either by significant mechanical problems or because they were being used as a source of spare parts to keep the other aircraft flying. The four operational machines—*Hobo Queen II*, *Harriet's Chariot*, 544, and 578—therefore became the mission aircraft by default, despite the fact that each had a variety of what were considered to be "minor mechanical defects."

The son of Italian immigrant parents Emelia and Raffaelle (Ralph) Marchione, Anthony James Marchione was born in Pottstown, Pennsylvania, on August 12, 1925. Tony, as he was always known to family and friends, grew up dreaming of a career as a musician until war drew him far from home. *(Courtesy Theresa Marchione Sell and Geraldine Marchione Young)*

In this informal family portrait taken while Tony was home on leave after basic training, the young airman-to-be stands between his parents. The older of his two sisters, Theresa, is next to her mother while younger sister Geraldine kneels in the foreground. Both girls thought the world of their easygoing and supportive brother. *(Courtesy Theresa Marchione Sell and Geraldine Marchione Young)*

Always fascinated by airplanes and the technical aspects of aviation—and knowing that he was certain to get drafted—on November 20, 1943, Tony joined the U.S. Army Air Forces. He is seen here in an official portrait taken soon after he completed flexible gunnery training at Tyndall Army Airfield, Florida, proudly wearing the wings of a qualified aerial gunner. *(Courtesy Theresa Marchione Sell and Geraldine Marchione Young)*

In November 1944 Tony Marchione (kneeling, second from right) joined a B-24/F-7 crew led by First Lieutenant Robert W. Essig (standing, at left). The crew also included Rudolph Nudo and Frank Pallone (kneeling, second and third from left, respectively). The crew was initially bound for Italy but was diverted to Oklahoma for photo-reconnaissance training. *(Viracola Collection)*

Upon arrival at Will Rogers Army Airfield, Bob Essig's crew transitioned into the F-7B, likely the very aircraft shown here. The photo-reconnaissance version of the B-24 retained its full defensive armament but carried no bombs, its primary "weapons" being aerial cameras. Tony Marchione and his crewmates spent nearly three months at Will Rogers, and their "final exam" was a complex photo-mapping mission that took them from Oklahoma to Colorado and back. *(USAF via Theresa Marchione Sell and Geraldine Marchione Young)*

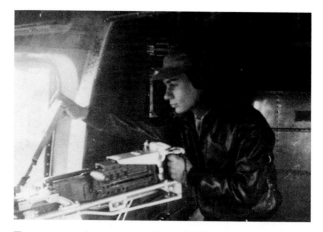

Tony scans the surrounding sky from the waist-gun position of an F-7B during a training flight from Clark Field soon after he and the other members of Bob Essig's crew joined the 20th Combat Mapping Squadron in the Philippines in May 1945. *(Frank Pallone Sr./Viracola Collection)*

The combat-ready Dominator was a formidable aircraft, as this in-flight shot shows. The B-32 could carry up to forty 500-pound general-purpose bombs, and was armed with ten .50-caliber machine guns in five powered turrets. Like the earlier B-24, the Dominator had a shoulder-mounted, high-lift, low-drag Davis wing. *(National Archives)*

Ground personnel inspect *Hobo Queen II* soon after the aircraft's arrival in the Philippines as part of the Dominator combat test. Most people in the USAAF had never even heard of the B-32, and anywhere they appeared Dominators were sure to draw curious onlookers. *(National Archives)*

Considered by many of his subjects to be the direct lineal descendant of Amaterasu, the Sun Goddess of Shintoism, Emperor Hirohito came to believe that the only way to preserve Japan as a sovereign nation—and to protect the hereditary monarchy—was to end the war as quickly as possible. The August 15 announcement of his decision to surrender to the Allies sparked an attempted coup and prompted restive Japanese fighter pilots to attack the B-32s that appeared in the skies over Tokyo. *(National Archives)*

Douglas MacArthur, left, and George Kenney formed an effective team in the fight against Japan. Kenney lobbied hard to bring the B-32 to the Pacific Theater, and MacArthur ultimately decided that the Japanese attacks on the Dominators over Tokyo did not warrant a resumption of hostilities. *(National Archives)*

Shown here during training in the United States, Joseph Lacharite was the twenty-nine-year-old 20th Reconnaissance Squadron aerial photographer tapped to fly the August 18 mission. Tony Marchione was assigned as Lacharite's helper, and together the two were to load and unload the cameras in First Lieutenant John Anderson's Dominator. *(Courtesy Rich Lacharite)*

Twenty-nine years old in August 1945 and an ace many times over, Saburo Sakai was one of the Yokosuka Kokutai's most formidable pilots. During his August 17 attack on a B-32 the aircraft accelerated away so quickly that the legendary fighter pilot wondered whether the bomber was equipped with some sort of auxiliary rocket engine. *(National Archives)*

One of several high-scoring pilots assigned to the Yokosuka Kokutai, twenty-five-year-old Warrant Officer Sadamu Komachi was a highly professional and experienced fighter pilot whose first combat mission was the 1941 attack on Pearl Harbor. He'd downed some forty Allied aircraft by the time he encountered the B-32s over Tokyo. *(National Archives)*

Though by August 1945 it was one of the older types in service with the Imperial Japanese Navy, the Mitsubishi A6M (known to the Allies by the reporting name "Zeke") remained a formidable interceptor and was in service with both the 302nd Kokutai at Atsugi and the Yoko Ku at Oppama. *(National Archives)*

Designed specifically to intercept enemy bombers at high altitudes, the Mitsubishi J2M-series land-based Raiden single-engine fighter (known to the Allies as the "Jack") made up in performance and armament what it lacked in maneuverability. In the hands of a good pilot it was extremely dangerous to high-flying Allied aircraft—including the B-32. *(National Archives)*

Heavily armed and ruggedly built, the Kawanishi N1K-J Shiden ("George") interceptor was more than a match for late-war Allied fighters and was particularly lethal against the hordes of B-29s that daily appeared over Japan. The type was in the Yoko Ku inventory and may have been the aircraft Sadamu Komachi flew during the August 18 engagement. *(National Archives)*

A photo officer in the 20th Reconnaissance Squadron, Second Lieutenant Kurt F. Rupke was assigned to supervise the photo runs made by Anderson's aircraft on the August 18 mission. Tony Marchione died in Rupke's arms. (*Courtesy Theresa Marchione Sell and Geraldine Marchione Young*)

George Davis (right), the flight engineer on one of the Dominators involved in the August 17 mission, proudly points to the three victory symbols added to the aircraft's nose. Despite the gunners' claims, surviving Japanese records list no fighter losses on that day or the next, and the claims are not reflected in the official USAAF record of confirmed World War II air-to-air kills. (*Ralph T. LeVine Collection via Roger LeVine*)

Gunner Sergeant Burton J. Keller (left) and flight engineer Sergeant Benjamin J. Clayworth of Anderson's crew stand below the hole in the B-32's fuselage (just above and to the left of the observation window) made by the 20mm cannon round that killed Tony Marchione. *(Ralph T. LeVine Collection via Roger LeVine)*

Crewmembers indicate the damage inflicted on John Anderson's 578. The man on the left is pointing to the small optical-glass port and the holes next to it made by the machine-gun bullets that wounded Joe Lacharite. The other man is indicating where the 20mm cannon round that killed Tony Marchione punched through the fuselage. The thin metal framework to the second man's right is the folded-up settee, minus its thin cushion, and the large hole in the floor is the belly entrance hatch that also served as a mounting for the aerial camera. *(Ralph T. LeVine Collection via Roger LeVine)*

After initial processing by the 3063rd Quartermaster Graves Registration Company, Tony Marchione's body was wrapped in a shelter half and buried on August 19, 1945, in Plot 2, Row 1, Grave 4 at Okinawa's Island Command Cemetery. There the young airman's remains would rest until disinterred on July 7, 1948, in preparation for their repatriation to the United States. *(Frank Pallone Sr./Viracola Collection)*

The burned-out remains of Leonard Sills's 544 lie in the coral pit at the end of Yontan's runway. The August 28 crash killed all thirteen men aboard. *(Ralph T. LeVine Collection via Roger LeVine)*

American personnel look on as one of two Japanese aircraft carrying Lieutenant General Torashiro Kawabe's delegation taxies after landing at Ie Shima on August 19. The arrival of the Japanese party helped convince MacArthur that the attacks on the Dominators—and the death of Tony Marchione and wounding of Jimmy Smart and Joe Lacharite—had been the work of a relatively few diehards and did not require the Allies to resume hostilities. *(National Archives)*

The short, troubled operational life of the B-32 came to a swift end following Japan's surrender. The Dominator program was canceled, all flyable aircraft were sent to disposal sites and demolished, while nonflyable machines and those still under construction were scrapped in place. Though initially intended for exhibition at the U.S. Air Force Museum the sole remaining B-32, 42-108474, was scrapped in August 1949. *(National Archives)*

On March 21, 1949, more than four years after his death in the skies above Tokyo, Anthony J. Marchione—the last American killed in air combat in World War II—was laid to rest in the cemetery of Pottstown's St. Aloysius Roman Catholic Church. *(Stephen Harding)*

Several of these "minor" issues were to become the source of major problems in the hours to come.

The one resource the 386th had in abundance was B-32 crewmen. The Dominator conversion courses the squadron had been running since before the move to Okinawa had produced more than enough qualified pilots, copilots, and flight engineers, and most of the other crew positions—navigator, radio and countermeasures operators, and gunners—could be readily filled by men who in most cases had racked up many hours of B-24 time before transitioning to B-32s. Because the Army Air Forces still planned to convert the entire 312th Bomb Group from A-20s to Dominators, between the end of the combat test and the beginning of operations from Yontan Tony Svore and Selmon Wells had instituted a crew-pool system intended to give as many men as possible some operational time in the B-32s. For most missions personnel were therefore drawn from daily rosters as needed, meaning that on any given flight the pilot and copilot might never have flown together, and the gunners and other crewmembers might have only a passing acquaintance. There were exceptions to this policy, however, in that at least three combat-experienced B-24 crews transitioned intact into B-32s.[2]

The four crews tapped to fly the August 18 mission gathered in the 386th's makeshift briefing tent at 5:30 in the morning, sunrise still half an hour away. Clasping canteen cups full of steaming coffee the men settled into rows of wooden folding chairs facing several bulletin boards, each of which illustrated a different aspect of the mission upon which they were about to embark.

On one board a length of string anchored by pushpins traced the flight path the aircraft would follow from Yontan to Tokyo and back, essentially the same track followed by the aircraft on the previous day's mission. The route kept the big bombers far offshore from the southeastern coasts Kyushu and Shikoku, a precaution that had been in place for all Allied aircraft since the atomic bombings of Hiroshima and Nagasaki and which was intended to keep aircrews safe from any potential radiation hazards. After takeoff the Dominators would shape a direct course for the 880-mile leg to Miyake-jima, the large island directly south of Tokyo Bay and, upon reaching it, would turn further to the north toward Chosi. Still some twenty miles offshore they would then proceed up the east coast of the Boso Peninsula to a point almost due east of Chiba, where they would turn inland to start their photo runs. Attached to a second bulletin board was a map encompassing the area from Okinawa to southern Honshu, upon which the 312th Group's meteorologist had annotated the latest weather information. A third bulletin board bore a large-scale map of the Kanto region, marked with the various airfields to be photographed and the Japanese units thought to be based at each. The map also indicated the positions of known early-warning and gun-laying radars—including the sites at Shira-hama, Choshi, and Hiraiso—and their frequencies. This latter data would assist the countermeasures operators aboard the Dominators in jamming the radars, if the need arose.

The question of whether such measures would be necessary and, indeed, if the Japanese could be expected to oppose the day's mission as they had the previous one was obviously a topic of immense inter-est to the crewmen gathered in the briefing tent. They had, of course, all heard about the fighter interceptions the day before, and at least three men present for the briefing had been aboard the B-32s that were attacked. When the squadron intelligence officer, Bill Barnes, stepped forward to address the issue of possible enemy action, he could add little more to what most of those present already suspected. Nobody on the Allied side really knew with any certainty who was in charge in Tokyo, or whether the Japanese could be trusted to lay down their arms and abide by the ceasefire. The best advice he could give, he said, was for the B-32 crews to be ready for anything.[3]

No one in the tent that morning relished the idea of getting shot at by the Japanese, and it's fairly certain that Tony Marchione in particular was regretting his decision to volunteer for the mission. Though as an airman with three combat missions and countless training flights under his belt he was no stranger to the idea of his own death or maiming, he undoubtedly had no wish for either of those possibilities to occur when the war was all but over. What had sounded like a milk run on August 16 was now likely to turn into something quite different.

And it is entirely possible that twenty-nine-year-old Staff Sergeant Joe Lacharite, an aerial photographer and one of the eleven other 20th Recon Squadron members sitting next to Tony during the briefing, was feeling equally unsettled by his decision to get himself assigned to the flight. Lacharite had been grounded because of a bad chest cold when his regular F-7 crew had flown a photo-recon mission over Japan, something he had always wanted to do, so when the Dominators were not attacked on August 16 he decided that perhaps the best way to see the Japanese capital was from a B-32. Lacharite had put his name on the volunteer list but had not been needed for the August 17 mission. Now, however, his services *were* needed, and his opportunity to fly over Tokyo was soon to become an experience from which he would never fully recover.

JOSEPH M. LACHARITE WAS born in Sherbrooke, Quebec, in January 1916 and was brought to the United States by his parents soon after. One of seven children, he grew up in Holyoke, Massachusetts, where his father first worked in a textile mill and later opened his own building-maintenance business. Life was not particularly easy for the family, and Joe left high school before graduating in order to help his father, but he also worked part-time as a spot news photographer for a local newspaper and even briefly ran his own small photo studio. He was fascinated by cameras and the ways in which photos could be enhanced in the darkroom, and those interests ultimately allowed him to do something most World War II draftees couldn't—he spent his military time working at something he loved.[4]

Inducted into the Army Air Forces in March 1944, Joe left his wife, Ruth, and their infant son in Holyoke and traveled to Sheppard Field, Texas, for basic training. It was during his time there that he made his photographic skills known, and when he completed basic in May he was sent to Lowry Field in Denver, Colorado. The base had been home to the Aerial Photography School since 1938, and by the time of Joe's arrival the institution was training both officers and enlisted men. For the latter, the two main courses of instruction were initially in photo laboratory work and the repair and maintenance of cameras, with each subject lasting ten weeks. Early in 1944 the two courses were combined, with enlisted students first mastering laboratory techniques and then progressing to the camera-technician training.

Although these courses prepared students to develop the images captured by cameras mounted in aircraft, and to service those cameras, combat operations in Europe and the Pacific eventually proved the need for more men qualified to actually operate the cameras in the air. As a result, in July 1944 the Photography School instituted a program to train aerial photographers and aerial photographer-gunners. Men who had successfully completed the combined laboratory-camera technician course and who were physically and psychologically suited for aircrew duty were given two additional weeks of training in such things as photographic-mission planning and camera operations while in flight. They also put their new skills to the test during actual aerial photography missions flown in Lowry's fleet of obsolescent Douglas B-18 Bolo twin-engine medium bombers. And, finally, those individuals tapped to be photographer-gunners underwent an abbreviated gunnery course at Lowry's Armament Technicians' School.[5] Joe Lacharite was a member of the first class to complete the laboratory-camera technician-aerial photographer-gunner course, graduating in November 1944.

Upon leaving Denver, Joe was posted to the Combat Crew Training Station-Photo-Reconnaissance at Will Rogers Field in Oklahoma City. It was, of course, the same organization at which Tony Marchione and the other members of Bob Essig's crew were making the transition from bombardment aviation to reconnaissance. Joe was assigned to a different crew, but he and Tony came to know each other and, although the two were not close friends, Joe later remembered that the young Italian-American gunner impressed him with his own knowledge of cameras and photography.

On joining what at the time was still the 20th Combat Mapping Squadron, Joe Lacharite flew three combat missions in F-7s, all from Luzon. His first, on May 21, saw Joe serving as a waist gunner as he and his crew journeyed to the same Balete Pass area that Bob Essig's aircraft would visit just over a week later, though bad weather made photography impossible. Joe was the assigned photographer on both his second mission, a fourteen-hour round-trip to Hainan Island, off the Chinese coast, and on the third, an only slightly shorter journey to Formosa's northwest coast to photograph the Japanese navy airfield at Taichu.[6] None of these flights encountered any serious enemy opposition.

Lacharite and his crew flew several training missions following the newly redesignated 20th Recon Squadron's move to Okinawa, but surviving records do not indicate that Joe participated in any further F-7 combat sorties with the squadron. This may have been because of the cold he'd developed just after arriving at Yontan, which by the first week in August had become severe enough that the flight surgeon grounded him. It was during this period of Joe's enforced idleness that his crew flew the mission to Japan, which in turn led the aerial photographer to volunteer for a B-32 flight. Joe, like Tony Marchione and probably every other American service member in the Pacific Theater, believed that the August 15 ceasefire was exactly what it purported to be—the end of armed conflict with Japan. And Joe, like Tony, was likely shocked to discover that the mission he'd believed would be something of a milk run might well turn into something far more threatening.

TONY MARCHIONE AND JOE LACHARITE were not the only men from their unit who would be participating in the August 18 mission, though as far as we can tell they were the only two who had actually volunteered. In keeping with 20th Recon Squadron's policy, each B-32 would carry a three-man photographic team: a photo officer, who would be stationed in the Dominator's nose and who would use the Norden bombsight to steer the aircraft over the correct photo path; the aerial photographer, who would install, load, and maintain the K-22 camera in the B-32's rear cabin; and a gunner, who would act as the photographer's assistant but would not be responsible for manning a weapon. Twenty-eight-year-old Second Lieutenant Kurt F. Rupke—the navigator on Tony's F-7 crew and a man who had known the young Italian-American since combat crew training in Oklahoma—would lead a team consisting of

himself, Joe, and Tony. The second 20th Recon team would be led
by First Lieutenant J. E. Stansbury, with Technical Sergeant G. L.
Chartier as photographer and Sergeant H. G. Thorsvig as the assistant. The names of the members of the other two teams have, unfortunately, not survived.

The men from the 20th Recon were given their aircraft assign-
ments at the end of the preflight briefing. Rupke's team would fly in
578, which for the day's mission would be piloted by twenty-seven-
year-old First Lieutenant John R. Anderson, whereas Stansbury and
his two men would be aboard *Hobo Queen II*, flown by twenty-four-
year-old First Lieutenant James L. Klein. The other two photo teams
were assigned to *Harriet's Chariot* and 544.

When the briefing ended the men of the photo teams joined the
B-32 crewmen in walking to the aircraft, parked on hardstands
some 200 yards away. As Anderson and his crew began their preflight checks, Rupke boarded 578 through the small stair-equipped
hatch on the left side of the aircraft's fuselage just forward of the
nose wheel. Tony Marchione and Joe Lacharite, between them carrying the K-22 camera in its case and a barracks bag bearing each
man's fleece-lined flight pants and jacket, personal oxygen masks,
small tool kits, film canisters, and other items, stopped near the
rear of the aircraft, marveling at the machine's sheer bulk. Neither
man had ever been that close to a B-32, and compared to the B-24s
and F-7s they were used to, the Dominator was a behemoth. After a
moment they climbed into the plane's rear compartment through a
belly hatch just aft of the retracted ball turret and stowed their gear
next to a fold-down settee attached to the port side of the fuselage.
They were soon joined by Sergeant Jimmie F. Smart, the rear upper
gunner, and Sergeant John T. Houston. The latter was normally the
aircraft's ball turret gunner, but he announced to Tony and Joe that
the unit's retraction mechanism was inoperative and the ball could
not be lowered, so on this flight Houston would man the tail turret.
The news that the aircraft's belly would be defenseless should the
Japanese prove hostile struck Lacharite as an ill omen.

Nor was the balky ball turret the B-32's only mechanical difficulty. Sergeant Burton J. Keller announced over the intercom that

his nose turret was partially inoperable; he could elevate and depress the two .50-caliber machine guns hydraulically, but they had to be traversed from side to side manually. Moreover, only one of the guns was actually capable of firing.[7] And, as if weapon issues weren't enough, when Joe and Tony attempted to seat their K-22 aerial camera in its mount—which attached to the inside of the belly entrance hatch above a hole covered by a detachable metal disk—they discovered that several of the springs intended to hold the camera upright and steady were broken. Moreover, the electrical junction box attached to the camera mount—through which Rupke would remotely operate the camera from the nose compartment—didn't seem to be working. When Joe informed the photo officer of the issues over the intercom, Rupke told him it was too late to do anything about it, and to just do the best he could.[8]

Tony and Joe then pulled on their leather flying helmets, attached their oxygen masks, and connected the masks' long, ribbed, rubber hoses to the regulator panels just above the settee. After ensuring that oxygen would flow on demand, the men disconnected the hoses and removed the masks and then pulled their fleece-lined pants over the single-piece, tropical-weight, belted flight suits that were their normal working uniform. Sitting on the ground with various entry hatches open the B-32 was fairly hot and humid, but within a half-hour after takeoff the aircraft's interior temperature would drop significantly despite the heated air from ducts scattered throughout the fuselage. Then, having completed their preflight rituals, Tony and Joe seated themselves on the folded-down settee and attached their seatbelts, to be joined for takeoff by Smart and Houston.

The four B-32s trundled from their hardstands just after 6:30 and the final aircraft lifted off from Yontan's runway fifteen minutes later. The big bombers assumed a loose echelon formation as they set a course for Japan, their crews settling in for what they undoubtedly hoped would be a routine and trouble-free mission. Barely two hours later that hope died, however, for within minutes of each other both *Harriet's Chariot* and 544 developed serious engine oil leaks that forced them to abort the flight and return to Okinawa.

Their departure was a serious blow, for it not only cut by half the defensive firepower that would be available should the Japanese prove hostile, it also meant that each of the remaining two aircraft would have to prolong its time over Japan to photograph additional targets. James Klein, pilot of *Hobo Queen II* and now the de facto mission commander, had no choice but to lead his diminished force onward. Senior leaders in FEAF and V Bomber Command had decided that the images the recon flight would produce were potentially important enough to send the Dominators back over Japan despite the possible risks. Like all good soldiers Klein and his fellow aviators would do their best to follow the orders they'd been given, though as they flew on they were all undoubtedly wondering just what sort of reception awaited them.

As THE TWO DOMINATORS droned on toward their landfall at Miyake-jima, some of the men best prepared to ruin the American aviators' day were dealing with their own apprehensions.

The navy pilots at Atsugi and Oppama who had participated in the previous day's attacks on the four B-32s had done so either because they believed that the *Bushido* code forbade Japan from ever surrendering to a foreign power under any circumstances, or because they felt that the nation's sovereignty—and thus its airspace—should remain inviolate until the surrender document had actually been signed. Moreover, as many of either persuasion would certainly have pointed out, the orders that had filtered down from IJN headquarters regarding the ceasefire had stated that units could defend themselves if attacked.

No matter which of the two positions an individual pilot might have supported, however, the fact remained that the August 17 attack on the Dominators had been in direct disobedience of both Emperor Hirohito's clearly expressed wishes and the explicit orders of the navy's most senior officer. While Saburo Sakai, Ryoji Ohara, and the others were not the only Japanese military personnel to have ignored the ceasefire—anti-aircraft units throughout the Kanto region had fired on American aircraft on August 15, 16, and 17, after all, and Vice Admiral Ugaki had himself attempted a final kamikaze attack—the 302nd Air Group and Yoko Ku pilots were undoubt-edly aware that they had disobeyed orders in a most dramatic and flagrant way. They could not even legitimately claim to have acted in self-defense, because the Americans had *not* attacked any Jap-anese installations and had only defended themselves against the intercepting fighters. Although the more glib among the naval avi-ators might have argued that it would have been pointless to attack a bomber *after* it had proven to be hostile by dropping its ordnance, the fact remained that the actions of the Japanese fighter pilots in-volved in the August 17 action against the Dominators technically constituted mutiny no matter what its moral or ethical underpin-nings might be, and in Japan's armed forces at that point in time that most uniquely military of crimes was punishable by death.

And yet, as far as most of the participants in the August 17 attack would have been able to tell, their actions either had gone largely unnoticed or had been purposely ignored. Messages from Tokyo continued to deluge the communication centers at both Atsugi and Oppama demanding the grounding of all aircraft and the unques-tioning observance of the ceasefire, but no truckloads of heavily armed troops had yet appeared at either installation's gates to force compliance. Indeed, the 302nd Air Group's increasingly malaria-crazed Captain Yasuna Kozono still held court in his barricaded command bunker as the sun rose on August 18, and the Yoko Ku's Lieutenant Commander Masanobu Ibusuki was still ordering that aircraft be fueled and armed and made ready for takeoff at any mo-ment. The pilots at both Atsugi and Oppama must have understood only too well that, whatever their motivation, they would ultimately be held personally responsible for their continuing determination to engage American aircraft and several—most notably Sakai—decided for their own reasons that the August 17 fight was their last and grounded themselves.[9] Many others, however, awoke on August 18 determined to continue the battle if the opportunity presented itself.

And in just hours, it would.

Hobo Queen II AND 578 passed over Miyake-jima just after noon and in what Rudy Pugliese's later mission report termed "excellent flying weather" with "unrestricted visibility."[10] The Dominators were then at about 18,000 feet, with their crews on oxygen and wearing their full, fleece-lined, high-altitude gear. As the aircraft turned slightly to the north to parallel the coast of Chiba Prefecture the gunners aboard each B-32 tested their weapons, at which point the men in 578 learned that they had yet another problem.

When tail gunner John Houston depressed the triggers on the twin .50s in his tail turret, he found that, for some reason he couldn't immediately diagnose, the guns were firing far more slowly than their usual cyclic rate of between 450–550 rounds per minute.[11] When he announced this over the intercom, Burton Keller—in the partially disabled nose turret—suggested to pilot John Anderson that because the Dominator's two top turrets seemed to be the only ones working normally he, Anderson, should take the aircraft to a lower altitude as quickly as possible if enemy fighters attacked. That way the B-32's belly, defenseless because of the inoperable ball turret, would not be exposed. The nose and tail gunners would do what they could, Keller said, but it would be up to the two upper turret gunners—Jimmie Smart aft and flight engineer Sergeant Benjamin F. Clayworth forward—to provide most of the aircraft's defense.[12]

Whether it would actually be necessary to defend either Dominator against attacking fighters remained an open question as the two aircraft flew northeast, paralleling the east coast of the Boso Peninsula. But it had already become clear that the Japanese were aware of the B-32s' presence. Soon after the aircraft had passed over Miyake-jima the countermeasures officer in Klein's *Hobo Queen II*, Second Lieutenant John R. Blackburn, had picked up the characteristic "whoop-whoop-whoop" sound of a Japanese early-warning radar in search mode—most probably the army site at Shirihama. Almost as soon as Blackburn heard the emission it changed to the steady hum that indicated the radar had detected the B-32, and the young officer immediately began jamming the signal. He was rewarded by the Japanese radar's immediate return to search mode, but the respite didn't last long. As the two Dominators turned east at 12:30 and crossed the coastline south of Chosi they separated to begin their initial photo runs; minutes later Blackburn picked up the ominous sound of gun-laying radar. He again immediately jammed the signal and dropped "rope," but also keyed his intercom and said to Klein, seated just ahead of him, "something's wrong here, they haven't stopped the war yet."[13]

By this time John Anderson's 578 was two or three miles away, just beginning a photo run. The aircraft's countermeasures operator, Staff Sergeant Frederick C. Chevalier, had detected occasional gun-laying radar emissions, but none had lasted very long and the young airman had not needed to jam them. A veteran of fifteen missions in B-24s of the 90th Bomb Group, Chevalier wasn't particularly concerned by the fact that his aircraft was being "painted"—indeed, he was relaxed enough to notice the extraordinary steel-blue color of the clear, unclouded sky above the Kanto region, a sky in which his aircraft and the other Dominator seemed to be the only things moving.[14] Though Chevalier didn't realize it at the moment, that beautiful and apparently empty sky was about to get dangerously crowded.

AT OPPAMA, SADAMU KOMACHI and other pilots of the Yoko Ku were also gazing at the sky, though not in appreciation of its beauty.

Shortly after John Blackburn in *Hobo Queen II* had begun jamming the Shirihama early-warning radar, the communications center at the navy base had apparently received telephonic warning that American aircraft were inbound toward the greater Tokyo region. This initial alert may actually have been caused by the appearance over the Yokohama area of the four F-7s of the 20th Recon Squadron, but the practical result was the same. The Japanese fighter pilots, several of whom had taken part in the previous day's attacks on the four B-32s, were watching the sky for any sign of what they still considered to be enemy airplanes. They would not be hard to spot, given that the grounding of virtually all Japanese military aircraft as a result of the ceasefire order—or because holdout pilots were attempting to conserve fuel—meant that the only machines flying about in Japanese airspace were almost certain to be Allied.

And, at about 1:00 in the afternoon the gathered Yoko Ku pilots spotted the telltale glint of sun reflecting off aluminum, so high

above them—Komachi estimated its altitude at about 18,000 feet—
that it could not be anything but an American bomber. The aircraft
was clearly visible with the naked eye, and the apparent noncha-
lance with which it serenely cruised above war-battered Tokyo
incensed Komachi. He later wrote that he "could not take it any-
more" and, seething with frustration, he burst out, "I've got to go
get them!" He ran to a nearby fighter—most probably a J2M Jack—
fired up the engine and quickly taxied to Oppama's main runway.
Then, not waiting for any sort of clearance, he roared into the sky,
followed by several of his comrades.[15]

Much the same scene was playing out at Atsugi, which had apparently also received the warning of incoming Allied aircraft. Several pilots of the 302nd Air Group—men presumably as outraged
as Komachi by the reappearance of enemy bombers over Tokyo—
hurried to their aircraft and also charged aloft.

The Japanese pilots who took to the air on August 18, whether
from Atsugi or Oppama, had no intention of simply shepherding
the American aircraft out of Japanese airspace. Their purpose was
far more direct: they were fighter pilots, and they were on the hunt.

THE FIRST B-32 CREWMAN to realize that something was seriously
amiss was most probably John Blackburn. As *Hobo Queen II* pulled
off its final photo run, the countermeasures officer picked up the
emissions of another gun-laying radar, but this time the steady
hum in Blackburn's earphones indicated that the radar had already
acquired them. As he began jamming the signal Japanese 120mm
anti-aircraft guns sited between Chiba City and Chosi immediately
opened fire on the Dominator. The tail gunner, Staff Sergeant J. R.
Baker, called out that the bursts were at the same altitude and about
1,000 yards astern.[16]

Seconds later another of the B-32's gunners shouted over the intercom that he could see Japanese fighters taking off from a field to
the south of the bomber's track, and Klein banked the plane slightly
to starboard so he could see them. The interceptors were clearly visible as they clawed for altitude, and Klein ordered his radio operator to contact Anderson and warn him that fighters were in the

air. When there was no response from the other Dominator, *Hobo Queen II's* pilot turned the B-32 southeast and headed for the sea.

The big bomber had barely made it to the coast, however, when about twenty miles south of Chosi Sergeant Billy J. Osborne, the forward upper gunner, yelled, "there's fighters coming in!"[17] The first Japanese aircraft—a Zeke, most probably from the 302nd—bored in at *Hobo Queen II* from one o'clock high, firing as it came. Osborne slewed his turret around and sent thumb-sized .50-caliber rounds streaming toward the incoming fighter. The gunner and the plane's copilot, First Lieutenant Glen W. Bowie, both saw the bullets hitting the forward fuselage and cockpit area of the Zeke, which suddenly rolled inverted and headed down at a steep angle, its engine emitting puffs of oily black smoke. Though neither man could follow the enemy fighter's fall all the way to impact, Bowie later verified his gunner's claim of a "definite" kill.[18]

That presumed victory was only the start of *Hobo Queen II's* fight, however. Over the next twenty-five minutes, ten or more Japanese fighters came at the B-32 from ahead, behind, and above. Fortunately, as soon as the first attacker had appeared Klein had put the Dominator into a fairly steep dive and opened the throttles to the stops, knowing that few single-engine aircraft would be able to keep up. He was right, and the bomber's rapid acceleration—combined with the volume of defensive fire put out by her gunners—prevented the Japanese pilots from making more than one pass each and ultimately kept them from inflicting any damage on *Hobo Queen II* or any injuries to her crewmen. The only drawback to Klein's defensive tactic was the stress it put on the Dominator's airframe. The speed and steepness of the dive made the aircraft shake and buffet so much that at one point Blackburn leaned forward and shouted to Klein, "I think we're going to come apart!" The B-32 remained intact, however, and at about 1,000 feet above the sea Klein leveled out and set a course for Okinawa, the Japanese fighters now miles behind and unable to catch up.[19]

WHEN THE GLINTING SUN had first drawn Sadamu Komachi's eye toward the high-flying American bomber it had clearly still been on a photo run, for it was flying from east to west from the direction of Kujukuri Beach, on the Pacific coast side of Chiba Prefecture, toward Tokyo. By the time Komachi and his compatriots had gotten their fighters airborne however, the aircraft—which Komachi believed was a B-29—had reversed course and was headed southeast toward the sea.

Komachi was an extremely competent and highly experienced fighter pilot, and he'd been engaging multi-engine Allied aircraft since his time at Rabaul. One technique he'd used quite successfully was to fly far out in front of his intended target while at the same time gaining altitude, then make a snap turn and come back in from twelve o'clock high with all guns blazing. This sort of attack—which was the same tactic German Luftwaffe fighter pilots had often employed against Allied bombers over Europe—had two main advantages. First, the attacking pilot could concentrate his fire on the enemy bomber's cockpit and the leading edges of its wings, thereby either killing the pilots or knocking out the engines. And second, because the attacker and his prey were flying toward each other, the high converging speeds made it difficult for the bomber's gunners to keep the fighter in their sights as it flashed pass. While there was always the risk of a midair collision if the attacker misjudged his angle or was himself injured by enemy fire, the tactic could be highly effective when used by a formidable fighter pilot such as Komachi.

As the veteran Japanese aviator raced to get himself into position in front of and above the lone American bomber, however, he ran into an unexpected obstacle: his fellow Japanese pilots. In their eagerness to engage the B-32 Komachi's comrades—some of whom were coming off earlier attacks against *Hobo Queen II*—were launching attacks from twelve o'clock level, from both beams low, and from six o'clock high. The sky around the Dominator was thus filled with aircraft, making it highly likely that if Komachi employed his favored strategy he would run the very real risk of ramming one of the other Japanese interceptors. He pondered the situation for a moment as he flew above, parallel to, and slightly ahead of the American aircraft and then, characteristically, threw caution to the wind and wrenched his aircraft into a wing-over to begin his attack.[20]

ALTHOUGH IT IS UNCLEAR why John Anderson did not respond to James Klein's initial warning about the Japanese fighters, it is most probably because the pilot of 578 was already aware of the enemy aircraft. At about the same time that the men aboard *Hobo Queen II* spotted the Japanese interceptors taking off, John Houston—Anderson's tail gunner—came on the intercom and said he saw fighters at six o'clock low, and they seemed to be gaining altitude quickly. One of the B-32's other gunners asked what they should do, and from the nose turret Burton Keller responded, "You do the same thing we've always been told to do: if any of them come in pointing their noses at us, you fire away."[21]

Just minutes later, the gunners aboard 578 had more than enough reasons to "fire away." The first to do so was tail gunner Houston. The planes he'd seen earlier had reached the Dominator's altitude in what seemed just minutes, and three or four of the fighters rolled in on the bomber from his eleven o'clock, sweeping from his left to right. One of the Japanese aircraft came in higher than the others, its right wing slightly up and left wing slightly down, firing as it came. Houston could see the flashes of its guns, and he held his own fire until the fighter was so close he could hardly miss. When the attacker's image filled his optical gunsight, Houston pulled the triggers on his twin .50s, and despite their slow cyclic rate they spewed out more than enough rounds to do the job. Houston saw his bullets chew into the fighter's engine, cockpit area, and forward fuselage, and at about 100 feet behind the Dominator the attacker exploded, seeming to disintegrate completely before Houston's eyes. The young gunner barely had time to exclaim "I got him!" over the intercom before turning his guns on yet another incoming fighter.[22]

In the nose turret, Keller was finding it harder than it should have been to engage fighters coming in from twelve o'clock. Although his guns would hydraulically elevate and depress normally, he had to rotate the turret itself by turning an auxiliary hand crank. He therefore tried to determine the incoming fighter's track, then cranked the turret into an area he knew the attacker would have to pass through and started firing the single operable .50-caliber machine gun just before the target filled his gunsight. He could not crank the turret fast enough to keep the fighter in the sight, however, and he later recalled that he was just trying to throw out rounds in the hope that his tracers would force attackers to "back off."[23]

Fortunately, things were going better for the top turret gunners. In the aft position Jimmie Smart had been "snap shooting" at enemy aircraft that flashed over the B-32 as they carried out beam attacks, but then concentrated his fire on a particular fighter that rolled in from three o'clock high. The plane seemed to hang in mid-air for a moment, its rounds flashing over the top of the Dominator, and Smart poured bullets into the left side of its fuselage. Rolling inverted, the fighter passed below the B-32 and as it disappeared from Smart's view Clayworth, in the forward turret, yelled over the intercom that he'd seen the attacker explode.[24]

It was at that moment that Sadamu Komachi rolled in on 578. The Japanese pilot screamed down almost vertically toward the B-32, opening fire with his 20mm cannon when the Dominator filled his gunsight. He could see his rounds pounding into the aircraft's wings—as though, he later said, they were being sucked in—and as he flashed past he saw that one of the bomber's engines was trailing a wispy stream of gray smoke.[25] What he didn't notice was that one of his rounds had shattered Jimmie Smart's turret, sending jagged plexiglass shards into the young gunner's forehead and temple. Smart immediately screamed "I'm hit!" and dropped from the shattered turret, startling Joe Lacharite and Tony Marchione. The two 20th Recon men had been standing with their backs to one another, looking out the small observation windows on opposite sides of the aircraft. They turned their heads toward Smart, now huddling on the fuselage floor barely ten feet in front of them and clutching his head, and then Joe turned back to look out the window on his side because a movement had caught his eye. To his horror, what he saw was a Japanese fighter coming right at him.[26]

WHEN JOHN HOUSTON SIGHTED the Japanese fighters closing on 578's tail, Joe Lacharite and Tony Marchione had been starting to stow the K-22 camera and its associated gear. Because of the problems with the camera's mount and its electrical control box, Rupke, the photo officer, and not been able to operate the camera remotely from his position in the aircraft's nose. As the B-32 had passed over its assigned photo targets Rupke had therefore simply used the intercom to tell Joe when to trip the camera's shutter. Tony had been helping to steady the mount, and had assisted in changing the film magazine as needed. It wasn't the ideal way to shoot aerial photos but it was better than nothing, and when the Dominator finished its final photo run, Joe mentioned to Tony that he thought they'd gotten some usable images.

Despite the closed bulkhead door that separated Houston's tail turret from the compartment where Joe and Tony were working, the two men could clearly hear the banging of the guns when Houston engaged the incoming fighters. Moreover, Smart's top turret guns were all the more audible for being barely ten feet away. Neither man was particularly bothered by the sound of the big .50-calibers pumping out rounds or the acrid smell of gun powder—both were, after all, qualified aerial gunners themselves—though the reality that they could not actively help defend the aircraft in the way that they had been trained to do would certainly have added to their anxiety and frustration.

One way to contribute, however, was to help the men actually on the guns to locate targets they might not otherwise be able to see. Because 578's ball turret was unmanned there was no way for the men in the operable turrets to know if an enemy fighter was coming in from beneath the aircraft. Tony and Joe were both hooked into the Dominator's intercom system, of course, and by peering out the observation windows on either side of the fuselage they could spot those aircraft and call them out to the appropriate gunner. That was what the two men had been doing when the injured Jimmie Smart unexpectedly dropped from his damaged turret.

The observation window Joe had been looking through was set into 578's aft fuselage about twenty-eight inches above floor level. It was some two feet forward of, and three feet below, the leading edge of the Dominator's starboard horizontal stabilizer. Roughly oval in shape and about thirty inches across at its widest point, the window was made of plexiglass and was intended as a way for crewmembers to scan the rear of the starboard wing, its two engines, and the main landing gear on that side. Directly below the window, right next to and just to the right of the belly entrance hatch that also served as the aircraft's main camera position, was a smaller optical-glass port intended for use with an obliquely mounted aerial camera.

Even as the image of the incoming Japanese fighter in the large observation window was registering in Joe's mind, 7.7mm machine-gun rounds from a second, unseen fighter coming in from three o'clock low punched through the lower right corner of the small camera port, shattered the optical glass, and slammed into Joe. One bullet tore completely through his left leg just above the kneecap, exiting out the back of his thigh, and four others lodged in his right leg between the ankle and knee. The impact spun the photographer around, and he fell to the floor of the aircraft just forward of the small door leading back to the tail and Houston's turret, blood already streaming from his mangled legs. The fall had jerked Joe's intercom cord from the jack it had been plugged into and Tony, who had been kneeling on the folded-down settee and looking out the portside observation window set into the fuselage just above it, was following the track of an incoming Japanese fighter and was momentarily unaware that Joe had been hit. But Jimmie Smart, still lying beneath his turret and attempting to stop the bleeding from his head wounds, saw Joe sprawled on the floor and called out to Tony over the intercom.

Luckily, Joe had fallen right next to the barracks bag carrying his and Tony's equipment, and he was able to yank the braided-cotton closure cord from the top of the bag and hurriedly tie it around his left thigh as a tourniquet. He was struggling to wrap the now-disconnected intercom cord around his right leg when Tony, having turned away from the observation window, carefully lifted Joe onto the settee and then, kneeling down, began tightening the second tourniquet himself. As he was doing this Tony announced over the intercom that Joe had been wounded, and from the cockpit Anderson said he would send Rupke back to help. Tony had just acknowledged the pilot's transmission when a 20mm cannon round punched a ragged, double-fist-sized hole through the B-32's thin aluminum skin just above and slightly forward of the port-side observation window. The projectile slammed into Tony almost squarely in the center of his chest, driving him backward. He hit the opposite side of the fuselage and crumpled to the floor, his legs splayed out toward the settee and his head resting near the shattered optical-glass port. Joe, immobilized on the settee and now also pierced by razor-sharp splinters of the Dominator's aluminum skin, could do nothing but gesture helplessly to Smart.

Seconds later Rupke, having made his way across the narrow bomb-bay catwalk that connected the forward and aft crew compartments, came through the bulkhead door forward of Smart's turret. Seeing that the upper gunner's injuries weren't life-threatening, the photo officer rushed past Joe to Tony, medical aid kit in hand, instinctively seeking to help the more badly injured, long-time crewmate he considered one of his own. When Rupke knelt next to Tony the young man was still alive and conscious, though he was surrounded by a spreading pool of blood, at least some of which was coming from a partial exit wound in his back. The 20mm round had struck him just below the sternum, shattering several of his ribs and shoving shredded bits of his fleece-lined flight jacket and the lighter clothing beneath it into the wound. Rupke looked down at Tony and despite the obvious extent and severity of the young gunner's wounds told him he everything was going to be all right.[27]

Likely aware that things *weren't* going to be all right, Tony looked up at Rupke and managed to whisper, "Stay with me."

"Yes, I'll stay with you," the photo officer replied, gently taking Tony in his arms.[28]

At that point Houston came through the small door from the tail section and he and Smart—himself still bleeding—did what they could to help Joe, applying compression bandages to his legs after attempting to get sulfa powder into his wounds despite the frigid wind blowing into the aircraft's fuselage through the bullet and cannon shell holes. Minutes later the B-32's navigator, Second Lieutenant Thomas Robinson, and radar officer, Second Lieutenant Donald H. Smith, arrived and covered Joe and Tony with blankets. They cut away part of the sleeve on one arm of the young gunner's flight jacket and started a line for blood plasma, then tried to stanch the bleeding from both the massive hole in his chest and the smaller exit wound in the middle of his back, just to one side of his spine.[29]

Despite everyone's best efforts, however, Tony Marchione died about thirty minutes after he was hit and just six days past his twentieth birthday.

EVEN AS RUPKE AND the others were dealing with Joe and Tony's wounds the men still in the forward part of the Dominator had their own hands full.

In addition to wounding Jimmy Smart, Sadamu Komachi's attack had knocked out the B-32's number 3 engine, which immediately started trailing smoke and throwing oil over the right side of the aircraft's fuselage. Under normal circumstances the pilot, John Anderson, would have feathered the propeller—that is, turned the blades edge-on into the airstream to prevent the prop from continuing to rotate and possibly further damaging the engine. But he didn't want to signal to the attacking Japanese that the engine was completely dead, so he triggered the power plant's internal fire extinguisher and let the propeller windmill. The tactic wasn't quite as successful as Anderson had hoped it would be, however, for the pilots of several of the fighters saw the smoke before it dissipated and quickly launched the concentrated attacks that resulted in the injuries to Joe and Tony.[30]

Realizing that more radical measures were required, Anderson and copilot Second Lieutenant Richard E. Thomas advanced the throttles on 578's three remaining engines and put the B-32 into a steep descent, like Klein in *Hobo Queen II* hoping to outrun the enemy interceptors. As 578 dropped, rapidly picking up speed, the Japanese fighters fell further behind. They tossed rounds at the big bomber from increasingly longer range, hoping for a lucky hit, then gave up the chase one by one and turned back toward Atsugi and Oppama.

But Sadamu Komachi wasn't so easily deterred. After completing his near-vertical attack on the B-32 the Japanese ace had needed several minutes to pull his fighter out of its dive, reverse direction, and head back toward the rapidly disappearing American plane. His pullout and course reversal had put Komachi off to the side of the Dominator's track rather than directly aft of the bomber, and by "cutting the corner" at maximum speed he was able to gradually gain on his quarry. By the time Komachi came within firing range of 578 the Dominator was barely 1,000 feet above the water and well out to sea to the east of Oshima Island. Because there was not enough room to make another vertical attack and recover in time to avoid crashing into the water, Komachi decided to come in on a beam run. The maneuver was probably not his best decision, however, for in swinging his fighter wide in preparation for the attack he lost position and airspeed relative to the B-32. Komachi thus ended up having to fire from beyond the ideal range, and only managed to put a few rounds into 578's rudder trim tab before the Dominator again accelerated away from him. Alone and vulnerable to any Allied fighters that might be in the vicinity, Komachi finally gave up and turned for home.[31]

Though John Anderson and the men aboard his B-32 were obviously relieved by the departure of their last dogged pursuer, they were by no means out of the woods yet. They were still facing another six hours in the air, at least, and the Dominator was down to three good engines. After radioing Yontan with news of the attack, the wounding of Smart and Lacharite, and the death of Tony Marchione, Anderson warned his crew that they might have to bail out and directed everyone to put on their parachutes.

But as the hours passed it seemed more certain that the aircraft would make it all the way back to Okinawa, and everyone tried to relax as much as possible. Conversations sprang up over the intercom, with one of the prime topics of discussion being the reason why the Japanese pilots had seemed to concentrate their most determined attacks on the Dominator's waist section. The best answer, the crewmembers agreed, came from Burton Keller. The nose gunner expressed the opinion that the enemy attackers must have either mistaken the B-32 for a B-29, or at least assumed the Dominator had the same sort of unmanned gun turrets. The Superfortress's gunners sat behind large plexiglass observation bubbles in the aircraft's waist, Keller reminded his listeners, and acquired and tracked targets with sights that remotely controlled the guns. Japanese pilots had learned that by concentrating their initial attacks on the B-29's waist bubbles they could kill or disable the gunners, thereby rendering the Superfortress defenseless. Other than the B-29 the only Allied bomber most Japanese pilots had encountered in any numbers in the previous three years was the twin-tailed B-24, and when they saw the tall single tail on the B-32 they probably assumed it was a variant of the B-29.[32]

Robinson and Smith spent the return flight to Okinawa in the Dominator's aft compartment caring for Joe Lacharite. The photographer's injuries were extremely serious—he'd lost a lot of blood and the bones in both of his legs had been splintered by the Japanese bullets—and his pain was so intense that the two young officers had injected him with at least two morphine syrettes. Joe was in and out of consciousness for several hours, and at one point his respiration was so shallow it appeared he might not survive.[33]

After reverently wrapping Tony Marchione's body in blankets and helping to lay it carefully near the bulkhead door leading to the B-32's bomb-bay catwalk, Kurt Rupke had returned to the cramped nose compartment. Heartbroken by the death of a young man with whom he had trained and flown for months—someone he considered a good friend despite the difference in their ranks, ages, and backgrounds—Rupke was also angry beyond words. From the moment he'd climbed aboard the Dominator that morning the young photo officer had believed that the aircraft was totally unsuited for the mission it was tasked to undertake. The inoperable or mechanically impaired turrets and guns were bad enough, he believed, but sending an airplane on a photo-recon mission when its camera mount and vital associated systems were essentially out of commission was almost criminally stupid. The airplane may have been fit for flight, Rupke seethed, but that was all it was fit for. Tony had been one of "his boys," and his death had been completely avoidable and absolutely unnecessary.[34]

THE CREW OF 578 sighted Yontan air field almost exactly twelve hours after taking off on their ill-fated mission. Anderson wanted to avoid banking his damaged aircraft into the dead engine, so he flew a nonstandard approach and ended up coming in a little higher and faster than usual. As the aircraft rolled out and turned slowly onto the taxiway several field ambulances fell into line behind it. Anderson stopped the aircraft before reaching its assigned hardstand, and medics jumped from the ambulances and swarmed aboard through the Dominator's belly hatch. They helped Jimmie Smart out the same way, then carefully took Joe Lacharite and Tony Marchione's body out through the opened bomb bay. As they were doing so the B-32 was surrounded by a huge crowd of people—a crowd that, as Keller later remembered, included reporters, GIs, and "every colonel in the Fifth Air Force."[35]

The Dominator's tired, dispirited crewmen were hustled from their aircraft and into the same briefing tent they'd sat in what seemed like days earlier, but had in reality been just that morning. There they joined the men from *Hobo Queen II*, which had landed earlier, and once settled with mugs of coffee and plates of sandwiches the young airmen faced a barrage of questions intended to answer one very important question: was this attack just another aberration carried out by a few diehards, or was it an indication that the war wasn't over?

CHAPTER 6

PEACE, OR WAR?

THE CROWD THAT THRONGED 578 upon its return to Yontan had begun gathering hours earlier in response to contact reports sent even as the attack on the two B-32s was still underway. When the first Japanese fighter rolled in on *Hobo Queen II*, James Klein had ordered his radio operator, Technical Sergeant Leslie Christenson, to send an "in the clear" (non-encrypted) message to the 386th Bomb Squadron's communications center announcing the interception. Minutes later, as 578 came under fire, John Anderson had issued similar orders to his radioman, Sergeant Darrell Champlin. A second transmission regarding the wounding of Jimmy Smart and Joe Lacharite and the death of Tony Marchione followed, and by the time the two Dominators had shaken their pursuers and begun the long flight back to Okinawa news of the attack was pulsing across the airwaves from Yontan to MacArthur's headquarters in Manila, and from Manila to Washington.

Rudy Pugliese, the 386th's assistant intelligence officer, was among the first people at Yontan to learn just how much anxiety the news had stirred up among senior leaders. Barely minutes after Klein's message was relayed up the chain of command, Pugliese—who was manning the incoming phone lines while Bill Barnes was briefing Selmon Wells, Frank Cook, and Tony Svore—took a call from FEAF commander George Kenney, who asked if there was any additional information about the attack. When the young intelligence officer responded that there was nothing yet, Kenney said he wanted to know immediately when the aircraft landed and, more important, what the aircrew debriefings revealed, and added that MacArthur was at his side. As Pugliese recounted later, "when a three-star general says a five-star general is waiting, you hop."[1]

The urgent concern shown by both Kenney and MacArthur regarding the interception of the B-32s and the casualties those attacks caused was heightened by the news that the 20th Recon Squadron F-7Bs dispatched to Tokyo had also encountered unexpected Japanese resistance. The three aircraft—a fuel leak had forced the fourth machine to abort—had been tracked by early-warning radars on the approach to their photo targets in and around Yokohama. As they started their runs they were painted by gun-laying radars and were then subjected to heavy, continuous, and unusually accurate 120mm anti-aircraft fire. The Liberators took evasive action but at least one suffered multiple hits. There were no casualties and no fighter interceptions, though it is possible that the F-7Bs had avoided the latter hazard because they arrived over their targets after the B-32s had drawn off those 302nd Air Group and Yoko Ku pilots still willing to take to the air.[2]

Kenney and MacArthur were not the only people anxious for information about the attack on the B-32s. Military and civilian reporters had descended on the 386th's headquarters compound the previous day in response to the actions involving the four Dominators, and they began returning as word started to circulate around Yontan that another attack had occurred, this time resulting in American casualties. Several of the newsmen sought out Rudy Pugliese, badgering him for details that he was honestly able to tell them he didn't yet have. They, like everyone else, the young officer said, would have to wait until the two B-32s had landed and their crews had been debriefed. Although it was almost certainly not the answer the reporters were looking for they, like everyone else, had no choice but to settle in and wait for *Hobo Queen II* and 578 to return.[3]

ARMY AIR FORCES POST-MISSION combat aircrew debriefings were conducted in much the same way in all World War II theaters, no matter what type of unit was involved. Also referred to as inter-rogations, the interviews were meant to provide both intelligence and operational information. The former would include such things as the number, type, and markings of enemy aircraft encountered; enemy losses, both confirmed and probable; the approximate loca-tion of friendly airmen forced to bail out; the damage inflicted on ground targets through bombing or strafing; new enemy instal-lations sighted; the accuracy of pre-mission briefings; and so on. The operational data sought, while somewhat less dramatic, was equally important in that it dealt with the mechanical reliability of the friendly aircraft; ways in which the airplane's systems or crew interactions could be improved; the accuracy of weather forecasts; and the like.

The officers on an individual crew were normally interviewed separately from their enlisted men, though before being debriefed every member of the crew, no matter his rank, was offered the same, small shot of whiskey. This last amenity was usually welcomed, for even those missions that did not provoke a hostile response or result in friendly losses could leave crewmembers physically ex-hausted yet so mentally keyed up that they were unable to relax. And, of course, if the mission involved enemy action or the injury or death of other crewmen the individual being debriefed might well be emotionally shattered.

The crews of *Hobo Queen II* and 578 faced all the usual questions during the interrogations that followed their return to Yontan, but they were also asked to respond to some decidedly out-of-the-ordinary queries: Could they somehow have avoided the attack? Did they think the Japanese pilots had been receiving instructions from ground controllers? Could they identify the individual mark-ings of the aircraft that had wounded Smart and Lacharite and killed Marchione? The men did what they could to answer the interroga-tors' questions despite being understandably bitter and emotional about the attacks—the Japanese government, after all, had publicly

accepted the Allied surrender terms and agreed to the ceasefire—
and the mood in the debriefing was decidedly dark. That changed
somewhat, however, when Selmon Wells asked the gunners from
both aircraft whether they truly believed they'd damaged or destroyed the Japanese fighters they'd claimed.

John Houston sheepishly raised his hand and said, "I'm pretty
sure I really got one, sir."

"What do you mean you're 'pretty sure,' son?" the 312th's commander replied.

"Well, sir," Houston said slowly, "I was shooting at him and he
blew up."

There was a moment of stunned silence, then laughter rippled
through the crowded room and quickly swelled to a crescendo.[4]

KENNEY, MACARTHUR, AND OTHER senior officers throughout the
Pacific Theater were more concerned by the attack on *Hobo Queen II*
and 578—and on the F-7Bs, for that matter—than they had been
about the previous day's incident involving the four Dominators.
The August 17 event could be explained away as the rash action of
several diehard pilots. But a second and far more serious attack—
which at first glance appeared to involve coordinated action by multiple fighters, radar sites, and anti-aircraft units and that resulted in
the death of one American and the wounding of two others—could
well be the beginning of an organized effort on the part of Japan's
military to repudiate Emperor Hirohito's decision to surrender.
The United States government was aware through both diplomatic
channels and neutral news sources of the August 15 attempted coup
in Tokyo, and Allied interception and decryption of encoded Japanese radio traffic indicated that there remained significant anti-surrender sentiment among senior army commanders.[5]

Yet though the events of August 17 and 18 might have been seen
as the first stirrings of a renewed Japanese war effort, MacArthur
decided to follow what at the time must have seemed to many of
his senior staffers to be a fairly risky course. Despite his very real
anxiety about the motives for the attacks the Supreme Commander
Allied Powers effectively chose to do nothing—at least for the mo-

ment. While the daily intelligence summary distributed within his command mentioned both days' incidents, and though Allied units throughout the Pacific Theater were cautioned yet again to be prepared to defend themselves, no retaliatory offensive military action was ordered against Japan or the deployed Japanese forces in MacArthur's area of command. There was no resumption of airstrikes, and no renewed bombardment of coastal targets in the Home Islands by Allied naval forces.

One possible explanation for MacArthur's decision not to immediately retaliate for either attack might have been the results of the debriefings following each mission. The crews who flew on August 17 reported that the attacks against them were "uneager" and seemed somewhat haphazard in their execution.[6] And though angered by the interception of their aircraft and saddened by the death of Tony Marchione and the wounding of Jimmy Smart and Joe Lacharite, the crews of 578 and *Hobo Queen II* agreed that the Japanese attacks against them did not seem coordinated or organized. Moreover, several of the crewmen from both days' flights pointed out that as they left the Tokyo area their B-32s had overflown several enemy airdromes where aircraft could be seen parked in alert revetments along the runways, yet no fighters rose from those fields to challenge the Dominators. Taken together, these observations strongly suggested that the pilots who shot up the two B-32s on August 18 were, as on the day before, diehards acting on their own initiative rather than as part of a larger, concerted, and ground-controlled effort. As soon as the debriefings ended Rudy Pugliese picked up the phone—a line to Kenney's headquarters had been kept open for him—and reported this key finding directly to the FEAF commander.[7] It is entirely conceivable that the information helped persuade MacArthur, who was presumably still at Kenney's side, that the day's events over Tokyo—despite constituting yet another breach of the ceasefire—did not warrant a resumption of Allied combat operations against Japan.

But there is another, far more likely explanation for MacArthur's decision not to react militarily to the attacks against the B-32s on either day.

In his initial August 15 exchange of radio messages with Tokyo, the supreme commander had directed that the Japanese send to Manila

> a competent representative empowered to receive in the name of the Emperor of Japan, the Imperial Japanese Government, and the Japanese Imperial Headquarters certain requirements for carrying into effect the terms of the surrender. . . . The representative will be accompanied by competent advisers representing the Japanese Army, the Japanese Navy, and Japanese Air Forces. The latter adviser will be one thoroughly familiar with airdrome facilities in the Tokyo area.[8]

MacArthur was equally direct in instructing the Japanese government on how the delegation was to make the journey:

> The party will travel in a Japanese airplane to an airdrome on the island of Ie Shima, from which point they will be transported to Manila, Philippine Islands, in a United States airplane. They will be returned to Japan in the same manner. The party will employ an unarmed airplane. . . . Such airplane will be painted all white and will bear upon the side of its fuselage and the top and bottom of each wing green crosses easily recognizable at 500 yards. . . . Weather permitting, the airplane will depart from Sata Misaki [airdrome, on the southern tip of Kyushu] between the hours of 0800 and 1100 Tokyo time on the seventeenth day of August 1945.[9]

And, in a truly MacArthurian touch, he added that in all communications regarding the flight Tokyo was to use the code designation "Bataan"—a reference, of course, to the Philippine peninsula on Luzon where on April 9, 1942, American and Filipino forces under Major General Edward P. King Jr. had surrendered to the invading Japanese.[10]

Over the two days following the initial transmission to the Japanese of MacArthur's directive there were various alterations in the delegation's itinerary, and a second appropriately marked aircraft was added for the journey. The day finally agreed upon for the flight was August 19, with the Japanese delegation slated to land at Ie Shima at about 1:30 P.M. None of the messages that went back and forth between Manila and Tokyo on the seventeenth mentioned the attack on the four B-32s over Tokyo, and it is likely that MacArthur was waiting to see if the Japanese canceled the delegation's trip following the August 18 interception of *Hobo Queen II* and 578. If that happened, he must have reasoned, it would be a strong indication that the attacks were part of a broader Japanese effort to repudiate the emperor's surrender decision and continue the war. In that case he could certainly order the resumption of offensive action against the Home Islands. But if, on the other hand, the Japanese delegation carried through with the trip to Manila, it would be a clear sign that the August 17 and 18 attacks on the two Dominators—and the death of Tony Marchione and the wounding of Jimmy Smart and Joe Lacharite on the latter mission—had been the work of a relatively few diehards. And if that were the case, it would be up to the Japanese to deal with the hotheads and any renewed Allied bombardment would likely only prolong the mutiny and further complicate the surrender negotiations and the planning for the occupation.

Although it was certainly something of a gamble, MacArthur's decision to delay any retaliation for the two consecutive days of attacks on the 386th's Dominators was validated on the morning of August 19. Just after 6 A.M. a sixteen-member delegation led by Vice Chief of the General Staff Lieutenant General Torashiro Kawabe boarded a Showa-Nakajima L2D twin-engine transport at Haneda airport on the west side of Tokyo Bay. Fourteen minutes later the aircraft—a Japanese version of the American C-47 transport—landed at the navy airfield at Kisarazu, just across the bay in Chiba Prefecture. There the Manila-bound delegates were split into two eight-man groups, with each then clambering aboard a navy Mitsubishi twin-engine aircraft known to the Allies as the "Betty." The two machines—a G6M1-L2 transport variant ("Bataan 1") and a demilitarized G4M1 bomber ("Bataan 2")—were both painted white and bore the green wing, tail, and fuselage crosses stipulated in MacArthur's directive. The planes lifted off from Kisarazu at 7:07 A.M. and flew southwest, skirting the southern coasts of Honshu, Shikoku, and Kyushu. Just after 11:00 the Japanese aircraft passed Sata Misaki—the southernmost point on Kyushu—and were joined by their American escort, two B-25J Mitchells of the 345th Bomb Group and a gaggle of P-38 Lightnings of the 49th Fighter Group. The onward flight to Ie Shima was uneventful, and the first Betty landed at 12:40. After a short time on the ground the sixteen delegates boarded an Army Air Forces C-45E four-engine transport for the onward flight to Manila.

MacArthur's gamble had paid off. The arrival of the Kawabe delegation in Manila was a certain indication that Japan would indeed surrender, and that the August 17 and 18 attacks on the B-32s had been the work of mutinous individuals rather than part of a larger conspiracy to renew hostilities. And while MacArthur couldn't have known it, the mere fact that the two Bettys bearing the sixteen-man delegation had made it to Ie Shima without being shot down by their own side was something of a victory as well.

THE PILOTS OF THE Atsugi-based 302nd Air Group who had taken part in the August 17 and 18 attacks on the B-32s over the Kanto Plain did so with the hearty encouragement of their commander, Yasuna Kozono. Though increasingly debilitated by both malaria and near-constant infusions of sake, the "Father of Japanese Night Fighters" had lost none of his anti-surrender zeal. Indeed, not only did the veteran aviator spur his pilots to continue the fight against the Allies, he took steps intended to prevent Kawabe's delegation from ever making what he saw as the "treasonous" journey to Manila dictated by MacArthur.

It is unclear how Kozono learned of the proposed trip, but we do know that on August 16 he contacted Captain Hiroshi Kogure—the Yoko Ku's chief flight officer and a fellow anti-surrender zealot—and suggested that between them they could keep the Kawabe delegation from dishonoring Japan. They would accomplish that patriotic act, he said, through the simple expedient of jointly establishing an aerial picket line over the Kanto Plain. Fighters from Atsugi and Oppama flying alternating patrols over the region would shoot down any aircraft that lifted off from a Tokyo-area airfield bearing the all-white paint scheme and green crosses mandated in the Allied *diktat*. Because the members of the delegation were, in Kozono's view, traitors to both the nation and the emperor, there would be no shame in killing them.[11]

Ironically, Kozono's scheme to prevent the Kawabe delegation from leaving Japanese airspace was discovered and ultimately thwarted by a man who until just days before had himself been conspiring with both the 302nd Air Group commander and the Yoko Ku's Kogure to prevent the nation's capitulation.

Captain Mitsuo Fuchida was a living legend in the Imperial Japanese Navy, renowned as the aviator who had led the first wave of the attack on Pearl Harbor and then participated in many of the early key battles of the Pacific war. By August 1945 the forty-three-year-old Fuchida was the senior aviation officer in the headquarters of the Combined Fleet, the navy's primary ocean-going component. Deeply patriotic, he was initially horrified when he learned of the emperor's decision to accept the terms of the Potsdam Declaration. On August 12 an army liaison officer with whom Fuchida worked, Lieutenant Colonel Yoshida, approached the naval aviator about joining a coup d'état intended to prevent the nation's surrender. Fuchida immediately threw his support behind the plot, and after securing the backing of Vice Admiral Takijiro Onishi—the vice chief of the navy's general staff and an ardent proponent of the kamikazes—the aviator reached out to his longtime friends Kozono and Kogure. Both officers readily joined the conspiracy, pledging that their respective units could be counted upon to continue the fight against the Allies and to offer whatever aerial support the coup plotters might require.

Fuchida's enthusiasm for the coup d'état died, however, within twenty-four hours of its birth. On August 13, as he was on his way to a meeting with Onishi, Fuchida was buttonholed in a corridor of the Naval General Staff building by Emperor Hirohito's younger brother, Prince Takamatsu. A navy captain himself and a classmate of Fuchida's years earlier at Eta Jima, the Japanese naval academy, the prince obviously knew of the planned coup and of Fuchida's role in helping to plan it. Gazing intently at the aviator, Takamatsu said he had just returned from a meeting with the emperor and was convinced of Hirohito's sincerity in wanting to pursue the surrender as the best way to prevent further bombings like those that had engulfed Hiroshima and Nagasaki. Fuchida had been part of the navy team sent to Hiroshima immediately following its obliteration, and Takamatsu's statement apparently struck home. Fuchida later recalled that at that moment he realized the only remaining thing in his life with any real meaning was his ability to help fulfill the emperor's will. To do that he would have to reverse course completely and help quash the revolt that he had helped put into motion.

Over the following two days Fuchida used his position and personal prestige to convince several fellow officers in key positions to withdraw their support for the coup, and his efforts may well have contributed significantly to the revolt's ultimate failure on the night of August 14–15. However, when on the sixteenth Fuchida was put in charge of arranging the details of the Kawabe delegation's flight to Manila, he had to directly confront the two men whom he himself had brought into the conspiracy.

Fuchida called the Yoko Ku's chief flight officer to requisition the unit's Showa-Nakajima L2D for the delegation's short hop across Tokyo Bay from Haneda to Kisarazu, and was stunned to learn that Kogure was still refusing to accept reality despite the failure of the coup. The men of the Yoko Ku would continue to engage any Allied aircraft that dared to violate Japanese airspace, Kogure said, and added that an aerial picket line intended to prevent the departure of Kawabe's delegation was even then being put in place in cooperation with Kozono's 302nd Air Group.

Realizing that Kogure was likely just following Kozono's lead, Fuchida decided to go to Atsugi personally to convince his hotheaded friend that further resistance to the emperor's wishes was dishonorable and that continued attacks on Allied aircraft despite the ceasefire could well result in the dropping of a third atomic bomb. Well aware that words would probably not sway the 302nd

Air Group commander, Fuchida climbed into his staff car just after noon on August 18 wearing his sword and carrying a loaded pistol. Though he hoped Kozono would see reason and cease his resistance to the surrender, Fuchida was willing to kill his old friend if it became necessary.

The inherent danger of the task ahead was brought home to Fuchida when his driver halted the staff car outside Atsugi's main gate. Sandbagged machine-gun emplacements manned by helmeted sailors guarded either side of the entrance, which was also blocked by wooden barricades strung with barbed wire. As Fuchida stepped from the car and slowly approached the gate, his hands in plain sight, the petty officer in charge of the gate guards walked forward and, noting his visitor's rank, saluted smartly. Encouraged by this sign of military discipline, Fuchida smiled, identified himself, and announced that he'd come to meet with Kozono. The petty officer replied that he knew who Fuchida was and turned to signal his men to open the gate and remove the barriers. As he was climbing back into the staff car the senior aviator asked that the petty officer not announce his arrival to Kozono, whom Fuchida assumed would not be overly pleased to see him.

Fortunately, the first man Fuchida encountered in the base headquarters building was Lieutenant Commander Toshio Hashizumi, an old acquaintance who also happened to be Kozono's executive officer. Initially somewhat startled at Fuchida's sudden appearance, the younger man quickly regained his composure and asked how he might be of service. When Fuchida said that he'd come to speak with Kozono and asked about the 302nd commander's state of mind, Hashizumi responded that Kozono was ill, had been drinking heavily, and seemed headed for a mental breakdown. Fuchida immediately saw a way to resolve the crisis at Atsugi without resorting to violence. He first secured Hashizumi's promise of support, then ordered the younger man to summon an ambulance.

That done, the two officers waited until the ambulance arrived and then walked to the door of Kozono's quarters. Pausing for a moment to steel themselves, the men then burst into the room, seized

Kozono, and wrestled him to the floor before he could draw his sword. Though bellowing like an enraged bull the 302nd commander could not free himself, and at Fuchida's command the ambulance orderlies stormed in, quickly buckled the "Father of Japanese Night Fighters" into a straitjacket, and then rushed him to the ambulance for the drive to the mental ward at Yokosuka naval hospital. In one stroke Fuchida had eliminated possibly the greatest obstacle to Japan's surrender, without drawing a single drop of blood.[12]

After a quick call to announce Kozono's departure to Kogure, Fuchida secured the latter's promise to stand the Yoko Ku pilots down, end the aerial picket line meant to stop the Kawabe delegation's departure for Manila, and disable all remaining flyable aircraft at Oppama. That done, Fuchida then assumed temporary command of Atsugi and ordered Hashizumi to call all of the base's personnel together in the vast open area behind the operations building. There, shortly before 2 P.M. Fuchida announced to the assembled men—some of whom had only just returned from the attacks on *Hobo Queen II* and 578—that they were to suspend all operations, give up their personal weapons, and begin removing the guns and propellers from all aircraft present on the sprawling installation. Fuchida remained on the base through the afternoon and into the evening to ensure that his orders were being followed and, after turning security for the airfield over to a loyal army unit, headed back to Tokyo.[13] Though eighteen of Atsugi's younger and more volatile pilots ignored Fuchida's orders and flew their aircraft to army bases where they believed—incorrectly, as it turned out—that they would find like-minded aviators willing to continue the fight, Atsugi itself was secure.

Several miles to the south, the pilots of the Yoko Ku were also in the final hours of their war.

By the time Sadamu Komachi had finally given up his pursuit of John Anderson's B-32 the Japanese pilot was some twenty miles off the east coast of the Boso Peninsula and near Oshima Island. Believing that he might at any moment be bounced by U.S. Navy carrier aircraft, Komachi had pushed his throttle to the stops in order to regain the relative safety of the Japanese mainland as quickly as he could.

On the flight back to Oppama the veteran pilot had time to consider the ramifications of the fight in which he'd just participated. The conclusion of every previous engagement in his eventful career—whether he'd downed an enemy aircraft or simply managed to make it back to base uninjured and with his fighter undamaged—had been cause for satisfaction. He'd always taken great pride in his skills, and in the fact that he'd put them to good use for his nation and his emperor. But something was different now. As he later expressed it, by taking part in the post-ceasefire interception he'd defiantly and enthusiastically disobeyed the direct orders of his military leaders—and far worse, he'd "become a traitor against His Majesty." The sense of pride, accomplishment, and exultation that he'd always felt after engaging his nation's enemies had evaporated almost as soon as he turned away from the damaged American bomber, to be replaced by an ineffable sadness and the growing realization that he'd allowed his hunter's instincts to dishonor him, his country, and his emperor.[14]

These thoughts were still with Komachi as he negotiated the tricky crosswind approach to Oppama. After landing he taxied his fighter to its revetment, noting as he did so that he was apparently the last to return from the sortie against the American aircraft. He shut down his plane's engine and climbed from the cockpit, then walked slowly back to the base command post, enveloped in silence and, as he later recalled, "recognizing the crime" he felt he had just committed.[15] His dark mood was matched by those of the other aviators and ground personnel gathered in the briefing area, for they had just been personally informed by both the Yoko Ku's Kogure and the admiral in charge of the entire Yokosuka naval district that their war was now definitively and irrevocably over: at that very moment ground crewmen were beginning to empty the fuel tanks and remove the propellers of all the base's aircraft. Although no charges were to be filed against the pilots who had taken part in the interceptions that day and the day before, the admiral said, any further acts of defiance against the emperor's decision and the orders of the navy's senior leaders would be considered mutiny and would be dealt with as harshly as naval regulations allowed.

The following morning—even as the Japanese delegation was winging its way to Ie Shima on the first leg of the flight to Manila—Komachi and his fellow Yoko Ku pilots got news none had ever expected to receive. Having been called together for another meeting with Kogure, the airmen were abruptly told that their naval careers were over as of that moment. They were directed to leave Oppama immediately and return to their home towns—an instruction Komachi and many of the others believed was specifically intended to keep them from undertaking any further mayhem against Allied forces. The commander did not express it directly, but he also implied that the men might want to destroy any official records in their possession in case the victors should decide to prosecute them for their wartime actions—or for their post-ceasefire interceptions of the American bombers. That chilling intimation was followed by what most of the aviators likely perceived as a final slap in the face—although they would be able to travel home by train for free if they wore their uniforms, they would not receive any final pay or allowances. They would walk out Oppama's front gate with only the money they already had in their pockets, which for most amounted to only a handful of increasingly worthless yen. It was an ignominious end to the careers of some of the finest and most combat-experienced aviators in the Imperial Japanese Navy, and one that most probably felt dishonored them and their years of service and sacrifice.[16]

For Sadamu Komachi, virtually penniless and seemingly without a future at the age of just twenty-five, the sad train ride to his parents' home in Ishikawa Prefecture—on the northwestern coast of Honshu—was made even worse by his growing fears that when the Allies occupied Japan they would come looking for him. His exploits as a fighter pilot had been widely publicized, after all, and he assumed that the victors would want to make an example of him. Perhaps, he thought, they would even execute him for his role in the post-ceasefire attacks against the giant aircraft over Tokyo. Gazing out the window at the passing landscape, he ultimately decided that it would be best for him and for his family if he simply disappeared for a while.[17]

AS THE NAVY PILOTS at Atsugi and Oppama were dealing with the harsh and growing realities of defeat, the airmen of the 386th Bomb Squadron were helping to prepare for the most visible manifestation of the Allies' victory—the occupation of Japan.

Planning for that momentous operation had begun, of course, long before Tokyo's acceptance of the capitulation terms set forth in the Potsdam Declaration. As early as May 1945 members of MacArthur's staff had begun formulating Operation Blacklist, a contingency plan that was to be put into effect should Japan suddenly collapse and surrender before the Allies could launch their planned two-phase invasion—Operations Olympic and Coronet.[18] Blacklist's primary goals were almost identical to those of the intended armed invasion, and included the "early introduction of occupying forces into major strategic areas; the control of critical ports, port facilities and airfields; and the demobilization and disarmament of enemy troops."[19] Moreover, Blacklist would use all the American forces available in the Pacific Theater at the time of its execution; just in terms of ground troops, this would amount to some twenty-two divisions and two regimental combat teams totaling more than 700,000 men. Japan proper was to be the first priority, followed by Korea, and then by Formosa and the Japanese-controlled parts of China. As Supreme Commander Allied Powers, MacArthur would have the final authority to designate the place and time of the actual surrender ceremony, as well as to set the date for the beginning of the occupation. Blacklist had been presented to, and approved by, the various Pacific Theater service commanders at a July 1945 conference on Guam.[20]

The details of Blacklist were communicated to the Japanese during the first night's session of the August 19–20 conference in Manila between Kawabe's delegation and MacArthur's team, headed by his chief of staff, Lieutenant General Richard K. Sutherland.[21] The Japanese were told that a small Allied advance unit would land at Atsugi on August 23 and would be followed two days later by the lead elements of the larger formations tapped for occupation duty. Kawabe was horrified by the thought that the largest kamikaze-training airfield in Japan was to be the first place Allied troops would set foot, but when he told the Americans that the air station had been in open revolt and was likely still a center of anti-surrender fervor he was merely given extra time to "get the situation under control." The arrival of the advance unit at Atsugi was therefore rescheduled for the twenty-sixth, with the large-scale landings to commence on the twenty-eighth.

The B-32s of the 386th Bomb Squadron were tapped to play a small but important role in the arrival in Japan of the lead occupation units. The Dominators' mission, as laid out by V Bomber Command, was twofold. The big bombers' primary task would be to help provide reconnaissance coverage of the Atsugi-Yokosuka-Yokohama area, the region that would be the first to come under Allied control. Images taken by 20th Recon Squadron photographers aboard the Dominators would help senior leaders determine if the Japanese were following MacArthur's orders to disable their anti-aircraft weapons and prepare the various installations for handover to the incoming occupation forces. Once those units had begun landing in Japan the B-32s would take on an additional mission; each aircraft flying recon over the Tokyo area from August 26 on would carry four 500-pound bombs. If the occupation troops encountered any armed opposition from Japanese forces the Dominators would drop their ordnance on preassigned targets throughout the Kanto Plain.[22]

The first B-32 sortie in direct support of the occupation was flown on August 25, the day before the scheduled landing of the advance party at Atsugi. Four Dominators—528, *Hobo Queen II*, *Harriet's Chariot*, and 544—were to photograph the navy airfield and the area between it and the sprawling Yokohama-Yokusuka harbor complex. In addition to documenting Japanese compliance with MacArthur's directives, the aircraft were also to record the condition of the major road and rail networks linking the Atsugi region with Tokyo, twenty-five miles to the northeast. This latter tasking was meant to help planners determine the most direct and least obstructed route by which the lead American units could make the journey from the airfield to the capital.

The August 25 mission started well enough, with all four Dominators airborne by 7 A.M. The gremlins that seemed to inhabit the 386th's big bombers soon reared their heads, however, for just minutes after lifting off from Yontan *Harriet's Chariot* was forced to abort the flight because its main landing gear would not retract. Barely a half-hour later the venerable *Hobo Queen II* also had to turn back because of a severe oil leak in its number 3 engine and a runaway turbo-supercharger in number 1. The other two B-32s plowed on, though as the flight unfolded they encountered increasingly bad weather from Typhoon Ruth, a category 1 storm that had originated in the Philippines on August 22 and was moving swiftly northward. The pilot of 528 chose to abort the mission about two hours short of the target area, and though 544 continued the flight her crew found that extremely heavy cloud cover over the entire Kanto Plain region made photography impossible. The Dominator turned back for Okinawa and managed to land just before Yontan itself was closed down by heavy rain, zero visibility, and winds gusting at more than 100 miles an hour.[23]

Typhoon Ruth's arrival over southern Japan had broader consequences for the scheduled beginning of the occupation, of course. The extremely high winds and complete lack of visibility would make it impossible for the cargo aircraft bearing the advance party to land at Atsugi, and the mountainous seas pounding the entrance to Tokyo Bay would not only hamper navigation through the twisting and relatively narrow channel, they could well set loose many of the sea mines anchored in protective fields off Japan's southern coast, endangering the Allied ships that would carry occupation troops. From MacArthur's point of view the only logical decision was to postpone both the landing of the advance party and the arrival of the main units. The former was therefore pushed back to August 28, and the latter to the thirtieth.[24]

The delay did little to improve the mechanical reliability of the 386th's Dominators, however. The diminishing effects of the typhoon allowed *Harriet's Chariot*—her gear issues supposedly resolved—and

578 to take off from Yontan early on August 27 in an effort to acquire the imagery that was not obtained two days earlier. But hardly had *Harriet's Chariot* lifted into the air when her crew realized that her main landing gear—which had operated perfectly on a post-repair test flight the previous day—would not retract, again. As the B-32 reversed course to reenter the Yontan landing pattern the men aboard 578 discovered that they had gear problems of their own—their aircraft's nose wheel was jammed in the down position, forcing the Dominator to return to base, and resulting in the mission's cancellation.

Though a cascading variety of mechanical problems increasingly dogged the 386th's small fleet of B-32s, operational necessity ensured that the squadron's maintenance personnel worked day and night to keep as many Dominators as possible fit for flight. The importance of the work done by the engine and airframe mechanics, electronics specialists, and other maintainers was underlined early on the evening of August 27, when a tasking order came down to the 386th from V Bomber Command. The two-part directive called for four Dominators to be in the air the next day in support of the arrival at Atsugi of the occupation forces' advance team.

The first part of the order directed that two B-32s orbit over Atsugi beginning at 9 A.M. on the twenty-eighth to act as radio-relay platforms to ensure uninterrupted communications between the advance team and higher headquarters on Okinawa and in Manila. The two Dominators tapped for the "commo" work—*Hobo Queen II* and 544—would carry full combat loads of ammunition for their gun turrets, but only long-range auxiliary fuel tanks in their bomb bays. The second part of the order tasked 528 and 578 to continue photographing key areas of the Kanto Plain, again giving priority to roads, railway lines, and other transportation infrastructure. Unlike the two radio-relay aircraft, however, the photo-recon Dominators would each be carrying four 500-pound bombs in addition to their loaded guns—just in case.

The arrival of the tasking order caused the usual flurry of activity in the 386th's headquarters as staff officers hurried to get all mission preparations under way in time for the required 5:45 A.M. takeoff of the two radio-relay aircraft. But the directive also piqued the curiosity of Wisconsin-born Captain Woodrow H. Hauser. As the 386th's long-time communications officer it was the twenty-six-year-old's responsibility to choose the radio operators who would fly aboard the two Dominators orbiting above Atsugi. He did so, but then made what was undeniably the worst decision of his life. Having never seen Japan from the air nor flown in a B-32, the young officer apparently decided that he could kill both birds with one stone simply by riding along on the radio-relay mission in his official capacity. Hauser chose to add his name to the crew manifest for 544 because he was good friends with the man chosen to pilot the Dominator, First Lieutenant Leonard M. Sill.

Friendship was also the presumed reason why Hauser then reached out to three friends and fellow 386th staff officers whose jobs normally kept them on the ground. The first two, twenty-four-year-old squadron intelligence officer Bill Barnes and twenty-seven-year-old gunnery officer First Lieutenant Kenneth C. Maule, both readily agreed to go along on the flight. Hauser and Barnes then broached the idea to their tent mate, Rudy Pugliese, saying it was a once-in-a-lifetime opportunity to see Tokyo from the air. They acknowledged that it would be a long flight, but pointed out there would be no danger from the Japanese. Pugliese was tempted to go along, but the fact that the man he'd replaced had been killed while flying on a supposedly "safe" mission helped to dissuade him, and he finally decided to stay at Yontan and "take care of the store" in Barnes' absence.[25]

The names of Hauser, Barnes, and Maule were added to 544's crew manifest for the radio-relay flight, which meant that, given the mission's noncombatant nature, two other men were scratched from the flight. One was the bombardier most often assigned to Sill's crew, and the other was Second Lieutenant John Blackburn, the young radar countermeasures officer who had flown aboard the B-32 piloted by James Klein during the ill-fated August 18 mission. They were not told of the change in plans until just a few hours before the scheduled takeoff time, however, and after stowing their flight gear Blackburn and the bombardier decided they were too keyed up to go back to sleep right away, so they repaired to Blackburn's tent to play bridge.[26]

The night of August 27–28 went quickly for the Dominator crews assigned to the radio-relay mission, and after a detailed predawn briefing the men walked to their waiting aircraft. When they arrived at the hardstand they found Frank Cook waiting for them. The man who had headed the B-32 combat test program and then stayed on as part of the command "triumvirate" had come to see them off. He first chatted with the crew of *Hobo Queen II*, whose copilot for the day's mission was Second Lieutenant Joe Elliot, the young man who had taken part in the August 17 fight as copilot of 539. Cook then walked over to talk with Leonard Sill, with whom he'd flown on several occasions, and the staff officers who would be flying with him.

After a few moments the crew of 544 began boarding. Cook reached up through the B-32's nose entrance hatch and shook hands with Sill, then stepped back to watch the start-up. Years later the older officer still recalled that the initial engine run-up was normal, and as the Dominator began to taxi toward the main runway Cook hopped into his jeep and drove to Yontan's control tower to observe the takeoff as he always did when "his boys" were launching on a mission.[27] He was not the only one who turned out to watch the takeoff for what promised to be a historic flight; hundreds of men had gathered along the edges of the runway despite the earlier hour.

Cook was standing on the narrow catwalk atop the tower by the time 544 reached the runway threshold, with *Hobo Queen II* behind her on the taxiway. The lead B-32 stopped briefly while Sill did a final run-up of each engine, then began to move. Despite a gross weight of more than 100,000 pounds—8,000 of it fuel—the bomber picked up speed surprisingly quickly.

As far as Cook could tell from his vantage point the initial takeoff roll was entirely normal, but when the Dominator reached a point about two-thirds of the way down the runway the full-throated roar of the four big Wright Cyclone engines suddenly died. Everyone watching could tell that Sill had intentionally chopped the power in an attempt to abort his takeoff, but it didn't appear that he had applied the brakes. The huge aircraft continued down the runway, slowing but not stopping, then ran out of concrete and crashed to the bottom of an eighty-foot-deep coral pit just past the runway's southeast end. To the horror of the many onlookers the fuel-laden aircraft immediately exploded in a huge fireball. The first personnel to reach the crash site could hear—mingled with the sharp detonations of exploding machine-gun ammunition—the screams of those aboard burning alive. All thirteen men on the aircraft died within minutes.

Hobo Queen II had moved from the taxi strip onto the runway when 544 began its takeoff roll, and the men aboard the second Dominator were making their last-minute checks when the massive explosion flared in the coral pit. Radio operator Staff Sergeant Robert Russell, seated just behind copilot Elliot, later recalled that the detonation lit up the still-dark sky, flooding the bomber's cockpit with light bright enough to make him wince.[28] As the initial fireball subsided a red beacon from the control tower signaled *Hobo Queen II*'s pilot to halt his takeoff, and minutes later Cook arrived in a jeep and ordered the plane's engines to be shut down. One after another the bomber's crewmen emerged, their eyes irresistibly drawn to the flames leaping into the sky at the other end of the runway. Several military and civilian news photographers who were aboard to record the events at Atsugi understandably chose to quit the flight at that point, and Russell helped them unload their gear. As they walked away from the B-32 the young radioman called out, "I wish I were going with you, but it looks like I'm going to Tokyo."[29]

The importance of the communications mission ensured that Russell was right, for *Hobo Queen II* didn't stay on the ground long. Barely twenty-five minutes after the disaster Elliot and the other crewmembers were back aboard their B-32, rolling down the taxi strip toward the same end of the runway where the crash had occurred. The depth of the coral pit kept the men aboard *Hobo Queen II* from seeing the wreckage as their Dominator turned onto the runway for a departure to the northwest, but the roiling flames were burning so intensely that Elliot and the others could actually feel the heat through their own aircraft's thin aluminum skin. As the B-32 started its takeoff roll Russell said two quick prayers—the first offered for Staff Sergeant Max Holben, a tent mate and one of the two radio operators aboard 544, and the second asking that he and his fellow crewmen might avoid the fate that had befallen his friend. The latter supplication seemed particularly apt just seconds after Russell uttered it, for as *Hobo Queen II* lifted off two sharp backfires barked from one of the Dominator's engines and a brief but brilliant flame illuminated the cockpit. Everyone on the flight deck inhaled sharply, Russell later recalled, but the engine quickly settled down as the B-32 gained altitude and turned north toward Tokyo.[30]

JUST AS THE CRASH of 544 was not allowed to prevent *Hobo Queen II*'s takeoff on her important task, the morning's disaster did not derail the second part of the mission. The departure times of the two pairs of Dominators had been staggered, so the crews of the photo-recon aircraft—528 and 578—were just getting out of their cots when the explosion and fire erupted at the end of the runway. Though they were obviously shocked by the catastrophe and saddened by the death of friends, they still had a vital mission to accomplish, so after a hushed meal in the mess tent the aviators gathered for the preflight briefing.

Though the first topic of discussion was obviously the crash of 544 and the possible cause for it—engine failure on takeoff? Flap malfunction? Pilot error? No determination could be made until the roiling flames subsided. Rudy Pugliese, his voice occasionally breaking, led the briefing in Bill Barnes's stead, laying out the operational details of the day's flight. The two photo-recon Dominators would follow the by-now familiar route from Okinawa to the Tokyo area, tracking northeast to Oshima Island and then turning due north for their photo runs. They were to fly the usual parallel lines, "mowing the lawn" as they photographed a series of targets between Yokohama and the capital. Frank Cook stepped in to remind the crews that they might be called upon at any time to bomb their preassigned targets if there was any sign of armed Japanese resistance to the arrival of the advance occupation unit, and if that order came they were to carry it out immediately. The senior officer also reminded the aviators that the skies above the Kanto Plain would be particularly busy, with Navy carrier-based fighters flying top cover for the many lumbering transports that would be bringing in the initial landing force and the equipment and supplies its members would require. And, finally, the navigators on each of the B-32 crews were given the coordinates of the Navy ships that would be providing air-sea rescue coverage along the routes to and from Japan.[31]

The photo-recon Dominators took off from Yontan just after 7 A.M., departing to the northwest so they would not have to fly through the thick column of greasy black smoke rising into the morning sky above the coral pit. After turning onto the heading for Oshima the B-32s climbed gradually to 3,000 feet and their crews settled in for what they fervently hoped would be an uneventful flight to the Japanese capital.

COLONEL CHARLES P. TENCH was also probably hoping for a day free of conflict. A member of MacArthur's operations staff, the forty-year-old officer had been tapped by the supreme commander himself to lead the advance group that would land at Atsugi. Given the historic nature of its mission and the very real possibility that it would receive a less-than-friendly welcome, Tench's group was surprisingly small. The force consisted of just 150 troops, only about 30 of whom were infantrymen. The remainder were the Army Airways Communications Systems radio operators, logistics personnel, air traffic controllers, navigation aids technicians, and other specialists required to prepare Atsugi for the impending arrival of MacArthur and the lead elements of the main occupation forces. Tench, his men, and the mounds of equipment they would need upon reaching Atsugi were loaded aboard sixteen C-47 transports of the 317th Troop Carrier Group, which began taking off from Kadena and other airfields on Okinawa at about the same time as Leonard Sill's B-32 was rolling from the taxi strip onto the main runway at Yontan.

The first indication the Japanese had of the advance force's impending arrival was the sudden appearance over Atsugi of Navy F4U Corsair and F6F Hellcat fighters, which had launched not long before from Third Fleet carriers approaching Sagami Bay. Although those on the ground probably could not see it, *Hobo Queen II* had also arrived and was flying in a lazy circle at 18,000 feet. At 8:20 Colonel

John H. Lackey Jr., the pilot of Tench's C-47, began his approach
from the south, touching down eight minutes later on the airdrome's
center runway. The lead plane was quickly followed by the other
fifteen transports, and by a few minutes after 9 A.M. Tench had officially taken control of the airfield from Lieutenant General Seizo Ari-
sue, chief of intelligence on the Imperial General Staff, and radioed
MacArthur—with assistance from *Hobo Queen II*—that the Japanese
were cooperating in every way. Over the following three hours a
further thirty C-46 Commando, C-47 Skytrain, and C-54 Skymaster
transports had landed at Atsugi, carrying additional equipment,
Army personnel, and members of Admiral William F. Halsey's staff.
With a determination and enthusiasm that stunned Japanese onlookers, the Americans set about preparing the sprawling airdrome
for the influx of occupation troops scheduled to arrive in less than
forty-eight hours.[32]

As THE MEN OF Tench's advance element were beginning to unload their equipment at Atsugi, the photo-recon Dominators arrived
over Honshu. The two B-32s initially took up a wide orbit above the
Kanto Plain as their crews waited anxiously to see if they would
actually have to drop the bombs nestled in each aircraft's belly, but
it soon became apparent that there was not going to be any Japanese
opposition to the first foreign occupiers. For the next several hours
the only excitement the crews of 528 and 578 encountered was the
arrival off their wingtips of Navy Corsairs and Hellcats, their pilots
politely asking variations of the same question: "Who the hell are
you and what kind of airplane is that?"[33]

Once Tench's Army Airways Communications Systems specialists were able to establish radio contact with Okinawa and Manila,
Hobo Queen II was released from her special tasking and turned for
home, leaving the other two Dominators to begin their assigned
photo runs. At that point, however, the gremlins that now seemed
to be permanent members of every B-32 crew got up to their old
tricks. As twenty-two-year-old Second Lieutenant Collins Orton
turned 528 onto the beginning of its third photo run at about 2:15
Second Lieutenant John L. Boyd, the 20th Recon Squadron officer

controlling the aircraft's K-22 camera from the bomber's nose compartment, announced that the device had failed. Despite the best efforts of the embarked aerial photographer, Sergeant Horace Butler, the camera refused to come back to life. When apprised of the camera problem the mission commander in 578 told Orton to "pack it up and head for home," and minutes later 528 was pointing her nose toward Okinawa.

Facing a long flight back to Yontan, Orton and his copilot, Flying Officer John Clark, decided to conduct an experiment. The men had flown B-24s together before transitioning to the Dominator, and during long-distance Liberator missions from the Philippines to China they had perfected the techniques of fuel conservation. By reducing the engine RPM and manifold pressure they'd been able to keep their B-24 in the air for nearly eighteen hours, its propellers turning so slowly that the crewmen could actually count the blades as they rotated. The aircraft would be flying so slowly that, as Orton recalled years later, if a man walked to the rear of the B-24 to use the relief tube, the small change in the center of gravity was enough to put the plane into a stall.[34]

To begin the experiment Orton and Clark first had the flight engineer, Master Sergeant Paul E. Fairchild, transfer all of the fuel from the B-32's bomb-bay tank into the main wing tanks, the only place from which the engines drew the high-octane aviation gasoline. It was something that they'd done all the time in their B-24, and they had no reason to think it would be a problem in the Dominator. Everything was fine for about two and a half hours, but then at about 5 P.M. the aircraft yawed slightly as the number 2 engine began losing power. As Orton later recalled, the power plant "just pooped out"—the cylinder head temperature went down, but the manifold pressure and RPMs stayed where they'd been set. Fairchild shut off the fuel flow to the engine and Orton feathered the prop, which seemed to solve whatever the issue might have been. But at about 6:45 the cylinder head temperature on the number 4 engine also inexplicably dropped, and seconds later the big Cyclone simply died.[35]

The loss of one engine was a not-uncommon irritation, but the failure of two was potentially disastrous. The Dominator could not maintain a safe cruising altitude on the two remaining Cyclones, and the big bomber was still some 200 miles from Okinawa and descending through 4,500 feet. A hurried discussion among Orton, Clark, and Fairchild pinpointed water condensation in the bomb-bay tank as the likely source of the problem,[36] and all three men agreed that the B-32 was almost certain to lose its two remaining engines sooner rather than later. Orton asked primary navigator Captain Roy C. Cunningham for a "steer" (course) to "Birddog," the nearest Navy plane-guard ships, and was pleasantly surprised to learn that the destroyers USS *John D. Henley* (DD-553) and USS *Aulick* (DD-569) were patrolling air-sea rescue station "Baker," almost directly ahead of the ailing Dominator. After ordering his crew to begin jettisoning everything but their parachutes, Orton directed radio operator Staff Sergeant Wiley D. Pringle first to communicate the aircraft's position and difficulties to V Bomber Command, and then to contact the destroyers on the "guard" frequency.

Henley and *Aulick* had steamed out of Okinawa's Buckner Bay on August 25 to take up station at "Baker," but by the evening of the twenty-eighth had not yet been required to undertake any rescues. That appeared about to change, however, when at 6:15 P.M. the air-search radar aboard *Henley*, the lead vessel, detected an airborne contact to the north of the ship's position. A half-hour later the destroyer's radio operator picked up Pringle's initial distress message, and just minutes after that the B-32 was circling the two vessels. Commander Simon Ramey, *Henley*'s captain, urged Orton to ditch the Dominator near the two Navy vessels, but the young pilot believed that his aircraft's long bomb bay and shoulder-mounted wings would cause it to disintegrate as soon as it hit the water. Orton therefore replied that he and his crew would bail out instead, and immediately ordered the men to begin preparations to abandon their doomed bomber.[37]

The bail-out process did not go quite as Orton had hoped, however. As he later recalled, he expected that the crewmen would exit the aircraft quickly and efficiently, "like paratroopers." Instead, he said, "each one would get to the [open] bomb bay or the rear [entrance] hatch, lick his finger to test the wind, straighten out his [parachute] harness, and then finally go. My God, it seemed to take forever." It didn't take quite as long as that, though. The first man leapt from the B-32 at 7:00 P.M. and Orton, the last to leave, took to his chute just four minutes later and hit the water thirty seconds after pulling the ripcord. He had barely popped back to the surface when 528 crashed into the sea some four miles away, almost exactly eight miles due north of the small island of Kikai-Jima and just over 195 miles northeast of Yontan.[38]

Although all thirteen men aboard the Dominator made it out of the aircraft, those watching from the two destroyers counted only twelve parachutes. Over the next several hours *Henley* picked up Orton and Cunningham, while *Aulick* retrieved all the others except armorer-gunner Sergeant Morris C. Morgan. Despite a search that continued well into the next day the young aviator was never found, and he was ultimately listed as "Missing in Action/Body Not Recovered." Sadly, Morgan was not the only casualty. Though gunner Staff Sergeant George A. Murphy made it out of the aircraft safely his parachute did not fully deploy by the time he hit the water. Despite the best efforts of *Aulick*'s medical officer, Lieutenant (junior grade) R. B. Laury, Murphy died at 11 P.M. of "traumatic shock complicated by massive internal injuries." His body was committed to the sea two days later following a burial service conducted by the destroyer's captain, Lieutenant Commander W. R. Hunnicutt Jr.[39]

Henley and *Aulick* were required to remain on air-sea rescue duty after picking up Orton and his crew, and the aviators therefore did not make it back to Okinawa for several days. While they were enjoying the questionable delights of life aboard a relatively small warship in unusually large seas, events moved on without them.

EVEN AS 528'S CREWMEN awoke to their first morning at sea the investigation of the previous day's fatal crash at Yontan had already begun.

Those attempting to determine the cause of the accident that killed all thirteen men aboard 544—the worst single loss of life in the troubled history of the B-32—had little to go on because the Dominator had been almost completely consumed by the fierce, fuel-fed fire that had engulfed it. Everyone who had witnessed 544's start-up, taxi, and initial takeoff roll agreed that nothing seemed amiss, and that the sudden reduction in engine noise was the first indication of trouble. Although several witnesses later said they heard the screech of the aircraft's brakes—indicating that Leonard Sill and his copilot were doing all they could to stop the aircraft—Frank Cook recalled years later that he had walked the entire length of Yontan's runway and had seen no indication of the skid marks that would have accompanied the application of the aircraft's brakes at that weight and speed. The mystery deepened when an inspection of one of the few unburned sections of the aircraft—the rear, inboard part of its right wing—indicated that the B-32's flaps had been correctly set for takeoff.[40]

In addition to attempting to find the cause of the crash—which was ultimately ascribed to "unknown causes"—investigators also had to try to positively identify the bodies of the dead. Squadron commander Tony Svore was part of the team that undertook that grisly task, which was made all the harder by the fact that most of the remains had been charred beyond recognition. Only four sets were ultimately identified, one of which was that of intelligence officer Bill Barnes. Svore later recalled that he was able to make that particular identification because Barnes, a close friend, always wore a unique ring that was easily recognized.[41] A memorial service for those lost was held at Yontan on August 30.

That same day the main units of the Allied occupation force began arriving in Japan—the bulk of the U.S. 11th Airborne Division landing at Atsugi aboard hundreds of transport aircraft while other Army, Marine, Navy, and British units went ashore at various points throughout Honshu and Kyushu. August 30 also saw MacArthur's arrival at Atsugi aboard his personal C-54 transport, *Bataan*.

The following day marked a suitably symbolic milestone in the history of the B-32. Just after 4:30 A.M. a single Dominator took off on a photo-recon mission to Tokyo, but its nose gear failed to retract and the aircraft returned to Yontan. The last operational mission flown by Consolidated's trouble-plagued super bomber therefore ended as so many earlier flights had—aborted due to mechanical difficulties.[42]

Nor did the B-32 have a chance to redeem itself. Within months the Army Air Forces cancelled all further development and procurement of the Dominator; those still under construction were dismantled and all flying aircraft were quickly scrapped. The venerable *Hobo Queen II* never even made it off Okinawa; severely damaged by a nose gear collapse, she was eventually scrapped in place. A single B-32 intended for ultimate donation to a museum was kept intact in Arizona for several years after the war, but it too was finally scrapped and the only artifacts remaining of the ill-starred Consolidated Dominator are an instrument panel, a single gun turret, and various odd pieces in private collections.

COLLINS ORTON AND HIS surviving crewmembers finally returned to Yontan on September 2, the same day that Japan formally surrendered during the ceremony aboard the battleship USS *Missouri* in Tokyo Bay.

When Second Lieutenant Elmer O. Jones, the bombardier on 528, walked back into his tent at Yontan he regaled John Blackburn and several other friends with the story of the bailout and ended by saying proudly, "look, I even saved the ripcord D-ring after I jumped." To which one of the men in the tent laughingly replied, "you damn fool, you were so scared you couldn't let go of it!"[43]

CHAPTER 7

HOMECOMING

GENERAL OF THE ARMY Douglas MacArthur's decision not to reignite hostilities against Japan because of the August 17 and 18 attacks on the B-32s over Tokyo is undoubtedly one of the most important, if perhaps least known, choices he made during the first weeks of his tenure as Supreme Commander Allied Powers. We can never be certain what might have happened had Allied forces resumed even a limited bombing campaign against the Home Islands in retaliation for the interception of the Dominators, but we can make some educated assumptions based on the available facts.

We know that in August 1945 the total number of Japanese military personnel remaining under arms both at home and across Asia and the Pacific was in the millions. Although many units were certainly ill-equipped, ill-trained, or decimated by disease or enemy action, others were highly experienced and remained both combat ready and highly motivated. By war's end the Japanese had amassed thousands of aircraft and as many small, fast boats for use in suicide attacks against Allied forces massing off the Home Islands. And millions of Japanese civilians were fully prepared to join in the defense of their homeland in the event of an Allied invasion.

Emperor Hirohito's decision to accept the terms of the Potsdam Declaration and surrender Japan to the Allies was so unpopular that it had provoked a major armed forces rebellion in Tokyo and minor ones elsewhere throughout what was left of the Japanese Empire. That such mutinies did not succeed in reversing the emperor's decision and lead to the installation of a fanatically anti-surrender cabinet is due in part to the Allies' suspension of offensive action after August 15. Senior military officers and government officials who might otherwise have chosen to break with the emperor and prolong the war were almost certainly swayed by the observable fact that the Allies were no longer pounding Japan with incendiaries or, for that matter, additional atomic bombs.

Given these realities—and the very real possibility that senior Japanese government and military leaders had not been told of the August 17 and 18 interceptions over the Kanto Plain—any resumption of hostilities by the Allies in response to the attacks on the B-32s would likely have been seen in Tokyo as a completely unwarranted abrogation of the cease fire. That, in turn, would certainly have strengthened the hand of the anti-surrender elements, fanning back to life the embers of rebellion that had been nearly extinguished following the unsuccessful August 14–15 coup. And had the *Bushido*-enflamed diehards in the Imperial Japanese Army and Navy managed to reassert their influence in Tokyo there is no doubt they would have immediately sought to cancel the ceasefire orders their senior leaders had already transmitted throughout what was left of the empire. And that, of course, would have inexorably led to a resumption of widespread hostilities between Japanese and Allied forces, which in turn could have had only two possible outcomes, either of them catastrophic.

In the first scenario the Allies would have resumed the atomic bombing of Japanese cities—as additional weapons became available—and continued the use of nuclear weapons until whatever government was then in power ultimately chose to surrender. This would have resulted in the death of hundreds of thousands, if not millions, of Japanese; the certain obliteration of Tokyo and other key metropolitan areas; and persistent radiation that would have produced horrific environmental and health effects both in Japan and likely throughout Asia and the Pacific for decades following the eventual end of the war.

The second scenario, though perhaps less apocalyptic, would have been disastrous nonetheless. If the United States had been unable to produce the number of atomic weapons required to bomb Japan into submission, the Allies would have been forced to go ahead with Downfall, the planned two-part invasion of the Home Islands. Operation Olympic would have kicked off in the fall of 1945 to subdue the southern part of Kyushu, followed in the spring of 1946 by Operation Coronet, the invasion of the Kanto Plain. Allied planners predicted that the Japanese defense would be both fanatical and prolonged, and based on the casualty rates for the invasion of Okinawa, predicted that the total number of Allied dead and wounded for both parts of Downfall could easily top 700,000. That number did not include the Japanese civilians and military personnel who would also be killed or injured.

In the end, of course, neither of these truly dreadful sequences of events played out. The Japanese surrendered; MacArthur effectively became the defeated nation's "American Caesar" and established the foundations for Japan's rebirth as a democratic society; and the men who took part in the last two Army Air Forces combat missions of World War II ultimately went home to live out the rest of their lives.

All but one.

THE CROWD OF PEOPLE that surrounded John Anderson's damaged Dominator upon its return to Yontan from the ill-fated August 18 mission included journalists from a number of civilian news organizations. Among them were Frank L. Kluckhohn, a star foreign correspondent for the *New York Times* who would later become the first American reporter to interview Emperor Hirohito; Sam Kinch of the Fort Worth *Star-Telegram*; and staff writers from the two then-dominant American news agencies, United Press and Associated Press. The newsmen watched intently as medics gingerly removed Jimmy Smart, Joe Lacharite, and Tony Marchione's body from 578. All three airmen were strapped to stretchers and then loaded aboard waiting vehicles of the Army's 556th Ambulance Company, Smart and Lacharite in one and Marchione in another. When the ambulances roared off, the reporters descended on John Anderson and his remaining crewmen, bombarding them with questions about the attack. Before the bewildered aviators could respond, however, they were hustled off for an in-depth debriefing. Two hours later the crewmen reappeared and, under the watchful eyes of Frank Cook and other senior officers, began answering the impatient reporters' questions.[1]

Though Anderson and the others withheld the details of Lacharite's wounding and Marchione's death—and, of course, operational information such as the targets they had been assigned to photograph— they were fairly candid in their responses to less sensitive questions and talked at some length. They were quick to credit Tom Robinson, the navigator, for the first-aid he provided to Jimmy Smart and Joe Lacharite, and were more than happy to give dramatic accounts of the aerial battle that emphasized their claims of enemy aircraft damaged and destroyed.[2] The nature and timing of the incident—coming just days after the ceasefire had supposedly gone into effect and less than twenty-four hours after the August 17 attack, which had also been reported in stateside newspapers—as well as the fact that an American airman had been killed and two others wounded, ensured that the story would be front-page news in the United States. And it didn't take long. The UP and AP wire stories began appearing in the morning editions of major newspapers on August 18 (which was August 19 on Okinawa); Kluckhohn's piece ran above the fold on the front page of the *New York Times* the next day.[3]

All of the stories about the August 18 attack that appeared in U.S. newspapers mentioned the names of Anderson and Robinson and repeated the claims of enemy aircraft shot down by Houston and Smart, but the identities of the casualties were not revealed. This was intentional, of course, because Army regulations forbade the release of the names of wounded or deceased personnel until after their next of kin had been notified.

In the case of the two wounded airmen the notification would not be made until after physicians had been able to fully evaluate each man's condition. That evaluation was made less than a mile southeast of Yontan's main runway, at the 381st Station Hospital. The facility's 500 beds were divided among more than 100 tents and small wooden buildings erected by the 801st Engineer Aviation Battalion in the weeks following the initial invasion of Okinawa. Upon arrival by ambulance from Yontan, Jimmy Smart and Joe Lacharite were hustled into the hospital's emergency triage area. Doctors quickly determined that Smart's head wounds were not as serious as they first appeared and would require only stitches, not surgery. Lacharite, on the other hand, had severe wounds to both legs and would require months of hospitalization followed by physical therapy. And despite their injuries the two young men were, of course, the lucky ones.[4]

THE AMBULANCE CARRYING Jimmy Smart and Joe Lacharite had driven straight to the low wooden building that served as the 381st's emergency room; the vehicle bearing Tony Marchione's body had gone a few hundred yards farther before pulling under a portico attached to a different structure. Though externally similar to the hospital's other buildings, the edifice did not house medical personnel dedicated to saving lives. It was part of a compound operated by the 3063rd Quartermaster Graves Registration Company, whose members were tasked with caring for the dead.

Though Tony had died very soon after being hit and hours before 578 landed at Yontan, the medic who had ridden with his body from the airfield had done a quick and thorough examination of his wounds. By the time the ambulance arrived at the 3063rd's compound the soldier had already signed the form that officially pronounced the young airman dead. This finding was confirmed by the enlisted mortician on duty, who then added his signature to the form already signed by the medic and thereby took formal possession of Tony's body.

As its designation implies, the 3063rd's ultimate purpose was to oversee the interment of U.S. Army personnel who died on Okinawa, and it and a sister unit, the 3008th, had detachments all over the island. By June 1945 there were eight temporary cemeteries on Okinawa, the largest of which had been established in April by the garrison force formed to manage post-invasion administrative and logistical operations, Island Command Okinawa. Located on the island's west coast, seven miles southwest of Yontan, it was the designated resting place for Army Air Forces personnel and it was there that Tony Marchione was destined to be interred.[5]

But several things had to happen before that burial could take place, the first of which was the positive identification of Tony's body. This may seem in hindsight to be an unnecessary step, given that Kurt Rupke had identified him to the medics before the ambulance left Yontan and his death had been officially confirmed, but it was required by regulation. The 3063rd mortician first checked the name, Army serial number, blood type, and religion stamped on the two dogtags hanging next to the crucifix on a light silver chain around the body's neck, verifying that they were indeed Tony's. The technician then fingerprinted the body, and a forensic dentist checked the teeth to ensure that they matched those on the dental records in Tony's personnel file—a copy of which had been obtained from the 20th Recon Squadron.[6]

Once the body was considered positively identified, the mortician and his assistant went through the pockets of the flight suit, removing Tony's wallet and other items, then took off the necklace bearing his crucifix and dogtags. The men next cut away and discarded Tony's torn and bloodied clothing, recorded the nature and exact location of his wounds, and washed the body before wrapping it in the shelter half in which it would be buried.[7] The technicians then placed the corpse on a gurney and moved it into an adjoining building that served as the 3063rd's morgue. Despite the fact that fighting had officially ended on Okinawa some two months earlier, Tony's was not the only body in the storage area; in war zones military personnel die from a range of causes other than hostile action. At that time the graves registration unit was processing the corpses of men killed in automobile and aircraft accidents,[8] by the various tropical diseases endemic to the Ryukyu Islands, and, in older personnel, by such "peacetime" causes as heart attack and stroke.

Owing to limited refrigerated space for the storage of bodies, the 3063rd performed interments as soon as possible. The commanders of the 20th Recon Squadron and 386th Bomb Group were therefore notified early on the morning of August 19 that Tony's burial would take place that afternoon at 3 P.M. A hastily convened Roman Catholic funeral Mass conducted in the main chapel at Yontan before the burial drew some thirty of Tony's friends, as well as senior officers from the 20th Recon Squadron and its parent organization, the 6th Photographic Group; the 386th Bomb Squadron and 312th Bomb Group; and V Bomber Command. Following the service Tony was laid to rest in the Island Command Cemetery—Plot 2, Row 1, Grave 4—between Technician Fifth Grade Roland Griffin and First Sergeant Francis T. McLaughlin.

The burial was not the end of the process, of course. On the day following the interment the 20th Recon Squadron's commander appointed Bob Essig to be the Summary Courts Officer for Tony's case, a position that made the pilot responsible for inventorying the young gunner's property and effects. Over the following six days Essig turned in all government-issued items and gathered personal materials for eventual shipment to Tony's family. The latter category included uniform shirts and pants, some civilian clothing and shoes, toiletries, souvenirs from Tony's time in the Philippines, and a watch and several rings. Not surprisingly, the young gunner's footlocker also held eighty-five letters and postcards he'd received from family and friends, as well as seventy-five black-and-white photos—some of relatives, others of his crewmates and the aircraft in which he'd flown. When Essig finished the inventory on August 26 he placed all the personal items in a single large cardboard box and turned it over to the 3063rd for onward shipment to the Army Effects Bureau in Kansas City, Missouri, the central clearing house for the personal property of deceased World War II soldiers.

The graves registration company's acceptance of Tony's personal effects triggered what was arguably the saddest aspect of the official process that followed the young man's death—the notification of his family. The Memorial Affairs Division of the Office of the Quartermaster General and the Casualty Affairs Branch in the War Department's Adjutant General's Office, both in Washington, received the 3063rd's notification of Tony's "Killed in Action" status on August 28. The following morning a special delivery telegram was dispatched to Ralph Marchione at the King Street home address, its opening words the stuff of every parent's nightmares: "We deeply regret to inform you . . . "

PRESIDENT HARRY S. TRUMAN's August 14[9] announcement that Japan had accepted the Allied surrender terms had sparked joyous celebrations across America. In Pottstown the news was greeted with a spontaneous parade through the center of town, and crowds of people cheering and waving flags gathered in front of City Hall. In the Marchione household the special radio bulletin was met with joy and tears of relief, and Ralph, Emelia, and the two girls went out to join the neighbors who were already dancing in the street. Over the following days the family waited expectantly for a letter from Tony that would announce the date of his homecoming, but nothing came.[10]

Though news agency reports of the August 17 and 18 attacks on the Dominators over Tokyo had run in the *Pottstown Mercury* and other local papers, they didn't arouse any concern for the Marchiones because they knew Tony was a crewman on an F-7, not a B-32, and because the unidentified crewman killed on the eighteenth was referred to as a photographer and not as an aerial gunner. The fact that no one in the family had received a letter from him since the one to Gerry dated August 17 also did not disturb them, because they assumed that Tony and all the other members of his unit were extremely busy making preparations to take part in the imminent occupation of Japan.

Just after noon on Wednesday the twenty-ninth, eighteen-year-old Terry Marchione got up from her desk in the front office of the Pottstown Manufacturing Company on South Hanover Street near the Schuylkill River and walked into the ladies' room for a cigarette break. She had not even lit up when one of her female coworkers came in and told her that their supervisor wanted to see her right away. When Terry walked into the man's office he said she had to go home immediately, but would not tell her why. She gathered up her things and hurried off on foot for King Street, several blocks to the north.

Across town, at the Sunnybrook community swimming pool, thirteen-year-old Gerry Marchione was spending time with several neighborhood friends when the mother of one of the girls arrived and said, "you have to go home, your Mom wants you." The woman gave no reason, but quickly bundled the teens into her car and drove them toward King Street. Gerry thought it odd that the woman let her off a block from the house yet kept the other girls in the car, but she forgot about it as soon as she saw the crowd of people gathered in front of her home. Gerry started running, and as she got closer she heard a heart-wrenching keening that she knew immediately was the sound of her mother screaming. Dashing up the few steps of the house's front stoop she burst into the living room, where she found her father and Terry, both sobbing and tightly hugging a nearly hysterical Emelia.

Her mother had been working in the kitchen, preparing lunch for Ralph, when the ring of the bell had drawn her to the front door. She opened it to find a young telegram-delivery boy standing there, his eyes downcast and a small envelope held tightly in his outstretched hand. Having already been the bearer of horrible news on more than one occasion, as soon as the boy had handed Emelia the telegram he turned, leapt onto his bicycle, and quickly pedaled away. Bewildered by the youth's abrupt departure but already beginning to realize that her entire world was about to change, Emelia tore open the envelope, read the dreadful words it contained and screamed. The sound brought Ralph running from the kitchen; he, too, read the lines that told him his only son was gone forever, and sobbed uncontrollably as he enfolded his wife in his arms. The sound of their grieving brought neighbors to the still-open door, and within minutes the news had traveled the length of King Street. At Ralph's urging a friend called Terry's boss, the neighbor woman went to pick up Gerry, and another man ran the few blocks to the nearby St. Aloysius parish church to summon a priest.

For all its tragic import, the War Department telegram was brief to the point of terseness. It said that Tony had been killed in action on August 18, but provided no details as to where or how and did not say that his body had already been interred on Okinawa. The final line expressed the deep sympathy of the official sender—Major General Edward F. Whitsell, the Acting Adjutant General of the Army—and said that an explanatory letter was en route. That letter arrived by special delivery on Friday, August 31, and added a few additional details. Tony had died in the performance of his duties, it read, and before his own death had provided first aid that helped save the life of a seriously wounded fellow crewmember. The letter added that Tony's personal effects would be returned after processing, and closed by saying that the Memorial Affairs Branch of the Office of the Quartermaster General would be contacting the Marchiones in due course. Again, the official signature block bore Whitsell's name.

It was in an early September letter from Memorial Affairs that Ralph and Emelia learned their son had been buried on Okinawa. Like many relatives of service members killed on distant fronts in World War II, they were shocked and extremely dismayed by the revelation that their loved one had been interred far from home. Their despair was somewhat relieved when they were told that Tony's burial in the Island Command Cemetery was considered "temporary," and that his remains would ultimately be transferred to "an appropriate location." No mention was made of where or when that might be, however.

In the weeks following the Marchiones' receipt of the official notification of Tony's death, letters from his friends filled in some of the details that the Army was unable or unwilling to provide. A letter to Terry written on September 6 by Frank Pallone was especially informative, if not entirely accurate:

Dear Terry,

I thought I'll [sic] take the liberty of writing you and telling the way in which your brother died. Being a real close friend and a member of his crew, I know that Tony would have done the same for me.

The last day he flew on August 18th, he flew with a B-32 crew from another outfit . . . on a mission over Tokio. Over the target fourteen Jap fighters came in on their ship. The first fighter that attacked, machined [sic] gunned one of the other gunners and hit him in the legs. Tony came to his aid with two tourniquets and stopped the bleeding in the gunners both legs. As [Tony] was leaning over the wounded fellow trying to comfort him another fighter attacked and hit Tony, he was killed instantly and he suffered no pain. The fellow who Tony treated was saved by his aid, and wishes to thank you for Tony.

Tony was really a swell fellow, the best I have ever met and lived with in my army career. Tony was a clean cut kid and they can't come any better. He was well liked by all the fellows that he associated with.

We had a military funeral and a Mass at the Catholic Chapel for him, with all his close friends and mostly all of the squadron turned out. . . . As close friends, the crew and I offer our sincerest condolences.
Sincerely,
Frank[11]

On September 17 the family received a letter addressed to Ralph and signed by a somewhat more august personage, Secretary of War Henry L. Stimson:

My dear Mr. Marchione:
You will shortly receive the Purple Heart medal, which has been posthumously awarded by the direction of the President to your son, Sergeant Anthony J. Marchione, Air Corps. It is sent as a tangible expression of the country's gratitude for his gallantry and devotion. It is sent to you, as well, with my deepest personal sympathy for your bereavement. The loss of a loved one is beyond man's repairing, and the medal is of slight value; not so, however, the message it carries. We have all been comrades in arms in the battle for our country, and those who have gone are not, and will never be,

forgotten by those of us who remain. I hope you will accept this medal in evidence of such remembrance.[12]

A few days after the arrival of Stimson's letter another tribute reached the Marchiones, this one a memorial certificate bearing the seal and signature of President Truman:

In grateful memory of
SERGEANT ANTHONY J. MARCHIONE
who died in the service of his country
IN THE SOUTHWEST PACIFIC AREA, AUGUST 18, 1945.
he stands in the unbroken line of patriots who have dared to die
that freedom might live, and grow, and increase its blessings.
freedom lives, and through it, he lives—
in a way that humbles the undertakings of most men.[13]

On October 3 a summary court-martial convened at the Kansas City Quartermaster Depot confirmed that Ralph Marchione was indeed entitled to receive his son's personal effects, though the single box containing those items did not arrive at the house on King Street until mid-February 1946. At about that same time the Marchione family received a small, ornate box containing an Air Medal that had been posthumously awarded to Tony by Far East Air Forces. The accompanying citation noted that the "courage and devotion to duty" the young airman had displayed during the August 18 flight reflected "great credit on the United States Army Air Force."[14]

The package containing the Air Medal would not be the last communication between the government and the Marchiones. For several months following the initial notification of Tony's death, Ralph and Emelia received occasional letters from various agencies within the War Department regarding such administrative decisions as the final amount to be paid out under their son's G.I. life insurance policy, the date the box containing his personal effects would be delivered, and so on. But then, in the fall of 1946, they received a letter from the Memorial Division of the Office of the Quartermaster

General that contained some truly momentous news: if they so desired, the body of their only son could come home.

THE VAST MAJORITY OF the several hundred overseas cemeteries established for America's World War II dead during the course of the conflict were always intended to be temporary. As had been done following World War I, the U.S. government planned to consolidate the remains in a few large memorial cemeteries that would be constructed overseas and maintained in perpetuity by the federal, civilian-staffed American Battle Monuments Commission. The contingency plans developed for the final disposition of the war dead recognized that not all of the remains could be accommodated in the memorial cemeteries, however, so the next of kin of those temporarily buried overseas were to be given three options. The remains could be interred in the overseas memorial cemetery established in the war theater in which their loved one died, or they could be returned to the United States for interment in either a national or private cemetery.[15]

On January 26, 1948, Ralph Marchione received a letter bearing his son's name at the top and the signature of Major General William B. Larkin, the Quartermaster General, below. The letter announced that

> the people of the United States, through the Congress, have authorized the disinterment and final burial of the heroic dead of World War II. The Quartermaster General of the Army has been entrusted with this sacred responsibility to the honored dead. The records of the War Department indicate that you may be the nearest relative of the above-named deceased, who gave his life in the service of his country.[16]

The letter went on to explain the options available to the family, but cautioned that if they chose to have Tony's remains returned for private burial they should undertake "no funeral arrangements or other personal arrangements" until they received further notification

about the status of their request. Not surprisingly, Ralph and Emelia
opted to have their son brought home for burial in the cemetery be-
longing to St. Aloysius Church, and they returned the form bearing
their choice within days of receiving it. Their rapid response was
not matched by the government, however, and it wasn't until June
10 that they received a letter from a Major Richard Coombs of the
Memorial Division acknowledging receipt and acceptance of their
"Request for Disposition of Remains." On that form Ralph had designated Fleischman's Funeral Home in Pottstown as the receiving
facility, and had then asked that Tony's remains be transported to
the house on King Street for a viewing. Coombs replied with what
was obviously a boiler-plate response:

> When the remains of your son are returned, the
> casket may not be opened while all custodial rights
> and responsibility for the decedent rests [sic] with the
> Department of the Army. However, upon delivery
> of the remains to the next of kin or the authorized
> representative of the next of kin, the Government
> relinquishes all rights and responsibilities. Therefore,
> if the next of kin so desires, the casket may be opened,
> providing such action does not violate federal or state
> public health law.[17]

Coombs's assumption that the Marchiones' use of the term *viewing* meant they intended to open Tony's casket is understandable.
Many family members of servicemen killed overseas were unaware
of the realities of mortuary operations in the theaters of war and assumed that their loved ones had been "prepared" in the same way
they would have been in a civilian funeral home. The reality was
quite different, of course. American military personnel who died
abroad during World War II, whether they were killed in action or
succumbed to illness or injury, were only very rarely embalmed.
The time and materials that would have been required to "prepare"
thousands of bodies would have been prohibitive, and the need to
inter corpses quickly in order to prevent outbreaks of disease meant

that the only "preparation" most bodies received before burial was a rudimentary cleaning. Moreover, very few corpses were buried in caskets—again, the logistics involved in getting caskets to the far-flung battlefields would have interfered with the shipment of ammunition, fuel, and other vital war supplies. Most of the deceased were, like Tony, therefore interred wrapped in canvas shelter-halves that did little to protect the remains. And in the Pacific, high temperatures and humidity, coupled with often very acidic soils, promoted rapid decomposition.

In keeping with Ralph and Emelia's wish that Tony come home, the Memorial Division issued a "Disinterment Directive" to the Island Command Cemetery as the first step in the repatriation process. Quartermaster Corps policy decreed that all of the deceased in a particular temporary cemetery be disinterred within the same relatively short time period which, of course, meant that several hundred to several thousand sets of remains then had to be dealt with. In Tony's case, this meant that though his "incomplete, badly decomposed skeletal remains" were disinterred on July 7, 1948, they were not processed (in this case an administrative term) and placed in a hermetically sealed casket until November 5.[18] The casket was enclosed in the standard compact shipping case and loaded aboard a C-54 transport with many other identically protected sets of remains and flown to the U.S. Army mausoleum on Saipan. On January 25, 1949, Tony's casket joined 4,500 others in the holds of the U.S. Army Transport *Dalton Victory*, which sailed the following day for Honolulu, where an additional 1,300 caskets were put aboard.

California's Oakland Army Base, just across the Bay Bridge from San Francisco, was one of fifteen designated distribution centers for repatriated remains.[19] *Dalton Victory* arrived at the huge port complex and logistics hub at 8:45 on the morning of February 16, the fourteenth "funeral ship" to offload its sad cargo at the installation since the beginning of the Pacific repatriation program in September 1947. A memorial service honoring the ship's "passengers, deceased" was held at Dock Three with Major General James A. Lester, commander of the San Francisco Port of Embarkation, as the principal speaker and with military personnel and relatives and friends of the deceased in attendance. The solemn event closed with military chaplains offering prayers and benedictions, and a bugler sounding Taps.[20]

Six days after the memorial service Tony's casket began the next leg of its journey to Pottstown. Before dawn on Tuesday, February 22, Master Sergeant Edward V. Trittenback, the senior noncommissioned officer designated as the escort for Tony's remains and those of eleven other individuals, supervised the loading of the shipping cases aboard a U.S. Army Transportation Corps funeral train made up of fifteen "mortuary cars." These were converted six-axle "heavy-weight" Pullman passenger carriages with the seats removed and a wide baggage door installed on one side, locking metal racks on the walls to securely hold the caskets in their shipping cases, and with all but two of the windows blanked out.[21] Each car carried between fifty and sixty-six caskets, and the remains aboard each car were grouped by the state or region that was their ultimate destination. In the case of the train bearing Tony's casket, the last six cars bore the remains of personnel from the Midwest and would be dropped in Kansas City, whereas the leading nine cars holding remains bound for East Coast cities would travel all the way to the New York Port of Embarkation.[22]

The funeral train's cross-country odyssey ended at the Brooklyn Army Base—Distribution Center No. 1—on March 2. There the caskets were removed from the mortuary cars and transported to a temporary mausoleum adjacent to the base's vast, eight-story-tall enclosed loading and transfer structure, Building B. Over the following weeks the individual caskets were sorted according to their final destinations, draped with American flags, then taken by hearse or military ambulance to local civilian railway stations and put aboard trains bound for the deceased's home town.

In Tony's case, the final leg of the long journey home from Okinawa began before dawn on Friday, March 18. Under the supervision of Staff Sergeant Luke E. O'Shaughnessy, an aerial gunner and combat veteran who would be the official individual escort from that point on, the casket bearing the young airman's remains was loaded into a military ambulance and driven from the Brooklyn

Army Terminal mausoleum to one of the Army piers on the east bank of the Hudson River. The vehicle drove aboard an Army-operated ferry for the two-and-a-half-mile passage across the river to the Navy pier complex at Bayonne, New Jersey, from where the ambulance departed for the short drive to Jersey City. The flag-draped casket was loaded aboard a baggage car of the Jersey Central Line's Train No. 601, which rolled into Pottstown's small central station at 11:38 A.M.

The Marchiones had been notified by telegram the day before of the time the train bearing Tony's remains would arrive, but had chosen not to meet it. They instead relied on two of Tony's friends and former crewmates, Frank Pallone and Rudy Nudo, to handle things at the station. The two men, both now civilians, had been contacted by the U.S. Air Force's Memorial Affairs Branch several weeks earlier and asked if they would "attend" Tony's remains once they reached Pottstown.[23] Both had readily agreed, and had arrived the day before to a warm, highly emotional welcome from Ralph, Emelia, and the girls. Pallone and Nudo introduced themselves to O'Shaughnessy on the station platform, and the three men shared a taxi as they followed the hearse bearing Tony's casket to the Fleischmann Funeral Home at 258 Beach Street. There the firm's director took official custody of the remains, the young escort departed, and Tony's two comrades settled down to wait as a mortician and his assistant moved the casket into a preparation room to perform the examination required by both state law and the military release form the funeral director had just signed.

The Marchiones planned to hold a visitation and Rosary service in their home the night before their son's funeral Mass, with Tony's casket resting on a flower-bedecked bier in the small living room. Although the June 1948 letter from the Quartermaster Corps Memorial Division's Major Coombs had stated that the casket could be opened once the Army had relinquished control, the initial examination at Fleischmann's put any such possibility completely out of the question. The mortician determined that the state of the remains—incomplete, disarticulated, and badly decomposed—made it impossible under Pennsylvania's public health laws. Fleischmann's funeral director passed the decision to Pallone and Nudo, who relayed it to Ralph and Emelia.[24]

In keeping with the Marchiones' wishes, Tony's casket was transported from Fleischmann's to the family home on King Street on the afternoon of Sunday, March 20. Throughout the day and into the evening relatives, neighbors, friends, parishioners, and members of the larger Pottstown community came to pay their respects. Framed pictures of Tony at various stages in his too-short life stood atop end tables and on window sills, and a vase of early spring flowers graced the small dining room table. Over the hours many fond stories were told, tears were shed, and quiet laughter at some remembered childhood antic of the young man who had gone to war occasionally lightened the atmosphere of loss that pervaded the small row house. At 7:30 the Reverend William M. Begley began the Rosary service, after which the home slowly emptied except for the family and Pallone and Nudo, who spent the night in Tony's old room.

The grief-tinged celebration of Tony Marchione's life continued the next morning at 9:15, when a hearse returned to the King Street house and loaded the casket for the short drive to St. Aloysius—the place where Tony had made his first communion, attended catechism, and may have hoped to be married one day. The Requiem Mass began at 10, with the Reverend John F. Campbell as celebrant, the Reverends George Hiller and David Leahy as concelebrants, and Pallone and Nudo among the pallbearers. The service was well attended, and many of those present added their cars to the procession that followed the hearse bearing the flag-draped casket to the older of St. Aloysius Church's two cemeteries.[25] There Anthony James Marchione—the young man who bears the sad distinction of being the last American killed in combat in World War II—was laid to rest with full military honors in the St. Paul's Section, Plot 68, Grave 3. As a bugler played Taps, Father Hiller intoned the traditional final petition: "May his soul and the souls of all the faithful departed through the mercy of God rest in peace."

AUTHOR'S AFTERWORD

ONE OF THE CARDINAL rules in both journalism and the writing of history is that one should never become emotionally involved with the people one is writing about. As reporters or historians we are supposed to remain detached and objective, weighing evidence and facts and following them wherever they may lead us regardless of our own beliefs, preconceptions, or prejudices. In more than three decades as both reporter and historian I have done my utmost to adhere scrupulously to that rule, and have—for the most part—succeeded.

But not in the case of Anthony Marchione.

I obviously did not know the young airman personally; he died seven years before I was born. But when I first heard about him—in the course of writing a long-ago small book about an odd and not very successful U.S. Army Air Forces bomber called the B-32 Dominator—I was immediately intrigued by his story. Here was a young man who, like millions of his contemporaries, was swept up in the national effort to defeat Japan and Nazi Germany. Like those many millions of others he was taught a deadly skill and then dispatched to faraway lands to employ that skill in the service of his country. And, like hundreds of thousands of other young Americans who'd put on the uniform, he'd been killed in the performance of his duty far from home and family. And yet, Tony Marchione was different from all the others who had died in that global conflict, because he holds the sad distinction of being the last American killed in combat before the September 2, 1945, surrender of Japan officially ended World War II.[1]

It was not merely Tony's enduring place as a footnote in the history of America's participation in World War II that captured my interest, however. Despite the many differences in our lives and backgrounds, I felt a close kinship with the young man from Pottstown. We both came from close-knit families, grew up in small towns, and entered the military at roughly the same age. And while serving our nation, Tony in World War II and I during the Vietnam period, we both suffered great misfortune. Though I survived mine—an armored vehicle accident that left me hospitalized for the better part of a year and disabled for life—I identified only too well with what Tony must have been feeling in those first few seconds after he was hit. The surprise, the blinding pain, the frenzied efforts of buddies trying their best to stop the bleeding and, worst of all, the sudden realization that this might actually be *it*, the unexpected end of a too-short life.

As I moved through my career—and the very interesting, joyous, painful, thrilling, and often calamitous events that have constituted my personal life—the idea of writing about Tony and the events surrounding his death never left me. Indeed, I wrote several short articles over the decades that touched on the events of August 18, 1945, in various ways, though always in the context of the B-32 and not focusing on Tony. I was able to locate and interview many of the people who took part in the final air combats over Tokyo at a time when their memories were still relatively clear and their willingness to provide documents and photographs was limitless—sadly, all but a very few are gone now—but owing to the "busyness" of life I did not attempt to tell Tony's story in detail until the fall of 2008. The resultant article, published in Smithsonian's *Air & Space*, only brushed the surface of what I knew to be a much broader and deeper story. I resolved to tell that tale as thoroughly and completely as possible, and this book is the result.

By the time I made that resolution I had already amassed several file cabinets full of pertinent information—official records, personal narratives, photographs, interview transcriptions, and, of course, reams of data on the aircraft with which Tony's life was briefly but inextricably linked, the B-32. But I knew I needed more, so I and my very able and dogged researchers, Thomas Culbert and Tetsuya Yamada, combed archives all over the United States and in Japan for any and all documents that might further illuminate the many aspects of this story. Although I could not personally examine a B-32— they were all scrapped soon after the war—I did go flying in the Collings Foundation's beautifully restored B-24 Liberator, the type of bomber Tony first crewed on and the basis of the F-7 in which he flew combat missions from the Philippines. That experience, combined with several previous flights in various B-17 Flying Fortresses, gave me insights about the conditions under which Tony and thousands of young airmen like him had to live and work. One especially insightful moment during the B-24 flight occurred as I stood at the left waist gunner's position, gazing out at the passing landscape with my hands resting on the twin grips of a .50-caliber machine gun. It suddenly struck me that I had a picture of Tony doing exactly the same thing—and for a moment I felt as though I had connected with him in some inexplicable way, despite the years and the distance.

In the end, of course, both the reporter and the historian—if they are serious about their craft—must put an end to the research and get the story on paper in the most honest, accurate, and complete way possible. I have attempted so to do, and I hope that Tony Marchione would approve of the end result.

Stephen Harding

ACKNOWLEDGMENTS

OVER THE COURSE OF my thirty-year search for information that would enable me to write the most accurate and complete account of the events surrounding the August 18, 1945, air combat over Tokyo that resulted in Tony Marchione's death I have been ably and generously assisted by a number of people. I sincerely appreciate their willingness to share documents, expertise, and memories with me, often despite the inconvenience and even emotional distress that cooperation caused. Any errors or omissions in this volume are, of course, mine alone.

First and foremost I wish to thank my most wonderful and truly amazing wife and muse, Margaret Spragins Harding. This book, and those that came before it, would not have been possible without her insight, intelligence, and unwavering support. Partner, best friend, assistant interviewer, and occasional translator, she is quite simply the best thing that has ever happened to me.

I would also like to thank aviation historian and illustrator James I. Long, with whom I once coauthored a small red book about the B-32 Dominator. That long-ago collaboration marked my introduction to Tony Marchione, and Jim's help and guidance over the years have been absolutely essential in my quest to tell the young airman's story in as accurate and honest a way possible.

Special thanks must also go to Theresa Marchione Sell and Geraldine Marchione Young, Tony's sisters. They provided extremely important and valuable documents and photographs, and gladly spoke at length about Tony despite the obvious sadness the reminiscences caused. They gladly opened their hearts to my wife and me when we visited Pottstown, as did Debra McNamara, Gerry's daughter.

I am also deeply indebted to the former members of the 20th Reconnaissance Squadron, 386th Bombardment Squadron, and 312th Bombardment Group (whose names are listed in the Bibliography) who patiently endured my many questions and who consented to interviews that have proved absolutely essential. Most have since passed away, but I believe their voices, speaking through this volume, will echo for years to come.

My sincere thanks also go to my agent, Scott Mendel, for his unwavering support and expert guidance; and to Robert Pigeon, my editor at Da Capo, for his continuing friendship and expert assistance in shaping and improving this manuscript—and those we both hope will follow it.

I would also like to thank:

My friends and colleagues at World History Group's *Military History* magazine: David Lauterborn, ace managing editor; Brian Walker, quite possibly the world's best art director; Sarah Cokeley, a delight of a senior editor who is destined one day to rule the publishing world; and Jennifer Berry, hands-down the best photo editor on the planet. No editor could ask for a better and more supportive staff.

Thomas Culbert, for his expert research on my behalf at institutions ranging from the National Archives to the U.S. Air Force Historical Research Agency to the Harry S. Truman Library.

Tetsuya Yamada, for his research in Japanese-language sources and expert translations. That Tetsuya lives in the small California town where I was born and that I left many years ago is one of those delightfully unexpected coincidences that life sometimes produces.

Henry Sakaida and Osamu "Sam" Tagaya, noted historians of World War II Japanese military aviation, who happily shared both their expertise on a host of topics and copies of documents that were simply unavailable elsewhere.

Chuck Varney, son of a 20th Combat Mapping Squadron veteran and founder of the unit's very useful website, for his willingness to share time, information, and insights about the unit and its members, aircraft, and operations. His wide-ranging and in-depth knowledge of World War II aerial reconnaissance cameras and related systems was especially useful.

James Zobel, of the MacArthur Library in Norfolk, Virginia, and David Clark of the Harry S. Truman Library and Museum in Independence, Missouri, for their tireless archival research assistance.

Paul Hoversten, of Smithsonian's *Air & Space* magazine, for his willingness to publish my article on Tony and the August 18 events.

And Richard Lacharite, for his willingness to share information about, and photos of, his father, wounded aerial photographer Joe Lacharite.

BIBLIOGRAPHY

PRIMARY SOURCES

Official Documents

Documents obtained from the National Archives and Records Administration's Modern Military Records Center in College Park, Maryland, are cited as NARA-MMRC; those obtained from NARA's National Personnel Records center in St. Louis, Missouri, are cited as NARA-NPRC. Other sources are as noted.

A History of Air Proving Ground Command Testing of the B-32, September 1944–October 1945. Two volumes, U.S. Air Force Historical Research Agency, Maxwell Air Force Base, AL.

Airplane Commander Training Manual for the B-32 (AAF Manual 51-126-7). HQs., Army Air Forces, 5 March 1945. USAFHRA, Maxwell AFB, AL.

Awards for Combat Crew, Mission 230-A-8. Office of the S-2, 386th Bombardment Squadron, 19 August 1945. NARA-MMRC.

Combat Test of the B-32 Airplane. Col. Frank Cook to Commanding General, V Bomber Command, July 17, 1945. USAFHRA, Maxwell AFB, AL.

Commander-in-Chief's Daily Intelligence Summary, 17/18 August 1945. Military Intelligence Section, General Staff, Headquarters, United States Army Forces Pacific, 18 August 1945. MacArthur Archives, MacArthur Memorial, Norfolk, VA.

213

Final Mission Report, Mission 190-Z-1, 9 July 1945. Office of the S-2, 20th
    Reconnaissance Squadron (LR, P-RCM), 9 July 1945. NARA-MMRC.
Final Mission Report, Mission 226-A-6, 14 August 1945. Office of the S-2,
    386th Bombardment Squadron, 15 August 1945. NARA-MMRC.
Final Mission Report, Mission 227-A-6, 15 August 1945. Office of the S-2,
    386th Bombardment Squadron, 15 August 1945. NARA-MMRC.
Final Mission Report, Mission 228-A-8, 16 August 1945. Office of the S-2,
    386th Bombardment Squadron, 16 August 1945. NARA-MMRC.
Final Mission Report, Mission 229-A-10, 17 August 1945. Office of the S-2,
    386th Bombardment Squadron, 17 August 1945. NARA-MMRC.
Final Mission Report, Mission 230-A-8, 18 August 1945. Office of the S-2,
    386th Bombardment Squadron, 19 August 1945. NARA-MMRC.
Final Mission Report, Mission 237-A-10, 25 August 1945. Office of the S-2,
    386th Bombardment Squadron, 25 August 1945. NARA-MMRC.
Final Mission Report, Mission 240-A-5, 28 August 1945. Office of the S-2,
    386th Bombardment Squadron, 28 August 1945. NARA-MMRC.
Final Mission Report—Supplement, Mission 240-A-5, 28 August 1945. Office of the S-2, 386th Bombardment Squadron, 28 August 1945.
    NARA-MMRC.
Flexible Gunnery Training in the AAF. Assistant Chief of Air Staff, Intelligence, Historical Section, March 1945. USAFHRA, Maxwell
    AFB, AL.
*General Order No. 2148, Award Citation, SSgt. Joseph M. Lacherite [sic] and
    Sgt. Anthonty [sic] Marchione.* HQs., Far Eastern Air Forces, 27 October 1945. USAFHRA, Maxwell AFB, AL.
History, 6th Photographic Group, Reconnaissance. Monthly reports,
    1 March 1944 through 30 September 1945. NARA-NPRC.
Individual Deceased Personnel File, Sgt. Anthony J. Marchione. The Adjutant
    General's Office, U.S. Army, Washington, DC, 1948. NARA-NPRC.
Individual Deceased Personnel File, Sgt. Morris C. Morgan. The Adjutant
    General's Office, U.S. Army, Washington, DC, 1948. NARA-NPRC.
Individual Deceased Personnel File, SSgt. George A. Murphy. The Adjutant
    General's Office, U.S. Army, Washington, DC, 1948. NARA-NPRC.
Narrative Mission Report, Mission 149-A-11, 29 May 1945. Office of the
    S-2, 386th Bombardment Squadron, 30 May 1945. NARA-MMRC.
Narrative Mission Report, Mission 163-A-6, 12 June 1945. Office of the S-2,
    386th Bombardment Squadron, 13 June 1945. NARA-MMRC.
Narrative Mission Report, Mission 164-A-13, 13 June 1945. Office of the
    S-2, 386th Bombardment Squadron, 14 June 1945. NARA-MMRC.
Narrative Mission Report, Mission 166-A-6, 15 June 1945. Office of the S-2,
    386th Bombardment Squadron, 16 June 1945. NARA-MMRC.

Narrative Mission Report, Mission 167-A-7, 16 June 1945. Office of the S-2, 386th Bombardment Squadron, 17 June 1945. NARA-MMRC.
Narrative Mission Report, Mission 169-A-4, 17/18 June 1945. Office of the S-2, 386th Bombardment Squadron, 18 June 1945. NARA-MMRC.
Narrative Mission Report, Mission 170-A-3, 19 June 1945. Office of the S-2, 386th Bombardment Squadron, 20 June 1945. NARA-MMRC.
Narrative Mission Report, Mission 171-A-3, 20 June 1945. Office of the S-2, 386th Bombardment Squadron, 21 June 1945. NARA-MMRC.
Narrative Mission Report, Mission 171-A-3, 20 June 1945. Office of the S-2, 386th Bombardment Squadron, 21 June 1945. NARA-MMRC.
Narrative Mission Report, Mission 173-A-3, 22 June 1945. Office of the S-2, 386th Bombardment Squadron, 23 June 1945. NARA-MMRC.
Narrative Mission Report, Mission 175-A-6, 23/24 June 1945. Office of the S-2, 386th Bombardment Squadron, 24 June 1945. NARA-MMRC.
Narrative Mission Report, Mission 176-A-1, 25 June 1945. Office of the S-2, 386th Bombardment Squadron, 26 June 1945. NARA-MMRC.
Narrative Mission Report, Mission 225-A-6, Office of the S-2, 386th Bombardment Squadron, 15 August 1945. NARA-MMRC.
Narrative Mission Report, Mission 226-A-6, Office of the S-2, 386th Bombardment Squadron, 15 August 1945. NARA-MMRC.
Narrative Mission Report, Mission 227-A-6, Office of the S-2, 386th Bombardment Squadron, 16 August 1945. NARA-MMRC.
Narrative Mission Report, Mission 229-A-10, 17 August 1945. Office of the S-2, 386th Bombardment Squadron, 20 August 1945. NARA-MMRC.
Narrative Mission Report, Mission 230-A-8, 18 August 1945. Office of the S-2, 386th Bombardment Squadron, 20 August 1945. NARA-MMRC.
Narrative Unit History, 386th Bombardment Squadron, July-August 1945. Office of the S-2, 386th Bombardment Squadron, 2 September 1945. NARA-MMRC.
Pilot's Flight Operating Instructions for Army Model B-32 (AN 01-5EQ-1). HQs., AAF, 5 March 1945. USAFHRA, Maxwell AFB, AL.
Report on Special Project 98269S. Lt. Col. Stephen D. McElroy to Assistant Chief of the Air Staff, July 2, 1945. USAFHRA, Maxwell AFB, AL.
Report to USAAF Proving Ground Command on the Combat Test of the B-32 Airplane. Major Henry S. Britt, Aug. 2, 1945. NARA-MMRC.
Reports of General MacArthur: The Campaigns of MacArthur in the Pacific, Vol. I, General Staff, GHQ, Tokyo, 1950. U.S. Army Center of Military History, Fory Lesley J. McNair, Washington, DC.
Reports of General MacArthur: Volume I Supplement, The Occupation: Military Phase, General Staff, GHQ, Tokyo, 1950. U.S. Army Center of Military History, Fort Lesley J. McNair, Washington, DC.

Summary of Accidents and Losses, 17–28 August 1945. Office of the S-2, 386th Bombardment Squadron, 28 August 1945. NARA-MMRC.

United States Strategic Bombing Survey, Summary Report (Pacific War), July 1, 1946, NARA-MMRC.

USS Aulick (DD-569), Deck Log, 28 August–3 September 1945. NARA-MMRC.

USS John D. Henley (DD-553), Deck Log, 28 August 1945. NARA-MMRC.

USS John D. Henley (DD-553), War Diary, 24–31 August 1945. NARA-MMRC.

Interviews

Amster, Howard J. 386th Bombardment Squadron. Audio-recorded March 16, 1997.

Anderson, John R. 386th BS. Audio-recorded Feb. 28, 1997.

Blackburn, John. 386th BS. Audio-recorded June 25, 1998.

Cook, Frank R. B-32 Combat Test Detachment. Audio-recorded July 12, 1998.

Chevalier, Frederick C. 312th Bombardment Group. Audio-recorded Feb. 24, 1997.

Houston, John T. 386th BS. Audio-recorded Feb. 28, 1997.

Keller, Burton J. 386th BS. Audio-recorded Feb. 24, 1997.

Klein, James L. 386th BS. Audio-recorded July 12, 1998.

Lacharite, Joseph. 386th BS. Audio-recorded Feb. 6, 1997.

Pallone, Frank J. Sr. 20th Reconnaissance Squadron. Audio-recorded Sep. 15, 1998.

Pugliese, Rudolph. 312th BG. Audio-recorded Feb. 1, 1997.

Rupke, Kurt F. 386th BS. Audio-recorded Feb. 5, 1997.

Russell, Robert. 386th BS. Audio-recorded Feb. 16, 1999.

Sell, Theresa. Sister of Anthony Marchione. Audio-recorded Feb. 1, 1997.

Svore, Ferdinand L. 386th BS. Audio-recorded Feb. 12, 1997.

Thomas, Richard E. 386th BS. Audio-recorded Feb. 28, 1997.

Wells, Selmon. 312th BG. Audio-recorded July 13, 1998.

Zimmerman, Kent. 386th BS. Conducted via email, Nov. 28, 2000.

SECONDARY SOURCES

Books

Bergamini, David. *Japan's Imperial Conspiracy.* New York: William Morrow and Company, 1971.

Birdsall, Steve. *Flying Buccaneers: The Illustrated Story of Kenney's Fifth Air Force*. Garden City, NY: Doubleday & Co., 1977.

Bix, Herbert P. *Hirohito and the Making of Modern Japan*. New York: HarperCollins, 2000.

Brooks, Lester. *Behind Japan's Surrender: The Secret Struggle That Ended an Empire*. New York: McGraw-Hill Book Company, 1968.

Chun, Clayton K. S. *Japan 1945: From Operation Downfall to Hiroshima and Nagasaki*. Botley, Oxford: Osprey Publishing Ltd., 2008.

Craven, Frank W. and James L. Cate. *The Pacific: Matterhorn to Nagasaki, June 1944 to August 1945*. Volume V in the series *The Army Air Forces in World War II*. Chicago, IL: The University of Chicago Press, 1953.

———, *Men and Planes*. Volume VI in the series *The Army Air Forces in World War II*. Chicago, IL: The University of Chicago Press, 1955.

Dorr, Robert F. *Mission to Tokyo: The American Airmen Who Took the War to the Heart of Japan*. Minneapolis, MN: Zenith Press, 2012.

Drea, Edward J. *MacArthur's ULTRA: Codebreaking and the War Against Japan, 1942–1945*. Lawrence, KS: University of Kansas Press, 1992.

Frank, Richard B. *Downfall: The End of the Imperial Japanese Empire*. New York: Penguin Books, 2001.

General Staff, GHQ, Tokyo. *Reports of General MacArthur: The Campaigns of MacArthur in the Pacific*, Vol. I, 1950. U.S. Army Center of Military History, Fort Lesley J. McNair, Washington, DC.

——— *Reports of General MacArthur: Volume I Supplement, The Occupation: Military Phase*, 1950. U.S. Army Center of Military History, Fort Lesley J. McNair, Washington, DC.

Griffith, Thomas E. Jr. *MacArthur's Airman: General George C. Kenney and the War in the Southwest Pacific*. Lawrence, KS: University Press of Kansas, 1998.

Hammell, Eric. *Air War Pacific: America's Air War Against Japan in East Asia and the Pacific, 1941–1945*. Pacifica, CA: Pacifica Press, 1998.

Hansell, Major General Haywood, Jr. *Strategic Air War Against Japan*. Washington, DC: U.S. Government Printing Office, 1980.

Harding, Steve and James I. Long. *Dominator: The Story of the Consolidated B-32 Bomber*. Missoula, MT: Pictorial Histories Publishing Co., 1984.

Hastings, Max. *Retribution: The Battle for Japan, 1944–1945*. New York: Vintage Books, 2009.

Hata, Ikuhiko and Yasuho Izawa. *Japanese Naval Aces and Fighter Units in World War II*. Annapolis, MD: Naval Institute Press, 1989.

Hopkins, William B. *The Pacific War: The Strategy, Politics and Players That Won the War*. Minneapolis, MN: Zenith Press, 2008.

Hoyt, Edwin P. *Closing the Circle: War in the Pacific, 1945.* New York: Van Nostrand Reinhold, 1982.

Houston, Major General John W. *American Airpower Comes of Age: General Henry H. "Hap" Arnold's World War II Diaries.* Montgomery, AL: Air University Press, 2002.

Kenney, George C. *General Kenney Reports: A Personal History of the Pacific War.* New York: Duell, Sloan and Pearce Publishers, 1949.

Kerr, E. Bartlett. *Flames Over Tokyo: The U.S. Army Air Forces' Incendiary Campaign Against Japan, 1944–1945.* New York: Donald I. Fine, 1991.

Kodaki, Naoki. *Zero Fighters of Our Grandfathers.* Tokyo: Kodansha, 1999.

MacEachin, Douglas J. *The Final Months of the War with Japan: Signals Intelligence, U.S. Invasion Planning, and the A-Bomb Decision.* Washington, DC: Central Intelligence Agency, 1998.

Manchester, William. *American Caesar: Douglas MacArthur, 1880–1964.* Boston, MA: Little, Brown and Co., 1978.

Matloff, Maurice, and Edwin M. Snell. *Strategic Planning for Coalition Warfare, 1941–1942,* in the series *United States Army in World War II: The War Department.* Washington, DC: U.S. Government Printing Office, 1980.

Miller, Edward S. *War Plan Orange: The U.S. Strategy to Defeat Japan, 1897–1945.* Annapolis, MD: Naval Institute Press, 1991.

Morison, Samuel Elliot. *The Rising Sun in the Pacific, 1931 to April 1942.* Volume Three in the series *History of United States Naval Operations in World War II.* Annapolis, MD: Naval Institute Press, 2010.

Nanney, James S. *Army Air Forces Medical Services in World War II.* Air Force History and Museums Program, Albert F. Simpson Historical Research Center, Maxwell AFB, AL, 1998.

Newton, Wesley P., and Calvin F. Senning, et al. *USAF Credits for the Destruction of Enemy Aircraft, World War II* (USAF Historical Study No. 85). Albert F. Simpson Historical Research Center, Maxwell AFB, AL, 1978.

Pacific War Research Society. *Japan's Longest Day.* Tokyo: Kodansha International, 2002.

Peattie, Mark R. *Sunburst: The Rise of Japanese Naval Air Power, 1909–1941.* Annapolis, MD: Naval Institute Press, 2002.

Perret, Geoffrey. *Old Soldiers Never Die: The Life of Douglas MacArthur.* New York: Random House, 1996.

Prange, Gordon W., and Donald M. Goldstein and Katherine V. Dillon. *God's Samurai: Lead Pilot at Pearl Harbor.* Washington, DC: Potomac Books, 2004.

Sakai, Saburo. *Zero-sen No Saigo*. Tokyo: Kodansha, 1995.

――― and Martin Caidin and Fred Saito. *Samurai! The Unforgettable Saga of Japan's Greatest Fighter Pilot*. New York: Nelson/Doubleday, 1978.

Sakaida, Henry. *Winged Samurai: Saburo Sakai and the Zero Fighter Pilots*. Mesa, AZ: Champlin Fighter Museum Press, 1985.

―――. *Imperial Japanese Navy Aces 1937–45*. Botley, Oxford: Osprey Publishing Ltd., 1998.

Smith, Jim, and Malcolm McConnell. *The Last Mission: The Secret History of World War II's Final Battle*. New York: Broadway Books, 2002.

Steere, Edward. *The Graves Registration Service in World War II*. No. 21 in the series *Quartermaster Corps Historical Studies*. Historical Section, Office of the Quartermaster General, Washington, DC, 1951.

―――, and Thayer M. Boardman. *Final Disposition of World War II Dead, 1945–1951*. No. 4 in Series II of *Quartermaster Corps Historical Studies*. Historical Section, Office of the Quartermaster General, Washington, DC, 1957.

Sturzebecker, Russell L. *The Roarin' 20's: A History of the 312th Bombardment Group*. Kennet Square, PA: KNA Press, 1976.

Tagaya, Osamu. *Imperial Japanese Naval Aviator, 1937–1945*. Botley, Oxford: Osprey Publishing Ltd. 2003.

Troiad: Yearbook of the 1943 Senior Class, Pottstown High School. Pottstown, PA: The Feroe Press, 1943.

U.S. Army Center of Military History. *Reports of General MacArthur: The Campaigns of General MacArthur in the Pacific, Volume I*. Washington, DC: U.S. Government Printing Office, 1966.

Watson, Mark Skinner. *Chief of Staff: Prewar Plans and Preparations*, in the series *United States Army in World War II: The War Department*. Washington, DC: U.S. Government Printing Office, 1950.

Weintraub, Stanley. *The Last Great Victory: The End of World War II, July/August 1945*. New York: Truman Talley Books, 1995.

Werneth, Ron. *Beyond Pearl Harbor: The Untold Stories of Japan's Naval Airmen*. Atglen, PA: Schiffer Publishing Ltd., 2008.

Werrell, Kenneth. *Blankets of Fire: U.S. Bombers over Japan During World War II*. Washington, DC: Smithsonian, 1978.

Wolk, Herman S. *Cataclysm: General Hap Arnold and the Defeat of Japan*. Denton, TX: University of North Texas Press, 2010.

Yoshimura, Akira. *Zero Fighter*. Westport, CT: Praeger, 1996.

Zaloga, Steven. *Defense of Japan 1945*. Botley, Oxford: Osprey Publishing Ltd., 2010.

Newspaper Articles

Argus Leader (Sioux Falls, SD), "Japs Attack U.S. Planes Over Tokyo." August 18, 1945.

Charlotte Observer (Charlotte, NC), "Charlotte Pilot Attacked While Flying Over Tokyo." August 19, 1945.

Daily News (Los Angeles, CA), "New Jap Attack, American Flyer Killed Over Tokyo." August 18, 1945.

Fresno Bee (Fresno, CA), "Zeros Attack B32s Over Tokyo, Killing Yank, Wounding Two." August 18, 1945.

Navy News (Guam, Mariana Islands), "Flyer Killed As Nips Jump Photo Plane." August 20, 1945.

New York Times (New York, NY), "U.S. Airman Killed By Foe Over Tokyo; Big B-32 Crippled." August 19, 1945.

———, "Saburo Sakai is Dead at 84; War Pilot Embraced Foes." October 8, 2000.

Pottstown Mercury (Pottstown, PA), "Sgt. Marchione Killed by Japs After Surrender." August 30, 1945.

———, "Air Medal Posthumously Awarded to Pottstown's Last Casualty of War." April 26, 1945.

———, "Full Military Rites Accorded Soldier Killed After V-J Day." March 22, 1945.

Star-Telegram (Houston, TX), "Jap Planes Attack B-32s on Photo Trip." August 17, 1945.

———, "Japs Again Attack B-32s; Texans Bag 2." August 18, 1945.

Transcript-Telegram (Holyoke, MA), "Japs Hit U.S Planes, Kill 1 Yank." August 18, 1945.

———, "Holyoker Injured in Last Plane Hit Over Tokyo." August 19, 1945.

———, "Sergt [sic] Lacharite Wounded Four Days after Japs Fell." August 19, 1945.

———, "Wounded Long After V-J Day." August 30, 1945.

———, "Airman Hit Four Days After V-J Is Expected Home Soon." September 15, 1945.

Monographs

Huber, Thomas M. "Japan's Battle of Okinawa, April–June 1945." Leavenworth Papers No. 18, U.S. Army Command and General Staff College, Fort Leavenworth, KS, 1990.

MacEachin, Douglas J. "The Final Months of War With Japan: Signals Intelligence, U.S. Invasion Planning, and the A-Bomb Decision."

Center for the Study of Intelligence, Central Intelligence Agency, Washington, DC, 1998.

Military History Section, "Homeland Defense Naval Operations, Part III, Dec 41–Aug 45," No. 124 in the series "Japanese Monographs." HQs., U.S. Army Forces Far East, 1949.

———, "Homeland Air Defense Operations Record," No. 147 in the series "Japanese Monographs." HQs., U.S. Army Forces Far East, 1948.

———, "Air Defense of the Homeland," No. 23 in the series "Japanese Monographs." HQs., U.S. Army Forces Far East, 1956.

Rodman, Captain Matthew K. "A War of Their Own: Bombers over the Southwest Pacific." Air University Press, Maxwell AFB, AL, 2005.

Magazine/Journal Articles

Hasegawa, Yoshiaki. "The Last Air Superiority Group Has Yet to Surrender." *Maru Extra*, Volume 79, October 1981.

Hata, Dr. Ikuhiko. "The Combat of August 15: The Last of the Japanese Air Force" (Hachi Gatsu Ju Go Nichi No Ku Nippon Kugun No Saigo). Bungei Shunju, Tokyo, 1978: 250–255.

Komachi, Sadamu. "Becoming an Unusual Flying Ace After August 15." *Maru Extra*, Volume 62, December 1978.

Sakaida, Henry. "Honor or Dishonor?" *Banzai: The Newsletter for the Collector of Japanese Militaria*, February 1991: 43.

"Surrender on the Air." *Military Review*, Vol. 26, No. 2, May 1946.

Whittaker, Wayne. "Here's the B-32, Our Newest Super Bomber." *Popular Mechanics*, September 1945: 12–15.

Y'Blood, William T. "The Second String." *Journal of the American Aviation Historical Society*, Summer 1968: 80–92.

———. "Unwanted and Unloved: The Consolidated B-32." *Air Power History*, Fall 1995: 59–71.

"The Outlaw War." *Newsweek*, Aug. 27, 1945.

NOTES

Chapter 1: Son and Gunner

1. Details of Marchione family history are drawn primarily from interviews conducted with Theresa Marchione Sell in 1997 and 2013, and with her sister Geraldine Marchione Young in 2013. Hereafter cited as *Marchione Sisters Interview*. Other details as noted.

2. At that time high school in most parts of Pennsylvania was three, rather than four, years: tenth, eleventh, and twelfth grades. Ninth grade was considered part of junior high.

3. *Flexible Gunnery Training in the AAF*, pp. 11–13. Hereafter cited as *Flexible Gunnery Training*.

4. A demand-flow mask, as its name implies, provides oxygen when the wearer inhales. This type of mask was superior to the continuous-flow masks—those that continuously "pushed" oxygen to the wearer—that had been standard in the Army Air Forces until early 1944.

5. As a young soldier, the author learned all too well that when attempting to field strip a "Ma Deuce" it is imperative to ensure that the weapon's bolt is all the way forward before removing the backplate. If the bolt is to the rear, the machine gun's driving spring rod can shoot out the back of the gun like a harpoon, an event that is certain to lessen a soldier's popularity with his comrades—if it doesn't impale the soldier himself.

6. *Flexible Gunnery Training*, p. 44.

7. Letter from Tony Marchione to his parents, April 5, 1945.

223

8. Tony's class was the second to the last B-24 CCT class to graduate from Davis-Monthan; in January 1945 the 223rd shifted its focus to the training of B-29 Superfortress crews.

9. Letter of April 5.

10. "Just for You," written March 27, 1945.

11. Details of this and Tony Marchione's other 20th CMS combat missions provided by Chuck Varney, webmaster of the 20th CMS memorial page.

12. The modern names for the cities are, respectively, Shantou (in Guangdong Province) and Xiamen (in Fujian Province).

13. Letter from Tony Marchione to "Don," written July 29, 1945.

14. *Final Mission Report, Mission 190-Z-1*, 9 July 1945.

15. Letter of July 29.

16. Letter from Tony Marchione to "Dick," written August 15, 1945.

17. Ibid. In this sense "PFC" doesn't stand for the Army rank of private first class, it stands for "proud f***king civilian."

Chapter 2: The Second-String Super Bomber

1. Counted from the December 7, 1941, attack on Pearl Harbor, rather than from the United States' official declaration of war against Japan the following day.

2. *Flying Buccaneers: The Illustrated Story of Kenney's Fifth Air Force*, p. 9. Hereafter cited as *Flying Buccaneers*.

3. Fifth Bomber Command had originally been activated in the Philippines in late 1941, saw brief service in Java before its fall to the Japanese, and was essentially reconstituted by Kenney in Australia, at which time the "Fifth" was changed to the Roman numeral "V."

4. *MacArthur's Airman*, p. 175. Formed on New Caledonia in December 1942, Thirteenth Air Force had moved on to the Solomons. Seventh Air Force had originated in 1940 as the Army Air Corps' Hawaiian Air Force, and was redesignated in February 1942.

5. *World War II: The War Against Japan*, pp. 506–507. This is Chapter 23 in the volume *American Military History*.

6. The historian was Dr. James Lea Cate of the University of Chicago, and he expressed the opinion in *The Pacific—Matterhorn to Nagasaki (June 1944 to August 1945)*, p. 12. Hereafter cited as *Matterhorn to Nagasaki*.

7. *General Kenney Reports: A Personal History of the Pacific War*, pp. 529–530. Hereafter cited as *General Kenney Reports*.

8. Ibid., p. 531. This exchange is also dealt with in *MacArthur's Airman*, pp. 221–222.

9. *General Kenney Reports*, p. 532.

10. Ibid.

11. The Army Air Corps was redesignated the Army Air Forces in June 1941.

12. Details on the development and testing of the B-32 are drawn largely from the chapter "The VLR Project" in *The Pacific: Matterhorn to Nagasaki*; pp. 208–211 of *The Army Air Forces in World War II*, Vol. V, *Men and Planes*; and *A History of Air Proving Ground Command Testing of the B-32, September 1944 to October 1945*.

13. The "X" designates an experimental or developmental design.

14. Production B-32s were powered by four 2,200-horsepower Wright R-3350–23A Cyclones, a development of the earlier 3350-5, and retained the reversible-pitch propellers on the two inboard engines.

15. The company's San Diego plant produced only the three prototype XB-32s and one combat-equipped example; all the remaining B-32s and TB-32s that were actually completed were built in Fort Worth.

16. The aircraft's name was officially changed back to Terminator late in the war, but the change was widely ignored and the B-32 has gone down in history as the Dominator. That name that will be used throughout this volume.

17. Author interview with Frank R. Cook. Hereafter cited as *Cook Interview*.

18. The parachute-retarded fragmentation bomb, or parafrag, allowed attack aircraft to drop accurately at extremely low altitudes and relatively high speeds, thus minimizing the aviators' exposure to both the bomb's blast and to enemy ground fire.

19. Also referred to as "demolition bombs," these non–armor piercing weapons were normally fuzed for immediate, rather than delayed, detonation, and were intended for use against large concrete-reinforced structures such as factories, warehouses, barracks, bridges, and so on.

20. Details on this first combat strike are derived from *Narrative Mission Report, Mission 149-A-11, 29 May 1945*.

21. Cited in *The Roarin' 20's: A History of the 312th Bombardment Group, U.S. Army Air Force*, p. 208. Hereafter cited as *Roarin' 20's*.

22. Author interview with Ferdinand L. Svore. Hereafter cited as *Svore Interview*.

23. Author interview with Rudolph Pugliese. Hereafter cited as *Pugliese Interview*.

24. The island should not be confused with Luzon's Bataan Peninsula, west of Manila, the site of the infamous 1942 death march in which Japanese troops brutalized and murdered American and Filipino prisoners of war.

25. *Narrative Mission Report, Mission 163-A-6, 12 June 1945.*

26. Now Taiwan.

27. Koshun is now known as Hengchun, and it is still the site of Taiwan's southernmost airport.

28. *Gremlins* are mythological sprites rumored to cause mechanical problems aboard aircraft.

29. *Narrative Mission Report, Mission 164-A-13, 13 June 1945.*

30. Taito was the Japanese name for the town; after World War II it reverted to its Chinese name, T'aitung.

31. "Ack-ack" was the usual term for AA fire in the Pacific Theater; "flak"—a contraction of the German *Flugzeugabwehrkanone,* or aircraft defense cannon—was used in the European Theater. *Narrative Mission Report, Mission 166-A-6, 15 June 1945.*

32. *Narrative Mission Report, Mission 167-A-7, 16 June 1945.*

33. Today's Leizhou Peninsula in Guandong Province; Haikou on Hainan; and, of course, Vietnam.

34. The Beinan River is known in modern Taiwan as the Peinan Hsi; Kiirun is present day Keelung, and Shoka is now Changhua.

35. *Hobo Queen II* could only carry nine bombs because she was still fitted with the auxiliary bomb-bay fuel tank she'd needed for the previous night's long-range shipping-interdiction mission, from which she returned just two hours before the seventh mission's scheduled takeoff time. Why 528 carried only nine bombs rather than the twelve carried by *The Lady is Fresh* is unclear.

36. *Narrative Mission Report, Mission 170-A-3, 19 June 1945.*

37. Today the bustling commercial port of Su-ao.

38. Modern Taimali.

39. *Narrative Mission Report, Mission 171-A-3, 20 June 1945.*

40. Modern Pingtung.

41. The word *salvo* has two meanings in terms of World War II aerial bombardment. In the first sense it simply means releasing all bombs with minimum intervals between them, essentially "dumping" them. In such a case the bombs are armed and will explode as intended. The other meaning, relating to hung-up bombs that fail to drop when the bombardier presses the release switch, means that the shackle to which the bomb is attached in the bomb bay is itself jettisoned. In such a case the safety wire is not yanked free as in a normal drop, meaning that the bomb never arms and does not explode on impact. In the B-32 both the bombardier and the pilot could salvo the bombs.

42. *Narrative Mission Report, Mission 173-A-3, 22 June 1945.*

43. The Canton River is today known as the Pearl River, and Canton itself is now Guangzhou.

44. Now Sanzao Dao in Guangdong Province.

45. *Narrative Mission Report, Mission 175-A-6, 23/24 June 1945*. Additional details from *Svore Interview*, op. cit.

46. Now Yilan City.

47. *Narrative Mission Report, Mission 176-A-1, 25 June 1945.*

48. The representative from the Office of the Assistant Chief of Air Staff for Operations, Commitments and Requirements (OC&R).

49. This brief summary of the three reports and their conclusions is based on, respectively: Cook's *Combat Test of the B-32 Airplane,* July 17, 1945; McElroy's *Report on Special Project 98269S,* July 2, 1945; and Britt's *Report to USAAF Proving Ground Command on the Combat Test of the B-32 Airplane*, August 2, 1945.

50. Modern Kaohsiung City.

51. *Narrative Unit History, 386th Bombardment Squadron, July–August 1945.*

52. Two kamikaze units, the 951st Air Group and the Nansei Shoto Air Group, are known to have been on Okinawa at the time of the U.S. invasion. Although it is unclear if either actually used Yontan before its destruction by retreating Japanese forces, advancing U.S. forces discovered five Yokosuka MXY7 "Ohka" rocket-propelled suicide planes when they overran the field on the first day of the invasion.

53. The main Japanese forces defending Okinawa may have abandoned Yontan without a fight, but on the night of May 24 commandos of the IJA's Giretsu Kuteitai airborne special operations unit attacked the airfield, killing two soldiers and destroying nine aircraft before themselves being killed.

54. Issued jointly by the United States, the United Kingdom, and Nationalist China on July 26, 1945, the declaration called for the unconditional surrender of all Japanese armed forces. Continued resistance would result in the "prompt and utter destruction" of those forces.

55. *Narrative Mission Report, Mission 225-A-6, 15 August 1945.*

56. *Narrative Mission Report, Mission 226-A-6, 15 August 1945.*

57. *Narrative Mission Report, Mission 227-A-6, 16 August 1945.*

Chapter 3: Crisis in Tokyo

1. In keeping with Japanese tradition, Hirohito is today commonly referred to in Japan by his posthumous name, Emperor Showa.

2. The phrase regarding the unconditional surrender of *Japan's armed forces* was a modification of the language used in the 1943 Cairo Declaration, in which the United States, Great Britain, and China had called for *Japan's* unconditional surrender. The alteration was made, at least in

part, to persuade Japan's senior civilian leaders (and quite possibly the emperor himself) that the nation's traditional institutions, including the monarchy, would remain intact.

3. This translation is taken from *Japan's Longest Day*, pp. 209–211, hereafter cited as *Japan's Longest Day*. For a slightly different translation, see Herbert P. Bix's monumental (and Pulitzer Prize–winning) *Hirohito and the Making of Modern Japan*, pp. 526–528, hereafter cited as *Hirohito*.

4. *Japan's Longest Day*, p. 211.

5. Ibid., p. 212.

6. The threat is contained in the declaration's final paragraph, which reads in its entirety: "We call upon the government of Japan to proclaim now the unconditional surrender of all Japanese armed forces, and to provide proper and adequate assurances of their good faith in such action. The alternative for Japan is prompt and utter destruction." For the text of the entire document, see *Behind Japan's Surrender: The Secret Struggle That Ended an Empire*, pp. 158–159. Hereafter cited as *Behind Japan's Surrender*.

7. The hawks' terms—in addition to the retention of the monarchy—are outlined in *Downfall: The End of the Imperial Japanese Empire*, p. 291. Hereafter cited as *Downfall*.

8. *Polity* is one of several words used to define the Japanese concept of kokutai, an ambiguous concept that can mean "national character," "national identity," or even the "essence" of what it means to be Japanese. In the military sense, it is usually translated as "group."

9. This account of the momentous August 9 meeting is drawn from *Japan's Longest Day*, pp. 30–35, and *Behind Japan's Surrender*, pp. 104–109. Although these and various other accounts differ somewhat on the words Hirohito actually spoke (they were not recorded and were later reconstructed based on the accounts of those present), they all agree on the substance.

10. Lord Keeper of the Privy Seal was a non–cabinet level administrative post, whose occupant was the keeper of the emperor's official seal. For a more complete account of the February 1936 coup attempt, see Stanley Weintraub's *The Last Great Victory: The End of World War II, July/August 1945*, pp. 535–538 (hereafter cited as *The Last Great Victory*), and *Hirohito*, pp. 296–303.

11. *Japan's Longest Day*, pp. 36–37. For a slightly different version of this incident, see *Downfall*, p. 297.

12. As with other statements made by senior Japanese leaders during the last days of the war there are several varying translations of the "Anami Proclamation." This one is taken from *Japan's Longest Day*, p. 41.

13. Ibid., p. 42.

14. *Japan's Longest Day*, pp. 44–45. See also *The Last Great Victory*, pp. 534–535, and *Behind Japan's Surrender*, pp. 198–206.

15. *Behind Japan's Surrender*, pp. 215–216.

16. Ibid.

17. Ibid.

18. *Behind Japan's Surrender*, pp. 234–236.

19. Ibid., p. 239.

20. *Behind Japan's Surrender*, pp. 251–252, and *Japan's Longest Day*, pp. 73–74.

21. *Japan's Longest Day*, pp. 75–77.

22. *Downfall*, p. 314

23. Ibid.

24. *Japan's Longest Day*, pp. 81–83. See also *Downfall*, pp. 314–315, for a slightly different version of Hirohito's remarks.

25. *Japan's Longest Day*, pp. 87–88.

26. Ibid., pp. 141–142.

27. Also referred to as *hara-kiri*, this is ritual self-disembowelment performed with a knife or short sword.

28. *Japan's Longest Day*, pp. 305–306.

Chapter 4: Ceasefire, or Not?

1. *Homeland Air Defense Operations Record (Japanese Monograph 157)*, pp. 75–78, hereafter cited as *Homeland Air Defense*. See also the information provided by Major Hiroshi Toga, 10th AD staff officer (and a postwar contributor to *Homeland Air Defense*), during his October 23, 1945, interrogation in *U.S. Strategic Bombing Survey, Interrogations of Japanese Officials*. Hereafter cited as *Toga interrogation*.

2. *Homeland Defense Naval Operations, Part III, Dec. 41–Aug. 45 (Japanese Monograph 124)*, pp. 27–29. Hereafter cited as *Homeland Defense Naval Operations*.

3. *Homeland Air Defense*, op. cit., and *Toga interrogation*.

4. *Homeland Defense Naval Operations*, p. 29.

5. I have chosen to use the Allied code names for World War II Japanese aircraft in this text simply because most readers will be more familiar with them than with the Japanese names.

6. General background information on the organization, personnel, equipment, and operations of the navy fighter units discussed in the chapter is drawn primarily from *Japanese Naval Aces and Fighter Units in World War II; Imperial Japanese Navy Aces 1937–45*; and *Beyond Pearl Harbor: The Untold Stories of Japan's Naval Airmen*.

7. *Japanese Naval Aces and Fighter Units in World War II*, p. 215. Hereafter cited as *Japanese Naval Aces*.

8. *Japan's Longest Day*, p. 164.

9. Ibid., p. 214.

10. Ibid.

11. *Japan's Longest Day*, p. 183.

12. The figure 2,000 is quoted in *Behind Japan's Surrender*, p. 375; other sources provide alternate numbers ranging from 500 to 2,500, so I have settled on 1,000 as an approximate figure.

13. The 5,300-aircraft figure is quoted in *The Last Great Victory*, p. 627.

14. The admiral was the grandfather of Vietnam POW and current Arizona senator John S. McCain III.

15. *Air War Pacific: America's Air War Against Japan in East Asia and the Pacific, 1941–1945*. Hereafter cited as *Air War Pacific*. The F4U and FG-1 Corsairs were identical; the first was manufactured by Vought, and the second was a license-built version produced by Goodyear.

16. Although Moore's victory was the last scored by a Navy pilot before the Japanese signed the surrender document on September 2 aboard USS *Missouri*, many authorities actually credit the final Navy air-to-air victory of the war to Lieutenant Commander T. H. Reidy, commander of VBF-83, who while flying an F4U Corsair shot down a navy Nakajima C6N "Myrt" reconnaissance aircraft over Tokyo at 5:40 A.M., just minutes before the American carrier aircraft received the official recall notice. The rationale—that the ceasefire went into effect at that time and that any action after that was somehow "unofficial"—is difficult to fathom in that hostilities obviously continued after that.

17. *Behind Japan's Surrender*, p. 375.

18. A contraction of its designation in Japanese.

19. The B-17, piloted by Captain Raymond T. Swenson, was on final approach when it was attacked by Ibusuki and Lieutenant Commander Shigeru Itaya. The Japanese rounds ignited emergency flares stored aboard the Fortress, starting a fire that quickly consumed the bomber after it skidded to a halt. All of the B-17's eight crewmembers survived but a passenger, flight surgeon First Lieutenant William R. Schick, died later that day from a bullet wound to the head. After the war Ibusuki joined Japan's reformed Air Self-Defense force, reaching the rank of lieutenant colonel. He was killed on January 9, 1957, when the Sabre fighter he was flying collided with another aircraft.

20. Sakai is credited with shooting down the Boeing B-17C piloted by Captain Colin P. Kelly on December 10, 1941, an action for which Kelly was posthumously awarded the Distinguished Service Cross because

he continued to fly the doomed aircraft so his crew could bail out; the Flying Fortress exploded before Kelly himself could escape.

21. Details about Sakai's life are drawn largely from *Winged Samurai: Saburo Sakai and the Zero Fighter Pilots*, hereafter cited as *Winged Samurai*; with additional information from *Japanese Naval Aces* and *Beyond Pearl Harbor*.

22. USSBS (Pacific), *Japanese Air Target Analysis, Objective Folders, Tokyo area*, June 20, 1945, multiple citations.

23. Sadamu Komachi mentions this directive specifically in his article in Vol. 62, December 1978, issue of *Maru Extra* magazine, as translated by Osamu Tagaya. Hereafter cited as *Maru Extra Komachi*.

24. Text drawn from *Combat Chronology of the U.S. Army Air Forces*, August 15, 1945.

25. Ibid.

26. Ibid.

27. Though Gonoike is a more accurate transliteration of the Japanese name for this installation, I have chosen to use the more widely known English rendering, Konoike.

28. *Pugliese Interview*.

29. Details of this flight are drawn from *Final Mission Report, Mission 228-A-8, 16 August 1945*.

30. Exhaust collector assembly failures were an all-too-common occurrence in B-32s. Many pilots involved in both the testing and combat operation of the Dominator complained about the problem, which was generally held to be the result of either shoddy workmanship, poor maintenance procedures, or both.

31. These steps are outlined in AAF Manual 51-126-7, "Airplane Commander Training Manual for the B-32 Dominator," p. 98, which rather laconically states: "Although the foregoing steps are necessarily listed in sequence, they are actually done as nearly as possible all at once."

32. The Type B radar was developed by the Tama Army Technical Research Station in early 1942. It covered a 90-degree sector with a radius of 125 to 150 miles, gave relatively accurate information on the target aircraft's altitude and speed, and was used to supplement the earlier and less capable Type A system. See *Homeland Air Defense*, pp. 57–58.

33. Details of the flight are drawn from *Final Mission Report, Mission 229-A-10, 17 August 1945*.

34. Tomioka is routinely misidentified as "Tomika," largely because that is the way it is referred to in the final mission report for 229-A-10.

35. Aircraft figures for Imba and Matsudo are drawn from *Air Defense of the Homeland (Japanese Monograph No. 23)*, p. 71. Hereafter cited as *Air Defense of the Homeland*.

36. *Svore Interview*.

37. Details of the 302nd Air Group's participation in the August 17 action are drawn from Dr. Ikuhiko Hata's 1978 article, "*Hachi Gatsu Ju Go Nichi No Ku Nippon Kugun No Saigo*" (*The Combat of August 18: the Last of the Japanese Air Force*), hereafter cited as *Combat of August 18*; and from Yoshiaki Hasegawa's article in Vol. 79 (October 1981) of *Maru-Extra* magazine.

38. Sakai's personal account of the August 17 events is drawn from his 1992 book, *Zero-sen No Saigo*, which is usually translated as *Saburo Sakai: Air Combat Record* and is hereafter cited as *Sakai Combat Record*. It should be noted that most authorities consider this book to be a far more accurate account of the Japanese ace's wartime experiences than was *Samurai!*, the often-cited volume written in the 1970s by American aviation writer Martin Caidin with Sakai's input. Additional details of the Yoko Ku's participation in the August 17 interception are drawn from *Winged Samurai*, pp. 134–135; from *Imperial Japanese Navy Aces*, p. 29 and pp. 52–53; and *Rampage of the Roarin' 20's*, pp. 328–330, hereafter cited as *Rampage*.

Historians have long noted discrepancies among the various Japanese pilots' accounts of the August 17 and 18 encounters with the B-32s. For example, some sources say that Sakai flew on the 18th, rather than on the 17th, and at various points in his life Komachi said Sakai was his wingman, but then repudiated that in other accounts. I have chosen to relate the events in what I believe is the most accurate and factual way, based on a close reading and correlation of all the relevant sources.

39. The "clock" system allows an aircrew to call out the relative position of other aircraft in both the horizontal and vertical planes. The nose of the sighting aircraft is at twelve o'clock, its tail is at six o'clock, the right wingtip is at three o'clock and the left wingtip is at nine o'clock. If another aircraft is sighted above the horizontal plane it is "high"; if below the horizontal plane, it is "low."

40. Although some accounts of the August 17 interception have the majority of the attacks being made on the B-32s by Japanese army aircraft, it is highly unlikely that any army interceptors took part, given that virtually all the army units in the Kanto region had already complied with the order to disable their aircraft. Though it is certainly possible that one or two individual army pilots took to the sky that day, virtually all surviving Japanese records indicate that it was the navy

pilots from Atsugi and Oppama that carried out the attacks. Moreover, only a few of the American crewmen had ever experienced an enemy fighter attack, and they would therefore have had difficulty telling the difference between the navy's George and the army's Tojo in the heat of battle.

41. Author interview with Robert Russell, February 16, 1999. Hereafter cited as *Russell Interview*.

42. The report of a Ki-61 being involved in the attack on Svore's Dominator remains one of the unsolved mysteries of the August 17 mission. Though virtually all Japanese army aircraft had been grounded by the time the four B-32s arrived over Tokyo, it is always possible that a lone army pilot had flown his aircraft to either Atsugi or Oppama and joined the navy aviators in their attacks. There was a Tony-equipped army unit, the 244th Sentai (fighter regiment) at Chofu, and it is possible this was one of that unit's machines. It is also possible, however, that the Tony reported by the B-32 crew was actually a Judy night fighter, a type flown by the 302nd Air Group.

43. *Svore Interview.*

44. Elliot's memories of the August 17 mission are drawn from *Rampage*, p. 329.

45. *Commander-in-Chief's Daily Intelligence Summary, 17/18 August 1945.*

46. Despite the American gunners' credible accounts, surviving Japanese records do not indicate any losses of friendly aircraft on August 17. The official USAAF/USAF records of enemy aircraft downed during World War II also do not credit any of the B-32 gunners with either kills or probables on August 17 because those claims could not be substantiated. It is worth remembering, however, that the Japanese destroyed massive amounts of military records in the weeks following the surrender, and that information regarding aircraft destroyed or damaged by the B-32s could well have been among them.

Chapter 5: A Desperate Fight

1. *Pugliese Interview.*
2. *Svore Interview.*
3. *Pugliese Interview.*
4. Details of Joe Lacharite's life and military service are drawn primarily from the author's February 6, 1997, interview with him—hereafter cited as *Lacharite Interview*—and from information provided by his family.
5. *Men and Planes*, pp. 643–644.

6. Modern Taichung. The field was also referred to as Toyohara.

7. Author interview with Burton J. Keller, hereafter cited as *Keller Interview*.

8. Author interview with Kurt F. Rupke, hereafter cited as *Rupke Interview*.

9. As noted earlier in this volume, there has long been some question whether Sakai flew against the B-32s on August 17 or 18. I have determined that the evidence points to his participation only on the 17th.

10. *Narrative Mission Report, 20 August 1945.*

11. *Houston Interview*

12. *Keller Interview.*

13. Author interview with John R. Blackburn. Hereafter cited as *Blackburn Interview*.

14. Author interview with Frederick C. Chevalier. Hereafter cited as *Chevalier Interview.*

15. Komachi's account of his interception of the B-32 is drawn from his article "Becoming an Unusual Flying Ace After August 15," hereafter cited as *Komachi article*. There has long been confusion about the type of fighter Komachi flew during this engagement. In his article he states it was a Jack, though other sources—such as Henry Sakaida in his excellent book *Winged Samurai*—say it was an N1K Shiden Kai "George." The Yoko Ku had both types, as well as Zekes. I'm inclined to believe that the pilot had a fairly good idea of which type he flew.

16. *Chevalier Interview.*

17. *Blackburn Interview.*

18. *Final Mission Report, Mission 230-A-8, 19 August 1945.*

19. *Blackburn Interview.*

20. *Komachi article.* See also "The Combat of August 18," by Dr. Ikuhiko Hata, and the entry on Komachi in *Winged Samurai.*

21. *Keller Interview.*

22. *Houston Interview.* See also *Narrative Mission Report, 20 August 1945.*

23. *Keller Interview.*

24. *Narrative Mission Report, 20 August 1945.*

25. *Komachi article.*

26. *Lacharite Interview.* Details of Joe's wounding and Tony's initial injuries are drawn largely from this interview. Additional details are cited as necessary.

27. *Rupke Interview.*

28. Ibid.

29. *Narrative Mission Report, 20 August 1945.*

30. Ibid., and *Chevalier Interview, Anderson Interview,* and author interview with Richard E. Thomas, hereafter cited as *Thomas Interview.*

31. *Komachi article.*

32. *Keller Interview.* Although Japanese pilots would have encountered single-tail B-17 Flying Fortresses during the initial years of the Pacific war, that type was almost completely replaced by the longer-range B-24 beginning in late 1942.

33. *Lacharite Interview.*

34. *Rupke Interview.*

35. *Keller Interview.*

Chapter 6: Peace, or War?

1. *Pugliese Interview.*

2. *Narrative Mission Report, Mission 230-Z-5, 20th RS, 18 August 1945.*

3. *Pugliese Interview.*

4. *Chevalier Interview.* As with the August 17 mission, the Japanese reported no aircraft losses resulting from the August 18 encounter, nor were any kills or probables credited to the American gunners.

5. *MacArthur's Ultra,* pp. 223–225.

6. *Pugliese Interview* and *Final Mission Report, Mission 230-A-8, 18 August 1945.*

7. *Pugliese Interview.*

8. "Surrender on the Air," in *Military Review,* May 1946, pp. 32–33.

9. Ibid., p. 38.

10. Ibid. For a detailed account of the communications between MacArthur and the Japanese, and of the events between August 15 and the September 2 surrender ceremony in Tokyo Bay, see also *Reports of General MacArthur: The Campaigns of MacArthur in the Pacific,* Vol. I, Chap. 14, pp. 442–457. Hereafter cited as *Reports of General MacArthur.*

11. The account of Mitsuo Fuchida's initial support of the coup, his interactions with fellow conspirators Kozono and Kogure, Kozono's attempts to prevent the Kawabe delegation's departure from Japan, and of the 302nd Air Group commander's ultimate thwarting by Fuchida are based primarily on information in *God's Samurai,* pp. 162–172.

12. Kozono survived the war and died in 1960.

13. After the war Fuchida converted to Christianity and became a well-known evangelist. He died in 1976.

14. *Komachi article.*

15. Ibid.

16. Ibid.

17. According to Henry Sakaida, Komachi remained in hiding for several years before resuming a normal life. He died in 2012 at the age of 92. Saburo Sakai went into the printing business after the war, and wrote several accounts of his wartime activities. He died in 2000 at 84.

18. The planned Allied invasion of the Japanese Home Islands, Operation Downfall, was to have been conducted in two main phases. The first, Olympic, would have put troops ashore on the southern part of Kyushu in October 1945. The second, Coronet, was planned for the spring of 1946 and would have been focused on the Kanto Plain.

19. *Reports of MacArthur*, p. 444.

20. Ibid. For a more in-depth discussion of Blacklist, see also the Volume I Supplement to the *Reports*, titled *The Occupation: Military Phase*, pp. 4–18.

21. MacArthur himself chose not to attend, believing that by remaining aloof he would further impress upon the Japanese delegates that he was the emperor's successor and was therefore above such mundane negotiations. See *American Caesar*, p. 441.

22. Author interview with B-32 pilot Collins Orton. Hereafter cited as *Orton Interview*.

23. *Final Mission Report, Mission 237-A-10, 25 August 1945*.

24. *Reports of MacArthur*, p. 449.

25. *Pugliese Interview*.

26. *Blackburn Interview*. I have been unable to determine the bombardier's name from surviving records.

27. *Cook Interview*.

28. Author interview with Robert Russell, hereafter cited as *Russell Interview*.

29. Ibid.

30. Ibid.

31. *Pugliese Interview, Cook Interview*, and *Orton Interview*.

32. *The Occupation: Military Phase*, pp. 24–25. Interestingly enough, although Tench and his men were the first members of the occupation force to set foot in Japan, they might not actually have been the first Allied personnel to land in the defeated nation. The official war diary of the U.S. Navy's Patrol Bombing Squadron 116 contains a cryptic entry stating that the Iwo Jima–based unit's commander, Lieutenant Commander Walter C. Michaels, landed his PB4Y2 Privateer (a Navy variant of the B-24) at Atsugi on August 27 after encountering "mechanical difficulties" during a patrol flight over Tokyo Bay. The plane was said to have been on the ground for less than an hour while the crew rectified the problem, and took off without ever being approached by the Japanese. Michaels later wrote that there were no problems with the

aircraft, and that he had faked the emergency so that he and his crew could claim to have been the first Americans to land in defeated Japan. Although this story has been widely repeated, the author has been unable to find any other official documentation proving that it actually happened.

33. *Orton Interview.*

34. *Orton Interview.*

35. Ibid. This account is also contained in Orton's official "Pilot's Statement," written on September 10, 1945, and included in Staff Sergeant George A. Murphy's Individual Deceased Personnel File.

36. *Orton Interview.* Water condensation in fifty-five-gallon aviation gasoline storage drums was a huge and well-documented problem in the Pacific Theater because of the high daytime temperatures and excessive humidity.

37. Details of the actions of *Henley* and *Aulick* during the rescue of Orton and his crew are drawn from the ships' respective war diaries, as well as from the Missing Aircrew Report produced following the incident.

38. *Orton Interview* and destroyer war diaries.

39. *Deck Log, USS Aulick, 28 August–3 September 1945*, pp. 1–2.

40. *Cook Interview.*

41. *Svore Interview.*

42. *Narrative Unit History, 386th Bombardment Squadron, July–August 1945.*

43. *Blackburn Interview.*

Chapter 7: Homecoming

1. *Cook Interview, Pugliese Interview,* and *Anderson Interview.*

2. At some point one of the aviators—it is not clear who—provided an odd tidbit of fanciful information that was quickly seized upon and repeated by the reporters in their various stories. When the Japanese fighters rolled in on Anderson's aircraft and shot out an engine, this story went, the young pilot radioed Klein in the other Dominator and asked him to slow down. At that point one of the enemy pilots supposedly cut into the radio transmission and said, in English, "Yes, please slow down so I can shoot you down." I asked Anderson, Klein, and other participants in the August 18 incident about this bit of lore, and all said it did not happen and they did not know how the story got started.

3. Among the other papers that gave the story front-page treatment in the days following the attack were the *Los Angeles Times* and the same city's *Daily News* and, of course, Kinch's *Star-Telegram.* Interestingly,

Kinch's reports made no mention of the Japanese pilot breaking into the conversation.

4. After his return from overseas Joe Lacharite spent nearly a year in the hospital before returning to his civilian life. He died on September 28, 2000, in Holyoke, Massachusetts.

5. *The Graves Registration Service in World War II*, pp. 158–162. There was also a cemetery for Japanese military and civilian dead, though the large numbers of the former—more than 110,000—resulted in the majority being interred in mass graves.

6. This documentation is included in Tony's Individual Deceased Personnel File, a copy of which is in the author's possession. His most recent dental examination had been performed at Will Rogers Field on February 30, 1944.

7. Wooden caskets were generally not used in the Pacific Theater because of the logistical difficulties associated with getting them to the islands (which usually did not have native woods suitable for casket construction) and storing them in the hot and humid climates. Shelter halves were the two parts of a "pup" tent.

8. Indeed, just ten days later the 3063rd would process the remains of those killed in the fiery crash of 544; those that were positively identified were interred in individual graves at the Island Command Cemetery.

9. August 15 in the Pacific Theater.

10. The following account of how Tony's family learned of, and responded to, his death is based largely on the *Marchione Sisters Interview*. The sisters also graciously provided a trove of Tony's letters, photographs, and official documents pertaining to his military service and death.

11. Letter from Frank Pallone to Theresa Marchione, September 6, 1945, a copy of which was provided to the author.

12. A copy of the letter was provided to the author by the Marchione family.

13. A copy of the certificate was provided to the author by the Marchione family.

14. A copy of the award citation was provided to the author by the Marchione family.

15. *Final Disposition of World War II Dead, 1948–1951*, pp. 39–40. Hereafter cited as *Final Disposition*. The program called for the final disposition of more than 280,000 individual sets of remains, some 171,000 of which were ultimately returned to the United States for final burial according to the families' wishes. The total cost of the program reached more than $163 million.

16. Letter to Ralph Marchione from Major General Thomas B. Larkin, dated 19 January 1948. A copy was provided to the author by the Marchione family.

17. Letter from Major Richard B. Coombs, QMC Memorial Division to Ralph Marchione, dated 10 June 1948, a copy of which was provided to the author by the Marchione family.

18. Regulations required that disinterred remains be "disinfested, disinfected and wrapped." Copies of Tony Marchione's Disinterment Directive and other documents pertinent to the repatriation of his remains are included in his Individual Deceased Personnel File, a copy of which is in the author's possession. Hereafter cited as *Marchione IDPF*.

19. *Final Disposition*, pp. 653–654. The other two West Coast distribution centers were at Auburn, Washington, and Mira Loma, California. Oakland Army Base would ultimately handle some 57,000 sets of repatriated remains, the majority from the Pacific Theater.

20. *Berkeley Daily Gazette*, Wednesday, February 16, 1949.

21. Most sources indicate that the Army had 118 mortuary cars, all of which had apparently first been converted from civilian passenger use into hospital cars in 1942–1943.

22. *Final Disposition*, pp. 654–655.

23. The U.S. Army Air Forces had, of course, become the U.S. Air Force as a result of the National Security Act of 1947.

24. *Marchione Sisters Interview*; author interview with Frank J. Pallone Sr., hereafter cited as *Pallone Interview*.

25. *Pottstown Mercury*, March 22, 1949.

Author's Afterword

1. Indeed, a strong case could be made that his was the final American combat death of any type in World War II—though other U.S. military personnel died fighting Japanese service members as late as 1946, the fact that their deaths occurred after the ceremony aboard USS *Missouri* in Tokyo Bay places them firmly in the postwar period.

INDEX